# TALES AND MAXIMS FROM THE MIDRASH

# TALES AND MAXIMS FROM THE MIDRASH

Samuel Rapaport

General Books

www.General-Books.net

***Publication Data:***

Title: Tales and Maxims From the Midrash
Author: Rapaport, Samuel, 1837-1923
Publisher: London : G. Routledge; New York, E.P. Dutton
Publication date: 1907
Subjects: Midrash

1

# TALES AND MAXIMS FROM THE MIDRASH

S)emcate

TO MT Son Isidore Rapaport 8,"JGÂ;;)5

THE MIDRASH

INTRODUCTION

Jl'st as the Written Law given by Moses emanates from God, whilst He Himse f only proclaimed the first two commandments of the Decalogue, owing to the Israelites being too terrified to hear God's voice (Deut. 20. 19), and the whole of the Torah was then conveyed to Israel by Moses, so he likewise received the Oral law, which he was not allowed to commit to writing. This Oral law had to be taught by word of mouth side by side with the Written law, and thus the former became an unfolding and sequel to the latter.

This, says the Midrash, is meant by the words: ' Only take heed to thyself, and keep thy soul diligently lest thou forget the wordsâ DHQl meaning " words " as well as" things"â which thine eyes have seen, and lest they depart from thy heart all the days of thy life ' (Deut. 4. 9). ' The words which thine eyes have seen ' means the Written words which can be seen, and ' lest they depart from thy heart ' refers to the Oral law, words conunitted to memory, laid up in the heart.

From time immemorial, during the time of the prophets and even earlier, the Israelites had established schools or assemblies for the teaching of the Torah. To the places of worship schools were invariably attached in which religion was taught, the Torah was read and exegetically expounded. Whenever a portion of Holy Writ was read a i:; il (Drash)â a searching ' Exod. Rabba, 46. 1-6 and 12.

inquiryâ into the meaning of every sentence was made, with explanations drawn therefrom, based on the Oral law. Not only was this the case on Sabbaths and Festivals, but on week-days too, especially so on Mondays and Thursdays, when a small portion of the Torah was read, an institution ascribed to Ezra. Later on â probably in the time of the Maccabeesâ the reading of the prophets was also introduced.

The dissertations and expositions which were held were known as tt "n; D (Midrash), and this term was originally applied to both the HDbn (Halacha) and the TM i (Agada).

The sermons, dissertations and expositions of whatever natureâ whether exegetical, homiletical or ethical â were always given by word of mouth, but were after delivery reduced to writing. A knowledge of the Scriptures on the part of the audience was assumed, as the study of the Law was looked upon as one of the highest religious duties. There was great anxiety on the part of these teachers that nothing should be added to the Written law, which is known to us as the lli 'i DHIi â the Canon of the twenty-four books.

There is this line of demarcation between nd"?;! (Halacha) and n"T i (Agada), which in course of time were separated from one another, though the former contains now and then a little of the latter, and vice versa.2 Halacha, derived from " n (to go, walk), is a term denoting laws regulating man's walk in lifeâ the performance of his religious duties. The Aramaic translation of Onkeles (Exod. 21. 9) gives il bn as an equivalent of toDIi Q. Halacha, when decided by a majority of the school, became incontrovertible, law that could not be gainsaid; and any one, no matter how great his reputation for piety and learning, who might attempt

Baba Kamma, 82.

' In the Mechiita, Sifra and Sifre, Halacha and Agada go together.

to impugn it, would be excommunicated. Thus we find such hghts amongst the Rabbis as Eleazer B. Hanoch, who, having questioned the Halacha on ' Purity," was put under the ban, in which he remained all his life, and a stone was thrown on his coffin, since he had died under sentence. Akabyah b. Mahalalel was similarly excommunicated for refusing to accept the decision of the majority on four questions, and Rabbi Eliazar b. Horkynas, too, was put under the ban for dechning to recognize the decision of the majority on some points. The names of the respective authorities in the Halacha were always retained.

The Agada, on the other hand, is a free interpretation of the Scriptures. As its name implies: ' It was said." Its assertions were not incontrovertible or not to be gainsaid. There was, on the one hand, strong opposition to the Agada; but, on the other hand, it was very highly esteemed by most, and not every one was considered quahfied to handle it. Even Rabbi Akiba received a mild rebuke when he tried to dive into the depths of this method of teaching. There grew up in the course of time a saying: ' If you desire to find the greatness of the Creator, study the Agada." The names of the Agadic teachers were not always mentioned, yet certain rabbis were known to have possessed an enviable capacity for this branch of religious instniction, such as Rabbis Abahu, Ishmael, Eliazar b. Azaryah, Eliazar b. R. Jose the Galilean, and others, and they were known as the Rabbis of the Agada.

The Agada, of which the various Midrashim contain collections, and which some of the Apocrypha have for their source, was written in the time of the Tanaim, and consequently before the Halacha, which was only taken in hand by the school of Rav Ash6.

Whilst the Agada seeks but free scope in its own

Sanhedrin.

teachings and in its own interpretation of Scripture, and does not intend to invade the domain of Halacha, it yet occasionally touches some legal points. It is the oldest exegesis of the Scriptures, and contains in its elevating teachings, sermons, prayers, homilies, historical records, exhortations, admonitions and consolations, conveyed frequently in allegories, legends, parables and similes.

From the time of Ezra there were many institutions for the diffusion of this kind of teaching by the Scribes and priests. It formed the vital element in the nation's morality. When the Scribes took the place of the prophets, their interpretation and exposition of the Scriptures also took the place of prophetic utterances. In prosperity the people's favourite was the Halacha, but in adversity they preferred attending Agadic expositions, containing as they didâ among much elseâ words of comfort and consolation, instilling faith in God and hope in His help and protection.

Rabbi Abahu and Rabbi Chanina b. Abbe were holding discourses at the same time; the former preaching on Agada and the latter on Halacha. Rabbi Chanina's audience, hearing of Rabbi Abahu's Agadic discourse, rudely left him, and went to hear the latter. This gentle sage, distinguished for his meekness and piety, felt aggrieved at the slight shown to his colleague, of which he was the innocent and unwilling cause. He went to see Rabbi Chanina and tried to assuage the grief caused him. ' It is hardly to be wondered at," he said, ' that the people come to hear me instead of craving for your words. For do we not find this folly in almost every walk of life? Let a man offer cheap and flimsy finery for sale, and he will find far more buyers than he who offers choice pearls and precious stones." The Rabbis knew well how to make their

Midrash Song of Songs j. Sota 40.

Agadic discourses as attractive as possible, and to awaken their audience from their lethargic condition when occasion arose. One device was to use words of foreign languages, Latin, Greek, Persian, etc., in order to provoke questions and further interest, and so well was the Agada known for its foreign words, that if one found in the Mishna a word of doubtful meaning, recourse was had to the written Agada for its elucidation.

Rabbi Akiba, once finding his audience drowsy and inattentive, used the following device: ' What," he asked, ' induced Esther to reign over 127 provinces? ' The question at once roused the attention of the whole assembly, who expected some subtle arithmetical solution, with which the Rabbi had no intention of edifying them. But finding his device successful and attention awakened, he answered the question by saying that ' it was proper for the descendant of Sarah, who lived 127 years, to reign over 127 provinces."

Rabbi Judah Hanasi, too, had recourse to enigmatical sayings: ' I know of a woman," he said, ' who bore 600,000 children at one time." This was enough to excite the curiosity of his congregation, who were depressed and in a dejected spirit owing to the havoc wrought by the ruthless Hadrian. Seeing that the assembly was quite puzzled at such a wonderful event. Rabbi Ishmacl b. Jose explained that that woman was no other than Jochabad, the mother of Moses, who was not only a host in himself, but also delivered 600,000 men from slavery.

Some of the Rabbis wrote down their notes on Holy Writ as they occurred to them. Rabbi Meir, who was a skilful Scribe and wrote a scroll of the Pentateuch for his own use, is said to have written on the margin thereof short notes for his discourses. A great many Agadic and other teachings were developed in the ' Gen. Rabba 58. j. ' Midr. Cantls. i. 27.

' Midrash Eccleii, 4, and Lamentations i.

b THE MIDRASH school of Yabne, or Jamnia, granted by Vespasian to Rabbi Jochanon b. Zakkai, the last pupil of Hillel, and to his friends as well as to Gamliel's descendants. This truly great load-star of the Jewish religion established his school there, and the place became a new Jerusalem and the new seat of a highly learned assembly. Of the Midrashic writings of the period between the Hashmo-neans and Hadrian, a period of some three hundred years, we possess but fragments, although that period may be said to have levelled the path from the Canon of the Bible to that of tradition.

What is known as the New Agada had its rise for the most part from the first to the fifteenth century. The reopening of the schools in Palestine in the year 520 c. e., and in Babylon in the year 589, gave rise to Midrash Rabba on Genesis, followed by that on Leviticus, then Exodus and Deuteronomy, the last of the five books being Numbers. Of the Midrashim on the five Megil-loth, that on Lamentations was the first, and that on Ecclesiastes was the last.

Midrash Tanchuma, or Yelamdenu, was most probably written in the last century of the Gaonim in Italy, about the ninth century c. e. These Gaonim were in constant communication with Palestine. Tanchuma was followed by Midrash 2110 ITIW on Psalms, Midrash on Proverbs and on Samuel.

I do not pretend to have explored for this little work (which I commenced in my sixty-ninth year, and hope to see published on or before my seventieth birthday) the Midrash in the whole of its scope. I have not even as much as touched the Pesikta (the oldest of all Midrashim) Mechilta, Yalkut, Sifra or Sifre; but have restricted myself to about nine hundred quotations from the following Midrashim, viz. Rabba on the five books of Moses and the five Megilloth, Tanchuma on

See Dr. Yost's Geschichte des Judenthums und seine Sekten vol. ii. pp. 13, etc.

the Pentateuch, and the Midrash on Psalms, Proverbs and Samuel.

Moreover, whilst I have here and there ventured to ' dress up ' the mere ' dry bones ' of simple quotations with a word or two of my own, according to the (dim) light that is within me, I have chiefly confined myself to the mere quotations only. I hope that the Eldorado which the intelligent reader will at once detect to exist in the somewhat untravcrscd highway of this wonderland of Rabbinical literature, may encourage an exploring thereof, and one is sure to find an inexhaustible deposit peppered with gold, to use the miner's phrase. The acquisition of a claim in this may not secure a residence in Park Lane, but it will ensure a habitation in the spheres which do not pass away. The whole realm of the moral code is represented in the Midrash; and there is not a point, whether on prudence, life's experience, or worldly wisdom, which the Midrash has left untouched.

The great conqueror Alexander the Macedonian, the son of Phihp, who, at the instigation of the Persians, was assassinated by Pisanius, when yet a boy showed great thirst for conquest. When he heard of his father's conquests he wept bitterly, complaining that by the time he assumed the crown there would be so little for him to conquer. He was barely twenty years old when he'ascended the throne, but he knew well how to make his power felt. He soon conquered the Thracians, as well as the rebellious Thebans, and his heroic qualities developed so rapidly that he was appointed by the Greeks as military chief in their wars against the Persians. Uninterrupted success followed his arms, and had he not died at a comparatively early age he would probably have conquered what was then known as the whole world. His victory over the Persian General Memnon, on the river Granicus, in the North-West of Asia Minor, opened for him the road into the interior of further Asia. He was not slow to take advantage of the opportunity, and pushed rapidly through the States of Asia Minor, through Lydia and Ionia to Pam-phylia. In the latter, near Issus, he gained a brilliant victory over Darius the Third, also known as Codo-manus, who narrowly escaped death, leaving his mother, his wife and his children in the hands of the conqueror. The Macedonian hero, with his troops intoxicated with victory after victory, now entered Syria, not so much in pursuit of Darius as with a view to extending his conquests. He took Damascus and Sidon, and attacked Tyre, so as to become master of the sea also.

That city, however, being very strongly fortified, and being on one side protected by the sea, offered a stubborn resistance, and Alexander found himself compelled to embark on a long siege. In order to prevent any untoward event during the siege, Alexander was anxious to ensure immunity from the neighbouring State.

He therefore sent a message to Jerusalem, with a letter to the High Priest Jedua with the following requests: (i) To supply him with troops; (2) to allow free traffic between the Macedonian army and Jerusalem; (3) to give him every possible assistance, such as had been granted to Darius. A hint was also thrown out that the High Priest would do well to consider whose friendship and goodwill was of greater valueâ that of the victor, or that of the vanquished.

The letter further expressed Alexander's anticipation of having these modest requests granted, and assured the Jews that they would have no reason to regret compliance. The Jews could not but know that it would be greatly to their advantage to be on good tenns with this famous hero, and that the beaten Persian could neither benefit nor injure them. Yet they did not feel justified in deserting the Persians. The High Priest therefore indited something like the following answer:â ' Recognition and high esteem are undoubtedly due to so glorious a hero, yet for the present the Jews of Jerusalem cannot comply with his wishes, for these reasons: We Jews have promised our loyalty, on our oath, to Darius. So long as that Prince lives the oath has its force and the Jews could commit no sin so grievous as wilful perjury, seeing that one of their commandments, with which God has entrusted them, is this: " Thou shalt not take the name of the Lord thy God in vain, for the Lord will not hold him guiltless that taketh His name in vain." ' The High Priest moreover mentioned instancesâ such as Zedekiah, the last King of Judah, who became disloyal to the Babylonian ruler, his former allegiance notwithstanding, and brought calamity upon himself and upon Judea. He further pointed out that Moses' teaching tends to show that the God of Israel is a God of Truth, that treachery and untruth bring misfortune on those who practise them, and that it is incumbent on every true adherent of the teaching of Moses to avoid all falsehood and duplicity. Alexander would perhaps have been satisfied with the explanation offered by the High Priest Jedua, had it not been for the Samaritans, who, whilst practising all sorts of idolatry, were at the same time anxious to unite with the Jews, and to be considered as a portion of that body. When the Jews repudiated them, they sought to set up a temple of their own on the model of the Jerusalem Temple. Menasseh, a brother of Jedua, formerly a priest, having married a Samaritan woman, the daughter of a Samaritan governor, was deprived of his office of priest in the temple, and was naturally all the more anxious to set up an opposition temple, in which he could exercise his priestly function. The Samaritans therefore strained every nerve to excite Alexander's illwill against the Jews, and to obtain his sanction for the erection of a temple on Mount Gerizim.

Sanblat, the Governor of Samaria, and father-in-law of Menasseh, the expelled priest, sought audience of Alexander, and took the opportunity to give his version of the motives of Jedua, the High Priest, in refusing Alexander's requests. He maintained that loyalty to Darius was not the motive of the refusal, as the Jews, he said, knew nothing of loyalty, but, on the contrary, would overthrow every throne not occupied by one of their own people if they had the power. He said that they were priest-ridden, and that if there were any who would join his (Alexander's) army, they dared not venture it, as that would exclude them from participating in the Temple service, which to them meant moral death. If he (the Macedonian) would only secure an alternative to the Jerusalem Temple by sanctioning the opposition Temple which the Samaritans were anxious to set up, this would bring large numbers from Jerusalem to the new Temple; and the newcomers, no longer fearing exclusion from the Jerusalem service, would gladly join with the Samaritans the banner of the great conqueror Alexander. It is perhaps not surprising that the Macedonian conqueror was much impressed with this plausible version, especially when the Samaritans, as an earnest of their acceptance of and adhesion to the new state of affairs, deserted en masse the ranks of the crushed Darius, and went over to Alexander's army.

The desired j)ermission for the building of the Gerizim Temjile was granted, and the work was taken in hand. Soon afterwards, however, the governor, who was a man of advanced age, died. Tyre could no longer resist the severe siege, and, as predicted by the prophet (Is. 27), it capitulated. Indescribable slaughter and ravage took place within its walls; the town was laid in ruins, and its heroes were either slaughtered or taken as slaves.

Alexander now turned his attention to the punishment of the Jews, and started with his ever-victorious army for Jerusalem. When tlie news of the approach of Alexander and his formidable army reached Jerusalem, there was consternation, and despair ruled supreme amongst the inhabitants, one and all. The Jews took refuge, as ever, in their religion; prayer, fasting, sackcloth and ashes were the order of the day. Confession of sin and repentance were practised daily by almost every person. When Alexander was but al)out one day's distance from Jerusalem, the High Priest and Elders of the Temple had the streets of the city beautifully decorated, the public buildings as well as the private residences were magnificently adorned, and they ordered the inhabitants to form two lines in the streetsâ one opposite the otherâ the people to appear in their holiday attire. The gates of the city were bedecked with garlands of the finest flowers, and triumphal arches were erected. The priests, the Levites and the Elders, at their head the venerable High Priest Jedua in full priestly robes, mitre, ephod and breastplate, made their way, towards evening, to the entrance of the city, cairying torches and candles in their hands, and a light was thrown on the brilliant assembly such as echpsed the noonday brightness of a magnificent summer's day.

Soon after their arrival at the gate, Alexander, at the head of his army, made his appearance. He was quite astonished at the sight that met his view, and seemed to be overwhelmed on beholding the grand and imposing assembly that came to meet him. When he saw the High Priest, who looked even as an angel in his garments, Alexander dismounted, as though impelled by an instinct, bowed himself reverently, and proclaimed aloud: ’ Blessed be the God whose servant you are." His army, however, having anticipated plunder rather than the sight before them, could ill conceal their bewilderment at the strange turn of affairs. They could hardly believe, on the evidence of their own senses, that their proud monarch should bend his head so humbly and so reverently before the High Priest. One of Alexander's confidential and favourite officers, Parmenion by name, ventured at last to ask the King why he, the proud conqueror, showed such marked honour and deference to the Jewish priest.

’ Listen, then," replied Alexander, ’ and I will tell you of a wonderful experience of mine. While I was still in Macedonia I often lay awake at night, when all else was at rest, thinking of a plan by which to gain mastery of Asia. One evening, when my thoughts were more than usually occupied with this fond scheme of mine, I fell, exhausted by this mental strain, into a deep slumber, and saw in a vision an awe-insi)iring man standing before me. The very sight of him seemed to instil into me courage and hope, and, as though reading my very thoughts, he advised me to cross the borders of Greece without further hesitation, and assured me of the success of my projected undertaking. That vision of mine was no myth, no nightmare, not the mere phantasy of a heated brain; for not only have I, since that vision, never met with anything but victory, but in the hoar-headed and venerable servant of the Jewish God, in his attire and in his bearing, I see no other than the man of my vision. Shall I not then revere the man who was the messenger of his God to lead me to victory? I am equally convinced that my destiny is to overthrow Darius, and for that purpose I was called to undertake this venture, and the appearance of this holy man foretells complete success." After this explanation, Alexander entered Jerusalem, accompanied by the Jewish dignitaries who came to meet him. He was welcomed and cheered throughout by the ix)pulation of the city. His first request was to be taken to the Temple, where he anxiously inquired concerning the ceremonies and sacrifices and the manner of the services.

His curiosity was gladly satisfied, and the High Priest directed his attention also to the passage in Daniel 8. 5, where it is foretold that a Greek ruler (which term the High Priest ajiplied to Alexander) would overthrow the Persian kingdom, and Alexander was exceedingly pleased with all he saw and heard. The following day the Macedonian hero summoned all the priests and elders, and asked them to tell him, without restraint and hesitation, what they wished of him as a token of his great satisfaction at the reception given him, and as a mark of his high estimation of their services and organization. The High Priest, who was the spokesman, asked his Majesty to grant them the free and unhindered exercise of their religious rites, and to waive the payment of taxes in the Sabbatical year, when, according to the law of Moses, no agricultural pursuits were allowed, and consequently there was no revenue from their lands. This was at once granted; but Alexander observed from Jedua's demeanour that there was some further favour he wished to obtain, but that the good man was reluctant to name it. He therefore requested the High Priest to lay all his wishes before him. The High Priest then ventured to ask that the great monarch might extend his permission regarding the exercise of the religious rites by his Jewish subjects to all other parts of his wide dominions, such as Babylon and Media, and this was also cheerfully granted by the great Alexander. At the express wish of the Macedonian warrior, a large number of the most valiant of the Jewish community joined his army, and he gave them permission to follow their religious observances in the camp. As a further favour, Alexander requested that his hkeness might be framed and placed in the Temple. It was pointed out to him that the Jews were strictly forbidden to have pictures and likenesses of anything whatever in their places of worship, and, in lieu of this, it was suggested (i) that all male children born in that year throughout Jerusalem should be named Alexander, and (2) that the Jews should adopt a new era called the Alexander Era. That era was to commence with October i of the year 312 before the Christian era. This suggestion met with Alexander's approval, and up to the eleventh century of the Christian era this method of reckoning the years was actually in force, and was known as the Era of Documents. With Alexander's entry into Jerusalem began a very 1 See Rapoport's Erech Millin, page 73.

considerable improvement in the condition of the Jows. The Samaritans used every subterfuge in order to be recognized as Jews by the Macedonian hero, so that they miglit enjoy the privileges and advantages bestowed on the latter, but they failed to convince Alexander, who remembered their efforts to prejudice him against the Jews, that they were of the same people. ' If you are indeed Jews," he asked, ' how is it that you are not known by that name? ' ' We are," they insisted, ' descendants of the Patriarch Jacob, and Israel's God is our God; but the Sidomites call us Samaritans, and we are also knowti to them by the name of Shechemites, after our ca )ital Shechem."

Alexander was not satisfied with their answer, and told them that he could not recognize them as Jews, and to the Jews alone he had granted the privileges which the Samaritans sought to obtain. He asked them to leave the matter in abeyance till his return from the long journey he was about to undertake, and on his return he would thoroughly investigate their claim, and then see that justice was done to them. The Samaritans were dissatisfied with Alexander's treatment of them, and they rebelled and burned the Governor Andromachus in his own palace. Alexander's anger at this was very great; he returned, put to death the leaders, exiled a number of Samaritans to Egypt, where they formed a colony in Thebais, and handed a large number of them over to the Jews as slaves, as a reward for their tried loyalty.

Alexander of Macedonia, be it remembered, was by no means a mere uncouth warrior whose knowledge did not extend beyond the narrow compass of the battlefield, for the vast dominion of art and science was an open book to him. From his thirteenth to his eighteenth

There is a difference in the dates mentioned in the Talmud. In Taanis it is stated as the 21st Kislev, and in Yoma 69 as the 28th of Tebeth.

year he was a pupil of Aristotle, who guided him through all branches of wisdom and knowledge, and inspired in him a love for Homer's works, which in fact he always carried with him. As a consequence, he naturally had a longing for intercourse with the educated and learned men of every place which he visited. Arrived in the South, his first step was to have the men distinguished for their wisdom brought before him. To them he put the following ten questions: (i) Which is the longer distanceâ from the earth to the skies, or from the east of the world to the west? Answer: The last-mentioned is the longer, because if the sun stands in the East or in the West, then he is perceived in the half of each sphere; but if he is in the centre of the sky, then he is not visible everywhere. Consequently he must be higher in the former case than in the latter. (2) Which was created firstâ the heavens or the earth? Answer: The Almighty clearly commenced His work with the heavens, for is it not said, ' In the beginning God created the heavens and the earth'? (3) Who is truly wise? Answer: He who can foresee the result of his acts is truly a wise man. (4) Who is truly strong? Answer: Strength is in the possession of him who can overcome his passions. (5) Who can be considered truly rich? Answer: Truly rich is he who possesses contentment. (6) How can man acquire true Hfe? Answer: True life can be obtained by deadening one's passions. (7) What hastens man's death? Answer: Indulgence in earthly pleasures. (8) How can man obtain the love of his fellow-men? Answer: By not seeking supremacy over them. Alexander felt himself hit by this answer, and said, ' I am not of your opinion in this respect. My idea is that, in order to obtain the love of one's fellow-man, one must acquire might and power, and use them with discretion." (9) Which is the more agreeable abodeâ on land or water? Answer: Surely on land, because seafaring men are not happy and con- tented till they reach land. (10) Who amongst you is considered the wisest? Answer: In this respect we are unable to give any one the preference, as you may have observed that our answers were unanimous and simultaneous.

Alexander proceeded in argument with the wise men. ' Why," he asked, ' are you so averse to heathenism, seeing that the heathens greatly outnumber you?" To which he received the reply that it is just the multitude, the masses, who are apt to lose sight of truth, and it is only given to a comparative few to perceive and understand pure truth. ' But," he continued, ' it is in my power to destroy the whole of you." ' No doubt," was the answer, ' you possess the power to do so, but we are not apprehensive on that point, having once received the promise of your protection." He then consulted them concerning his projected journey to Africa. The wise men answered, ' That you cannot reach, as it lies beyond the dark mountains, which no human foot can traverse."

The king seemed to be piqued by this, and said, ' I do not ask you whether I shall or can traverse those mountains. My mind is made up, and there is no resistance to my will. What I want to know is the best means known to man for undertaking this formidable expedition." The wise men advised him to the best of their knowledge. Part of their advice was to procure certain draught animals from Libya, which possess the faculty of seeing their way in darkness. The king, having adopted all the necessary measures, started for Africa. He arrived at a place called the land of Amazon, whose inhabitants consisted only of women, to whom he sent a declaration of war. The women sent a message to him that a war with them could only be an inglorious one, inasnuich as if he were victorious a victory over women could not bring him cither fame or honour; whereas if they should be victorious, that would surely bring disgrace uix)n him.

The king saw the wisdom of their argument, and gave up the idea of war, but bade them supply him with bread. The women brought him lumps of gold in the shape of loaves of bread. The king said in amazement: ' Do you use this metal as bread? ' They answered: ' You surely have not come all this distance merely for bread; is there no bread in your own country? '

Alexander took his departure thence, but, before starting, he wrote on the gate of the city: ' I, Alexander of Macedonia, was a simpleton until I arrived at this gate, where I learnt wisdom from women." He next arrived at Katzia, where also he was met with presents of gold. ' I want no gold of yours," said Alexander to the chief. ' And to what other purpose have you come all this great distance?" was the answer, given in the shape of a question. ' I have come," said Alexander," to become acquainted with your manners and customs, especially with your administration of justice."

A remarkable case of litigation happened to be in progress in the place at this time. A man who had bought a house of another found in its precincts a treasure-trove, which he took back to the seller, sapng: ' This is yours; I bought the house only, and not what may be found in it." The other, in refusing to accept the proffered treasure, argued that he sold the house, and the buyer was the rightful owner of all that might be found in it. The judge gave his decision that the son of the purchaser of the house should marry the daughter of the seller, and the young couple should receive the treasure as a dowry. As Alexander expressed his wonder at and approval of the wise verdict, he was asked by the judge how a similar suit would be decided in his own country. ' In my country," replied Alexander, ' the treasure would be taken by the Crown, and both parties would be deterred by the threat of death from laying any claim to it." ' How," said the judge, ' have you also rain and sunshine in your country?" ' Surely," replied Alexander. ' And you possess also animals and fowls? ' ' Why not? ' asked the Macedonian. Then," remarked the judge, ' I must suppose that the purpose of the rain and sunshine in your land is to sustain those harmless creatures; for you, the human inhabitants, judging by your perverse-ness and injustice, are unworthy of such blessed gifts of nature."

One day they arrived at a river, and as his servants were washing off the salt of the fish, which they carried with them for their august master, in the water of the river, they saw that life was returning to the fishes. When the marvellous event was reported to Alexander, he determined to find the source of that river. He pursued his way, and at last found a gate, where he demanded admittance. The answer he received to his demand was: ' This is the gate of the Lord; the righteous shall enter therein," and he concluded that it must be the gate of Paradise. As all his pleadings did not gain him admittance, he asked for some article from the place as a token of his having arrived there. A lump of gold in the shape of a human eye was handed out to him, and on putting it in the scales to ascertain its remarkable weight, he found that whatever weight he might put on the opposite scale, it would not turn the scale on which the golden eye was put. As soon as he met with the Rabbis again, he asked them to unriddle this remarkable thing. The Rabbis told him to put a little earth over the eye, and its weight would vanish. They explained that the eye was a perfect type of the human eye, which, as the wise king tells us (Prov. 27.), is never satisfied, until a little earth is put over it (in death), and its everlasting hunger ceases.

' This allt'Kory was conspicuously applicable to Alexander's career. ind character. However extensive were his conquests, be longcu for more and was never satislieu, not even after tlie

Alexander returned home from his great adventures through the wilderness and went to Egypt, where he built the city of Alexandria. He was anxious for the Jews, whom he held in high esteem for their bravery and loyalty, to be among the settlers of the great city. Once, some African tribe and some descendants of Ishmael laid complaints before him against the Jews. The Africans claimed the possession of Palestine, basing their claim on Numbers 34. 2 and on their being descendants of Canaan; they maintained that they had an undisputed right to the country of their ancestor. The sons of Ishmael, too, put in a claim to the possession of at least a portion of Palestine, as the land was promised to their grandfather Abraham (Gen. 25. 13). And so the Egyptians bethought themselves of their claim against the Jews, and referred also to a Scriptural passage (Exod. 12. 36).

Alexander had the elders of the Jews summoned to him, and mentioned the claims of the respective parties against them. The Jews selected one named Gebeha, son of Psisa, as their defender. He faced the plaintiffs, and said: ' You have each based your claims on Scripture; I, too, will plead against you out of the books of Moses, our lawgiver. Regarding the Canaanites, we have it in Genesis 9. 25 that Canaan was cursed and was made a slave to his brothers. A slave can possess no property of his own. As to the demand of the Ishmaelites, we have it also on the same authority (Gen. 25. 5) that Abraham presented Isaac with all his possessions, and to the children of his concubines he made presents and sent them away from his son Isaac.

' Against the claims of the Egyptians, we have a huge counterclaim. The second book of Moses mentions the plundering of Asia, not after receiving, in consequence of his great conquests, the appellation of ' the great." But with his death, his and his country's greatness ceased, the monstrous possessions were cut up, and none of his kin ascended the throne.

time of the Jewish compulsory servitude in Egypt as 430 years. We are fully prepared to restore the value of what we carried away from Egypt, if the Egyptians will pay us the wages of 600,000 men, whom they com- )elled to work for them for the period mentioned."

Alexander demanded a reply on the part of the three claimants against the Jewish arguments, within three days, if they did not wish to be punished for making fictitious claims.

Nothing more was heard of the claims. The Jews rose in Alexander's esteem daily, and he gave them the most beautiful part of the city, on the banks of the river, as their quarter, and granted them the full rights of citizenship. The Jewish community increased greatly in wealth and numbers. A year later, at the battle of Arbela, a town in Chaldea, Alexander entirely annihilated the Persian empire. After more wars and conquests, he died suddenly at the age of thirty-three. His death was brought about as much by revelry as by his many cares and bodily exhaustion. Some of his generals contended for his throne; he was left unburied for some time, and eventually no royal burial was his j)ortion. The Macedonian monarchy was divided amongst four of his generals.â Midr. Rabba Gen. 33; Lev. 27.; and Tanchuma Emmor, etc.

' Different dates are f iven for the above event. In Sanhed 91. it is given as the 24th of Nisson, and in Taanis as the 25th of Sivon.

The spirits of demons were created on the eve of the sixth day, but before their bodies were formed the Sabbath set in, when rest was proclaimed, and their formation was not consummated.â Gen. Rabba 7.

After Cain had killed Abel, Adam separated from his wife for the space of 130 years, during which time Adam emitted male demons and Eve female demons.â Gen. Rabba 20.

Eve, ' as the mother of all living," was also the mother of demons.â Gen. Rabba 20.

Four things were altered from their former condition in the time of Enos, son of Seth: the mountains became as hard as flint, dead bodies of man commenced to putrefy, which was not the case before; man began to resemble the ape, and demons commenced having power or dominion over man, of which they were deprived before the image of God in man was impaired. â Gen. Rabba 23.

From Adam to Enos man had God's image, then man formed the image of demons.â Gen. Rabba 24.

Noah took demons into the ark and thus preserved their species.â Gen. Rabba 31.

A demon named Shamdon went with Noah to plant the vineyard and made a condition with him (Noah) not to interfere in any way with his work, or he would injure him.â Gen. Rabba 36.

Demons are also known as the ' Hairy ones," as the prophet describes them (Is. 13.).â Gen. Rabba 65.

The flaming revolving swords were placed at the entrance of the Garden of Eden through the agency of demons. The word Jon"? means demoniac agency as well as ' flames." And when we are told that Pharaoh's magicians imitated Moses' performance of miracles Dn"'to'?3, it means that they did this through the agency of demons.â Exod. Rabba 9.

As Pharaoh's magicians worked their imitation of Moses' miracles through demons, they were unable to imitate the third plague, since demons cannot bring forth anything smaller than a barleycorn.â Exod. Rabba 10.

With the crow of the cock announcing the approaching dawn of day, the power of demons diminishes, their power being for the most part confined to night only.â Levit Rabba 5.

Religious men may gain power over demons and subdue them in various ways, as did King Solomon before his fall, before he was led astray by strange women. After his fall, though partly restored to his greatness, he not only had lost his power over demons, but was in terror of them, hence he had need of the sixty mighty men to surround his bed (Songs 3. 7).â Numb. Rabba 11.

The ninety-first psalm was composed by Moses as a sort of talisman or protection against demons whom he feared, when about to ascend Mount Sinai, as putting a stumbling block in his way. Agras, daughter of Machlas, is the name of a female demon who commands a large number of associates or assistants, and there is one great demon whose name is 2Dp (Kativc), in Hebrew ' Arrow." The Psalmist alludes to this when he says, ' The arrow that flieth l:)y day ' (Ps. 91.). This terrible demon has exceptional power l)etwcen the first six and the last nine hours of the twenty-four. His power is greatest neither in the shade, nor in the sun, but in the condition betwixt sun and shade. His physiognomy is described as follows: head similar to that of a calf, one horn rising out of his forehead in the shape of a cruse or a pitcher. No one beholding him, man or beast, can hve, but drops down dead at once, and several instances are given of men who on seeing him fell down dead immediately. There was one, however, Judah son of Samuel, who was proof against falling down at the sight of this demon, but he died shortly afterwards. There is a certain period of the year when this demon has special sway, and that is during the three weeks between the 17th day of Tamuz and the 9th day of Ab. So great indeed is his power for evil during the above-mentioned period, that the Rabbis prohibited the schoolmasters chastising naughty scholars during those days, lest ' Arrow' should avail himself of his propitious season and add mischief of his own to the beaten pupils, and the result should prove fatal. It is comforting to know that during the existence of the 2WD (Mishkan) Tabernacle, demons were removed from this globe because the Shechinah took up its abode in the Mishkan, which was erected by special command and design of the Lord.â Numb. Rabba 12; Midr. on Psalms, Lamentations, and Song of Songs.

There is not so small a space as a yard of ground upon which there are not thousands of demons ready to injure man, but a sort of mask or thick veil is put before their faces, which tends to dim their sight, so that they cannot look clearly at man, and thus injure him by their very stare. When, however, man incurs retribution for his misdeeds, the image of God on him is reduced (or eliminated), and this has the effect of lessening the dimness of the demon's sight, so that he then has the power of injuring man by merely looking at him.â Deut. Rabba 4.

Arginutin is the name of the demon who has dominion over bathing places.â Gen. Rabba 63.

Demons could not exist on earth while the Mishkan stood.â Numb. Rabba 12.

Mcin is above everytliiiigâ even over demons he can have dominionâ but when he falls (by sin), dominion is given over him.â Numb. Rabba 11.

The priestly benediction in which occur the words ll. i: '), ' and keep thee," refers to security from injury by demons.â Numb. Rabba 11.

A woman once sent her child to fetch her a candle. On his way to do her bidding a demon met him, and was alx)ut to inflict injury on him, when lo and behold a cock crowed, announcing the approaching dawn. The demon not only desisted from his pernicious intention, but told the child to inform his mother of the fact that if it were not for the dawn of the day he would not have returned to tell the tale.â Levit. Rabba 5.

Let no man disregard God's behests; they were the wisdom of Solomon, and his safeguard, but as soon as he lost hold of them, terror was his portion, and he was terrified by fear of demons.â Exod. Rabba 30.

The men of the Tower of Babel were divided into three sections in their work and were punished with three different punishments. One section became demons, another had their language confused, and the third were ' cast about."â Midr. Psalms i.

When Esau is styled the ' hairy man," this indicates tiiat he was a demon. The name of demons is ' hairy ones." â Gen. Rabba 65.

That demons themselves do not enjoy immunity from injury by other demons, the following story will illustrate. Rabbi Abba b. Dowsa passed by a well, when he was addressed by a demon, who solicited his and his pupils' help to ward off the attack of a more fierce demon. The demon suggested that the Rabbi and his disciples need do no more than meet at the place, i. e. the well, and when the attacking demon made his appearance his opponent would say to him, See that ' See Dr. Ludwig Philipsohn's Prophet Jeschajah, cap. 13.

there is a number of men waiting to take your life," and he would become so cowed that he would be slain with ease. And so it actually happened.â Midr. Psalms

The following is an instance where a demon rendered excellent service to the Jewish community. Diokletian, when he was tending a herd of pigs, was invariably persecuted by Jewish children, who never missed an opportunity of throwing missiles at him. When he rose to the dignity of king he was bent on having revenge on the Rabbis, who, he supposed, were those who had persecuted him when he and they were but boys. He sent a letter to them late on a Friday to appear before him on the following morning, well knowing that the message would not reach them in time to allow them to make preparation for their appearance without interference with the evening hjmin of the Sabbath. Rabbi Samuel, son of Nachmon, meeting Rabbi Judah Hanasi in the bathing house, saw that he was very sad, and on inquiry, he was told of the sudden summons to the unfriendly king.

Whilst they were conversing, Arginiton, the demon who has dominion over the bathing house, was dancing before them. Rabbi Judah Hanasi, not knowing him, and not being in a mood for dancing, was about to rebuke him, but he was prevented by his colleague (Rabbi Samuel) from doing so. But Rabbi Samuel himself addressed Arginiton, telling him that there was trouble in the community. The demon assured them that all would be well with them and they need not sadden their Sabbath.

When the Sabbath was over Arginiton laid hold of the Rabbis and placed them at the gate of the king's palace. When the latter was informed of their presence he ordered the gates to be fastened, lest the visitors should step inside and afterwards plead that they were there in good time, but had to wait for admission; but as the gate was being fastened the demon placed the Rabbis within. When the king was informed of this amazing fact, he concluded that miracles were performed for them, and when they came before him, his anger was considerably softened. Instead of dealing hardly with them, he began to converse about olden times, asking how it was that they used to treat him so contemptuously. They answered, Diokletian the swineherd was treated indifferently, but for Diokletian the great king there can be nothing but the utmost respect. The king dismissed them with a mild rebuke.â Gen. Rabba 63.

Demons offered their services to King Solomon in the erection of the Temple.â Song of Songs Rabba i.

After King Solomon had ascended his father's throne, he called all his counsellors together one day and addressed them as follows: ' As the wise and distinguished men of the people, you cannot but recognize that the time has now come when I have to discharge a deferred debt, which has been left to me as a legacy by my illustrious father, King David. It is the building of a Temple to the glory and worship of the Most High God, which would gladly have been undertaken by my father were it not for the message he received through Nathan the Prophet, that it was not to be he himself but his son and successor who should undertake the work.

I now desire to discharge that holy duty and to erect a structure worthy of its exalted purpose, and consecrate it to Almighty God. The condition of things is propitious; peace rules supreme, there is no lack of ways and means, and Hiram of Tyre has, in fact, already received instructions to fell cedars in Labonon, and marble and stone is also ready in abundance. But it requires your wise counsel to enable the building to proceed without the use of any iron. It would not be proper to employ an element of destruction in the erection of a structure which is to be dedicated to peace and harmony." At the end of the king's speech, the members of the Court looked at one another in perplexity for a while; then they began:â ' Wise King and Ruler! Moses, our teacher of blessed memory, found himself in similar perplexity when he wanted to engrave the names on the Ephod, but the Spirit of God enlightened him, and he soon found the marvellous worm called " Shomir," which possesses the wonderful power of cutting the hardest object known by a touch. If, O Glorious King! you succeed in obtaining that wonderful insect, you will have no need of iron or any element of destruction in the erection of the house which you wish to consecrate to the Most High God, and dedicate as the emblem of peace and harmony.

The king's countenance brightened at this information, and, lifting up his eyes heavenwards, he said, ' Verily, O God of Israel, thou hast granted wisdom and knowledge to my people Israel! You, my friends, have given me new life and fresh spirit. Now, can you tell me where the wonderful insect is to be found, so that I may have it brought and may utilize its power? ' ' That, mighty ruler," replied the wise men, ' is beyond our ken, and we doubt whether it is within the knowledge of any mortal man. It is supposed that the " Shomir " has its home in wild and desolate places which have never been traversed by human foot. We are therefore not able to comply with your wish, but if you have the advice of a male and female demon who traverse those wastes, we doubt not that they will be able to throw more light on this dark mystery."

Solomon then sent to Sichon, the rendezvous of demons, had a male and female demon brought before him, and addressed them as follows: ' It is said of you that you have a knowledge of mysteries which we do not possess. Tell me, therefore, where I could obtain that wonderful insect known as " Shomir "? '

They replied, ' We are aware of the existence of the marvellous " Shomir," but are unable to give anything like a near description of its abode; that is only known to our king and great master, Ashmedai. He alone would be able to gratify your wish." ' And," said

Solomon, ' where is the abode of your king and great master? ' His home," was the answer, ' is on a high mountain, far, very far, from Jerusalem, in a lovely and beautiful spot. There he has a well filled with cold clear water, covered with a wooden slab, sealed with his seal. Every day he leaves his terrestrial abode and flies heavenwards to hear the songs of the angels, who sing praises to the Great God.

Being refreshed with the heavenly hymns, he searches through the heavens, and casts his eyes on the various spheres within his view, and towards evening he returns to his abode. Arriving there, he looks carefully at the seal of his well to see that it has not been tampered with, and, finding it all right, he lifts the slab and refreshes himself with the cooling and refreshing liquid.

' More than this, O mighty king, we are not permitted to impart to you concerning our king and master." For a long time King Solomon allowed his eyes to wander about his great room, and at last fixed them on a youth amongst the assemblyâ a youth of powerful frame and lovely appearance, and with an expression of the most resolute and keenest spirit in his countenance.

' Benaihu, son of Jehoiada," exclaimed the king, ' long have I known you as the most courageous in all my legions! See now what a magnificent opportunity there is offered to you to prove the truth of the opinion I have formed of you. Will you venture to bring Ashmedai as a captive to me, and by such heroic deed not only to make yourself a hero amongst your people, but to do a great service to the holy cause of your religion? ' 'I will venture," cried the youth, ' any task your majesty may honour me with," his eyes shining brightly with delight. ' God be with you," said the king; ' He knows that we do all this to glorify His name; may He guide you and bless your undertaking." Benaihu left the assembly, and at his orders a chain was given to him upon every link of which was engraved the unspeakable name of God in the Chaldean language. He also ordered for his journey a large quantity of lambs' wool, spades and shovels, and a pipe of the most exquisite wine of the vines of ' Bal Hamon," a famous vineyard, the property of King Solomon.

Thus equipped, Benaihu staitcd with a few followers on the perilous expedition. After a long and adventurous journey through the desert, he reached the lovely spot on the mountain which was the home of Ashmedai. On the top of the mountain grew a cluster of lovely palms, on which an eternal summer seemed to rest. At its foot ran a clear brook, teeming with fish of all sorts; on the slope of the mountain could be seen the well of the great Ashmedai, as described by the two demons.

Benaihu mused a long while, then he said to his followers: ' My friends, we have now reached our destination, but not our aim. Now let us bear in mind that muscular power is now of no use to us when we have to deal with the master of demons, but God has granted us discernment and understanding, and with these divine gifts it should not be impossible to prevail over the mighty king of the demons. If only we contrive to empty his well of the water and fill it with the wine we have brought with us, then our task is an easy one; but to effect this is a formidable difficulty, because we must not lift the slab and break the seal, or we defeat our purpose."

He then commenced, during Ashmedai's absence, to dig a jnt under the well, and connected the two by boring a small tunnel, so that the water from Ashmedai's well ran into the newly made pit, then stopped up the small tunnel completely with the lamb's wool; then a similar jiit was dug above the well, and also connected with Ashmedai's well. The wine was poured in here, and found its way into the well. After this he had every possible trace of the fresh digging removed, and ordered his companions to go away from the place, but he climbed up one of the many palm trees, and sat there to watch events. When the shadows of the evening lengthened there was a fiery flush through the skies, and there came with it a monstrous creature with black wings, which gradually let itself down to the earth.

Ashmedai, for he it was, looked long on the seal of the well, and finding it untouched, broke it, lifted up the slab, and was about to refresh himself with the contents of the well. When he detected that it contained wine instead of the refreshing liquid which he had husbanded, he turned in disgust from it, exclaiming, ' Wine is a mocker, and every intoxicant confuses the senses. No! your flattering sweetness shall not lead me astray; as well would I suffer the tortures of un-quenched thirst as have your exquisite taste upon my palate." But after a while Ashmedai could not any longer withstand his craving for some liquid, if only to moisten his lips, and he said to himself, ' If I only sip at the accursed stuff it will have no power over me. I will touch of it no more than is sufficient to moisten my burning tongue." He drank at first very sparingly, but it was very, very sweet, and it seemed to give him a brightness and freshness he had never experienced before. ' Only a little, a very little more,' he said, ' not sufficient to overmaster me." But this very little was followed by few more ' very littles," till he became quite intoxicated, and fell asleep. This was quite satisfactory to the concealed young hero, who, climbing down from his hiding place, went cautiously forward until he reached the sleejiing demon, over whose neck he threw the chain with the name of God engraved on every link.

Ashmedai slept till the early hours of the morning, when he found himself heavily fettered, scarcely able tu turn round on his bed. He looked for heavy manacles, but found only a fragile chain round his neck, which he could not credit with such immense power. He tried his utmost to snap the frail thing, but without success.

He roared terribly, so that the very air was filled with the violent noise. ' O set me free; who will set me free from this hellish burden? ' ' No one," came the answer from the hitherto hidden Benaihu; ' all your efforts are fniitless; you are fettered, not indeed with iron manacles, only with a chain of softer metals, but that has the name of God engraved on it, and in the name of God you are my captive." Ashmedai, on hearing Benaihu's words, became quiet and resigned to his situation. One of Benaihu's men was ordered to take charge of him, and like a tamed lion he was led forth. Ashmcdai's concealed courage exhibited itself now and then on the journey towards Jerusalem. As they passed one day a gigantic palm tree, he asked for a rest under its shade, and when this was granted, he rubl)ed himself so violently against it that it was uprooted. Thereupon he passed a hut, the property of a poor widow, and was about to demolish it, when the woman, seeing the giant about to lean against the frail walls of her home, prevailed upon him to spare her hut.

One day they met a blind man who became entangled amongst some bushes and could not find his way out. Ashmedai took the man by the hand, and led him out of his perplexed situation into the highway. So also they met a man in his cups, who was nearing a precipice into which he was about to fall, when his demoniac majesty hastened to get him out of danger's way and l)laced him in a safe road. They passed one day through a town where he heard a man calling out to a shoemaker, ' Heda, friend, can j'ou make me a pair of boots to last me seven years? ' Ashmedai burst out laughing at this. They met also a wedding party, with music accompanying them. Ashmedai wept. They saw a wizard sitting on a large stone telling a patronizing clientele their future fate, and again Ashmedai laughed. Benaihu was curious to know the motives of the demon's conduct, but he could not be persuaded to explain himself, and said he reserved the explanation for King Solomon himself. When they arrived in Jerusalem, Benaihu brought his captive triumphantly before Solomon, who was sitting on his throne surrounded by his counsellors and elders. At the entrance of Ashmedai they rose from their magnificent divans. Ashmedai, however, in great excitement and anger took a long staff, and marking round himself a space of four yards in circumference, and pointing to King Solomon, exclaimed, ' Look at this man, a king of dust and ashes! When he dies, nothing will be his beyond a space of earth the size of which I have just marked out, yet he is not satisfied to have subjected all his neighbours and all the kingdoms as his tributaries, but he must needs try to wrench the sceptre from the king of the spirits. Otherwise, why have you, O great king, brought such contempt and dismay upon me? ' 'Be not angry with me," returned Solomon, ' king of spirits, and be assured that conquest is not the object of your captivity. It is a matter appertaining to the glory of my God, who is also your God. Tell me, then, where I can obtain the marvellous " Shomir," of which I have need to cleave the marble and stones for the House of God." ' If that is the object," returned Ashmedai, pacified and reassured by Solomon's reconciling words, ' then I willingly submit to my hard fate, and will also tell you where and how to obtain the much-sought " Shomir." The " Shomir " belongs to the lord over all seas and waters, but he has entrusted it for safe keeping to a mountain-bird in the desert. This bird is to be found in the desert on a very steep, barren hill; there in a cliff it has bored out a hole, and keeps the " Shomir," which was created in the evening of the sixth day of creation, before the Sabbath was proclaimed."

The services of the young hero Benaihu were again called into requisition. Solomon addressed the youth with his wonted eloquence, referring to the services he had rendered in the past, and entertaining no doubt of the hero's willingness to render this consummate national sersnce of obtaining the ' Shomir," the reward for which his royal master would not bestow niggardly or grudgingly.

Benaihu replied by a profound bow before his majesty, and left the palace to prepare at once for his hazardous journey. There is no need for details of the hardships the young hero had to encounter on his journey, where there was not a blade of grass, a drop of water, or a shade for shelter from the merciless rays of the scorching sun, nor is it necessary to relate all his adventures, and all the subtle designs adopted to wrest the ' Shomir ' from its guard. Suffice it to say that the hardships and adventures of our hero were rewarded by success, and the ' Shomir ' was at last in Jerusalem. Needless to say, there was great joy and festivity in the Holy City, and the work (which lasted seven years) now began in earnest, that of erecting, without iron or any other metal, a structure for the worship of the God of Israelâ a structure which was the admiration of the world, and which has never been equalled in majesty and splendour.

Ashniedai, the mighty king of demons, was all these years held captive by Solomon in Jerusalem. He was very desirous to be informed by the chief of the demons concerning the mystic spheres, but during the building of the Temple he was too much occupied with the sacred business to be able to spare time for anything else. After the consecration of the holy edifice, Solomon had Ashmedai brought before him, and explained the reason of his prolonged captivity, requesting him at the same time, first of all, to explain to him his inexphcable conduct whilst on the way to Jerusalem. ' What, for instance, prompted you to guide the blind man into safety, when he was entangled in a bush? Surely it could not have been compassion, a virtue to which a demon is a stranger? ' Ashmedai replied, ' That blind man is a most pious and righteous man, and I heard it proclaimed in the higher spheres that great reward should be his who should render that man a service."

' And why did you lead the drunken man into the road away from the precipice into which he was walking? ' That man," said Ashmedai, ' is very wicked, and if he deserves any reward for ever having done anything but evil, he should receive it here on earth." ' And what provoked your laughter when you heard a man inquire for boots to last him seven years? ' ' Simply," said the master of demons, ' that the man had but seven days more on earth." ' Why did you weep on meeting a bridal party with their music? ' ' Mighty King of Israel," exclaimed Ashmedai, ' this very moment the last shred of flesh is gnawed off the bones of that bridegroom; he died five days after I met the wedding party." ' Last of all," demanded Solomon, ' what was the cause of your laughter on seeing the wizard with the people who consulted him? ' ' Why should I not laugh when I saw a stupid person who professed to remove the veil of the hidden future, whilst he knew not that under the stone on which he was sitting there was hidden a kingly treasure? '

Demons resembk man in these respects, they eat and drink, are fruitful and multiply, and die. But they also somewhat resemble angels in so far as they have wings, flying to and fro all the world over like angels, and knowing a little of the secrets of the higher spheresâ not quite as much as angels, but generally the fate of men is known to them. Talmud. Chagiga 4t. Hence Ashmedai knew the fate of those he met on his way to Jerusalem.

King Solomon now intimated by a gesture that he wished to be left alone with the king of the demons, and all his counsellors, ministers, and high officials surrounding his throne left the palatial room. When the king was alone with Ashmedai he addressed him as follows: ' The fact that I carefully excluded all my advisers from hearing what there is between us will have shown you that I have an important matter upon which I crave information from you. I therefore want you, 0 Ashmedai, whose power is infinitely above mine, because you know what is going on in the higher as well as in the lower spheres, to tell me my own future." Ashmedai betrayed a satirical smile and said, 'It is perhaps not to be wondered at that a monarch as wise and mighty on earth as you are, who has acquired almost all the knowledge that it is possible for a mortal man to possess, should long for knowledge of the supernatural from the region of the unseen; but I must advise you to desist from this ambition: it will not be of any use or pleasure to you." ' No," insisted Solomon, ' nothing will induce me to abstain from increasing my knowledge, for it is that, and not silver or gold, that I have set my heart upon." ' If my advice is to no purpose," said Ashmedai, ' I will proceed to open for you the hidden secrets, but it will be necessary to release me from the chain I had put round me when I was made captive, and you will, instead, have to give me the chain that adorns your majesty's neck, and the ring with the name of God on it, which lies on the table before you."

Solomon did as suggested, took off his chain and jiut it on Ashmedai's neck, and placed the ring on his hand. Scarcely had the master of the demons closed his hand on the ring handed him by Solomon when a thunder clap passed through the room which made the whole place vibrate. At the same moment Ashmedai seemed to have grown into a terrible giant, his eyes looked like two great gleaming fires, his arms extended to enormous proportions, and looked as though they would catch hold of the extreme ends of the earth. Solomon trembled at the sight, his heart seemed to stand still from terror, and he was about to call for help; but his whole body was paralysed, his tongue refused its duty, and in the midst of this he was seized by Ashmedai by arm and neck and thrown into the air, and he became senseless. The men who had quitted the throne room at King Solomon's bidding were all the time impatiently awaiting the summons back to their king and master, but they remained in the ante-room longer than they ever had to wait, when at last they received the glad tidings, and the monarch summoned them to his presence. They found, on entering the throne room, King Solomon sitting as usual on his throne. They expressed their surprise at the absence of Ashmedai, whom they had left in the room on retiring, but no answer was vouchsafed to them. The king, however, took up the thread of conversation on the subject upon which he was consulting when they retired from the room. Yet they detected a marked change in the tone of the king's words, which lacked that mildness and gentleness for which the wise Solomon was so renowned.

Some of the ministers ventured to ask his majesty for the reason of this change, but, instead of a reply, they received a sardonic laugh. It occurred to some of the wise men that this might not be King Solomon, but Ashmedai, the king of demons, who usurped their monarch's position; but who could give expression to that dreadful thought?

King Solomon had been thrown by Ashmedai no less a distance than four hundred miles from Jerusalem. For a long time he laj in the open field, unconscious; as consciousness returned and he opened his eyes, he took in the situation, but happily his wisdom had not failed, amongst his other great qualities, to bestow on him the habit of practising abstinence in the midst of his splendour, and he occasionally used to subject himself to actual hunger, and deprive himself of the necessaries of life, so as to cultivate the habit of wanting things and not having them.

He now made up his mind to face his great calamity in the best way possible, and resolved that, if need were, he would be bent, but not broken totally by it. As a beggar he traversed the land over which he had ruled with such splendour and power, and he was often thrown on the mercy of one of his humblest subjects. Yet in the midst of this great sorrow he proclaimed himself, wherever he came, the great ' Koheleth," King of Jerusalem.

No wonder that he was everywhere looked upon as insane! But he struggled hard to make his way to Jerusalem, which he eventually reached, and on his arrival at his metropolis he asked to be brought before the Sanhedrin. He repeated to the Sanhedrin his assertion that he was King Solomon, and related to them all the events that had happened to him. His statement was received by the Sanhedrin, if not with derision, still, with great mistrust and incredulit ', and they were about to declare him insane, when one of the Sanhedrin, wiser and bolder than the others, rose and spoke as follows: ' Friends and worthy colleagues, whom the Lord has graced with wisdom and understanding, it will not be difficult for you to comprehend that any one afflicted with insanity would not be able to make so coherent a statement as we have now heard, but would wander about in his assertions incoherently from one subject to another. Now, this man who asserts himself to be King Solomon, has not spoken one incoherent word, and has given no indication of his insanity, except his assertion in general that he is the gre t king our master, and that assertion he made coherently enough. Besides this, there is no reason whatever, either in his demeanour, gesture or speech, to condemn him as insane. Would it be consistent with justice, as shown to us by our Great Lawgiver, to conclude that this man is insane, simply because he claims the throne as his own, without further investigation as to who is the one who now occupies the throne as King Solomon? Moreover, can we overlook the fact that when we left the throne room there were two individuals, and when we returned one had disappeared, without our being able to comprehend how that happened? My advice is, that we request Topos, one of King Solomon's many wives, that when the present king pays her a visit, she may notice his feet, and then on her report on this you can form your judgment in this matter." The Sanhedrin fell in with this suggestion, and when they appealed to Topos, she reported that the king, her husband, never entered her chamber without a cover over his feet. The Sanhedrin requested her to try and remove the covering from her husband's feet at the next opportunity. Topos did as requested by the Sanhedrin, and reported that, to her amazement and disgust, she found her husband's feet to resemble those of a cock.

The Sanhedrin were now concerned to have Ashmedai stripped of the chain and the ring by which he had subtly obtained the throne from King Solomon. In this they succeeded through a confidential servant of the demon, and these precious and holy things were handed over to the rightful owner, the real King Solomon, who now re-entered upon his glorious throne. The wise king had the chief of the demons brought before him, and exhibited to him the chain and the ring. The demon, amidst a peal of thunder, made his escape from the palace, and was seen no more.

Solomon was again in his former greatness, but was 1 The Rabbis say that the feet of demons resemble those of a cock.

till the end of his days in terror of demons; hence he had sixty of the most valiant men of his army surrounding his bed.â Midr. Rabba Gen. 7 and 36; Exod. 30; Num. 5 and 11; Lament. 3; Ruth, Eccles., and Song of Songs, and Midr. Tanchuma Emmor and Midr. Psalms 78.

Of the six things which existed before creation, when only ' the spirit of God moved upon the face of the waters," two, the Torah and the throne of God, were complete in every detail. The remaining four, however, viz., the Patriarchs, Israel, the Temple, and the name of Messiah, existed prior to the creation only in an incomplete form.â Gen. Rabba i.

From the time of creation constant reference is made in Holy Writ to Messiah and the Messianic hope of Israel. ' The Spirit of God moved upon the face of the waters '; the Spirit of God means Messiah.â Gen. Rabba 2; also Levit. Rabba 14.

When Eve at the birth of Seth exclaimed, ' God hath appointed me another seed." her underlying thought was the King Messiah.â Gen. Rabba 23.

He who knows how long the Israelites worshipped idols can learn therefrom when the Son of Davidâ Messiahâ will come. Three different prophets tell us this: (i) ' Like as you have forsaken Me, and served strange gods in your land, so shall ye serve strangers in a land that is not yours ' (Jer. 5. 19); (2) ' And I will visit her the days of Baahm," etc., (Hos. 2. 13); (3)' Yea, they made their hearts as an adamant stone lest they should hear the law, and the words which the Lord hath sent in his spirit by the prophets. Therefore it is come to pass that as he cried and they would not hear, so they cried and I would not hear, saith the Lord ' (Zech. 7. 12, 13).â Lament. Rabba i.

The great mountain spoken of by the prophet

Zechariah (4. 7) is no other than Messiah, Son of David, and he is called ' the Great Mountain," because lie towers above the Patriarchs, is greater than Moses, and is above the ministering angels. As Isaiah says 52. 10), ' Behold, my servant shall deal prudently, he shall be exalted and extolled and be very high."â Midr. Tan-chuma Toldos.

The word "Jlin (Hadrach), used by the prophet Zechariah (9.1), is one of the titles of Messiah. It is connected with the word ITT (leading), and is therefore applied to him who will lead man to repentance.â Midr. Song of Songs 7.

The ' four carpenters' to whom the prophet also refers, are Elijah, Melchizedek, the Messiah of war, called by some Messiah son of Joseph, and the true Messiah. These Messiahs are referred to in the 32nd chapter of Isaiah, and their existence is constantly mentioned. Seven or eight Messiahs are sometimes said to be promised in the words of the Prophet Micah (5- 5) ' Then shall we raise against him seven shepherds and eight principal men," but it is held that there will be but four (Zech. i. 20), and these are they: Elijah the Tishbite, an unnamed man of the tribe of Manasseh, Messiah of warâ an Ephraimite, and Messiah the Great, the descendant of David.â Midr. Song of Songs 2.

Two of King David's descendants were destined for universal dominion: King Solomon and King Messiah, to whom David refers in his seventy-second Psalm.â Numb. Rabba 13.

The whole of the 27th chajiter of Isaiah refers to the Messiah.â Exod. Rabba i.

Solomon's Song has also reference to Messiah. ' The voice of the turtle is heard in our land ' means the voice of Messiah.â Midr. Song of Songs 2.

When King Solomon speaks of his ' beloved," he usually means Israel the nation. In one instance he compares his beloved to a roe, ar. d therein he refers to a feature which marks alike Moses and the Messiah, the two redeemers of Israel. Just as a roe comes within the range of man's vision only to disappear from sight and then appear again, so it is with these redeemers. Moses appeared to the Israelites, then disappeared, and eventually appeared once more, and the same peculiarity we have in connexion with Messiah; He will appear, disappear, and appear again. â Numb Rabba ii.

The fourteenth verse in the second chapter of Ruth is thus explained. ' Come thou hither' is the prediction of Messiah's kingdom. ' Dip the morsel in the vinegar,' foretells the agony through which Messiah will pass, as it is written in Isaiah (cap. 53.), ' He was wounded for our sins, He was bruised for our transgressions." ' And she set herself beside the reapers ' predicts the temporary departure of Messiah's kingdom ' And he reached her a parched corn ' means the restoration of His kingdom.â Midr. Ruth 5.

To three individuals God said, ' Ask, and it shall be given to thee." These are Solomon, Ahaz, and Messiah, to the last of whom it was promised, ' Ask of Me, and I shall give Thee the heathens for Thine inheritance."â Gen. Rabba 44.

In a similar strain we read, Israel is to overcome ten of the heathen nations of the world; seven of them have already been conquered; the remaining three will fall at the advent of Messiah.â Gen. Rabba 44. But, despite all this, Messiah will not come till all those who are to be created have made their appearance in the world.â Gen. Rabba 24.

In tracing the descent and history of the Israelites, the Bible enumerates the generations of the heads of the families of the earth whose history touched that of the chosen people. ' These are the generations of the heavens and the earth' is the first instance of the use of the word Jin'?")D in such a connexion. If regard be had to the Hebrew text of the verse, it will be found that here the word referred to is written in full, i. e. spelt Jin"?"!!, with the additional whilst in all other places whore the word occurs the word is always spelt with one "I, thus, mi':'!. This, it will be found, is the invariable usage until we come to, ' Now these are the generations of Perez ' (Ruth 4. 18). Here we once again find the word nn"?!! spelt in full. These are the only two instances in the whole of the Bible. The first refers to the time before the sin and fall of Adam, which brought death into the world, and, in consequence, all succeeding mi' n, ' generations," were deprived of some of the possibihtics of life, and this is indicated by the omission of the 1. But the enumeration of the descendants of Perez. bringing appreciably nearer the promised abohtion of death through the agency of his descendant, the Messiah, is hailed as the occasion to celebrate the restoration to perfect man of what he had lost through the imperfection of the first of his kind, and hence the word Jin' in is here spelt in full.â Exod. Rabba 30.

A similar deduction is made with reference to the spelling of the word Dmli? ' he-goats." Each of the princes of Israel brought as a sacrifice at the dedication of the tabernacle five he-goats. This word is spelt without the 1, thus, Dnli, in all the numerous repetitions of the details of the offerings, which are identically the same in all instances. There is but one exception, and that is (Numb. 7. 17) in the account of the offerings brought by Nachshon, son of Aminadab, because from him were to spring six (the numerical value of 1) of the great men of Israel, who were each to be distinguished by six special attributes. The Messiah and his ancestor David are among the six, and Isaiah thus enumerates the six distinguishing traits in the character of the descendant of Jesse, whose coming he foretells. ' And there shall rest upon him (i) the

Spirit of the Lord, (2) the Spirit of wisdom and understanding, (3) the Spirit of counsel, (4) and might, (5) the Spirit of knowledge, and (6) the Spirit of the Lord."â Numb. Rabba 13.

Abraham, Job, Hezekiah, and Messiah found God out for themselves without being previously instructed.â Numb. Rabba 14.

The great gifts of God, of which Adam was deprived by reason of his sin and fallâ light being one of themâ will all be restored through Messiah, who will appear from the North and rebuild the Temple in the South.â Numb. Rabba 13.

The prophecy of Isaiah concerning Jerusalem, ' Behold, thy sons shall come from afar and thy daughters shall be nursed by thy side," could not be hailed with the same satisfaction as the words of Zechariah, ' Behold, thy King cometh unto thee; he is just and having salvation, lonely and riding upon an ass." This latter prophecy will bring it about that the daughter of Zion shall greatly rejoice in the Lord, her soul shall be joyful in her God.â Midr. Song of Songs i.

So greatly shall Zion rejoice and so glorious will be the restoration of the Temple service in the days of Messiah, that three additional strings will be required besides the seven that were formerly upon the harps used by the Levites. In this way only will it be possible for the whole people to give expression to the depths of reverence for their God that shall then stir their hearts.â Numb. Rabba 15. and Tanchuma Behaloscho.

It was indeed pre-ordained that Jerusalem should be lost to the Israelites, but only until the coming of him concerning whom it was said, ' Rejoice greatly, O daughter of Zion."â Gen. Rabba 56.

And so the destruction of Jerusalem is to be looked upon as an event bringing joy in its train rather than as an irreparable loss or sorrow, for through it the coming of the Messiah and consequent expiation of

Israel's sin were rendered possible. For, just as all sacrifices were formerly brought to Jenisalem, so in future shall messengers come with offerings to Messiah, and all kings sliall prostrate themselves before him.â Midr. Esther i.

As you brought Me the perpetual light in the Temple, says God unto Israel, so will I bring unto you Him, Messiah, who is the personification of light, ' the sun of righteousness ' promised through Malachi.â Midr. Tan-chuma Tetzava.

Our father Abraham, by his meritorious life, won for himself the blessing. ' Tell the stars, if thou art able to number them," He said unto him; ' so shall be thy children." Isaac's ready compliance with God's demand to sacrifice his life evoked the promise, ' I will multiply thy seed as the stars of heaven." Jacob was heartened with the prospect, ' And thy seed shall be as the dust of the earth." That which God promised to Abraham He has already fulfilled in that Moses was able to address to his people the words, ' The Lord your God hath multiplied you, and behold, you are this day as the stars of heaven for multitude."

Balaam was constrained to acknowledge the impossibility of ' counting the dust of Jacob," and it might seem as if the prophet Hosea looked fonvard to the speedy reahzation of the promise made to Isaac when he gave utterance to the sentiment, ' Yet the number of the children of Israel shall be as the sand of the sea, which cannot be measured or numbered." The fulfilment, however, will not come about until the time of the Messiah, when the heathen shall be altogether absorbed and God will pour out His Spirit upon all flesh.â Numb. Rabba 2.

The honour and majesty with which David tells us (Ps. 104.) that God is clothed, He will bestow on Messiah. As it is said, ' His glory is great in Thy salvation, honour and majesty hast Thou laid upon Him."â Numb. Rabba 14.

Seeing in his spirit of prophecy that the time would come when the Dti Q, ' Mishkan ' (the Sanctuary) would cease to exist and the Shechinah dwell no more in Israel's midst, Moses was anxious to know by what means the sins of his people would then be expiated. The Almighty vouchsafed the information that He would choose a righteous man from their midst, and make him a 21 f2 (pledge) for them, and through him their sins would be forgiven.â Exod. Rabba 35.

The prophets formerly recorded the good deeds performed by man, but now Elijah and Messiah record them and God puts His seal on the record.â Levit. Rabba 34.

' Fear not, Abraham; I am thy shield and thine exceeding great reward," refers to the glorious epoch of Messiah. The Patriarch was apprehensive lest the covenant made with him might not prove lasting because of the sins of his descendants. God here gave him the assurance that, though his descendants fall into sin, there shall be one great and noble amongst them, who will be qualified to say to the avenging angel, ' Stay thy hand." ' Him will I accept and he shall be a pledge for my people."â Midr. Song of Songs i.

' The sceptre shall not depart from Judah nor a lawgiver from between his feet until " Shiloh " come," refers also to Messiah, who is to enlighten Israel on the words of the Torah, and point out the errors of the people. Rabbi Chanan, on the other hand, holds that the teaching of Messiah will not be addressed to Israel, whose knowledge of the law of God will be all-sufficient. Rather will his task be to instruct the Gentiles: in the words of the prophet Isaiah (11. 10), ' To him shall the Gentiles seek, and he shall assemble the outcast of Israel."â Gen. Rabba 98.

The faithful of Israel are desirous of sepulture in the land of Palestine because, at the advent of Messiah, the resurrection will take place there before any other part of the world, but that will be the resurrection of the righteous only.â Gen. Rabba 96.

The general resurrection of the dead is appointed for the day of judgment, and when it takes place the revived souls will sing angelic songs.â Midr. Eccles. i.

The death of the righteous is even like the Day of Atonement, in that each secures forgiveness for the sins of Israel.â Levit. Rabba 20.

A time has been appointed by God for the coming of Messiah. Yet if Israel but repent his sins, the glorious redemption will be hastened, and Messiah will make His appearance before the appointed time.â Exod. Rabba 25.

Great indeed will be the time of the approaching advent of Messiah. The wicked will be trodden dow n as ashes under the feet of the righteous, the trees will send forth their fragrance, and concerning the righteous it will be said, ' He that is left in Zion and he that remaineth in Jerusalem shall be called holy."

The seven years preceding the coming of the Son of David will be distinguished by the following signs: The first year rain will be scarce and partial; in the second year pangs of hunger will be felt; during the third year a severe famine will be experienced, and many human beings will die; men of renown and piety will jierish, so that the Torah will be forgotten in Israel. This famine will be the last of the ten predestined for the world; the other nine occurred during the lives of Adam, Lemech, Abraham, Isaac, Jacob, Elijah, Ehsha, the Judges, and King David. The fourth year will be marked neither by famine nor by plenty, but the fifth year will be one of prosperity, when the earth will bring forth abundance. There will then be joy in all parts of the earth, and a revival of study and knowledge of the Torah will be noticeable in the ranks of Israel. The sixth year will be full of rumours of war, and the seventh year will see the actual dread visitation of war. After all these signs have come to j)ass, at the end of the seventh year, the Son of David will make His appearance. According to other opinions, prior to the coming of Messiah the world will be terribly corrupt; there will be no compassion amongst men, great derision and contempt for the Torah and for piety will be universal, and truth will be almost unknown. Men will be as shameless of their evil doings as the very animals, and the few righteous who still exist will be in exceeding great distress. Persecution will be rife everywhere, the youth will have no respect for the aged, so that the aged will even rise before the presence of the young. The daughter will rebel against her mother, and a man's worst enemies will be those of his own household. The reigning powers will become infidel, and none will be found to raise his voice in protest, so that mankind will seem to merit nought but extermination. If, therefore, we behold the generations becoming ever more corrupt, there is therein good reason to anticipate the advent of Messiah.â Midr. Song of Songs 2.

The ndli (' Zemach '), mentioned by Jeremiah (23. 5) and by Zechariah (6. 12) is the Messiah.â Numb. Rabba 18.

Unlike the kings of this earth, God bestows some of His possessions and dignities upon beings of flesh and blood. He set Solomon upon His own throne (i Chron, 29. 23). He caused Elijah to ride upon His own horse; that is to say, upon the storm and whirlwind. To Moses He gave God's rod, and upon the head of Messiah He placed His own crown.â Exod. Rabba 8. and Tanchuma Voera.

Many and varied are the things that in the Bible are designated ' the first." The month of the Egyptian exodus God named the first month of the year (Exod. 12. 2). He revealed Himself as ' the first' to the prophet Isaiah (44. 6). Zion, too, is styled ' the first' (Jer. 17). Of Esau also the epithet is used (Gen. 25.) And, lastly, Messiah is mentioned as ' the first' (Isa.

41. 27). There is this intimate connexion between thcni, that God, who is the lirst, will rebuild Zion the first, and bring retribution on Esau ( = Romc), known as the first, at the time of the advent of Messiah the first, in the month =Nissan) which was appointed as the first.â Exod. Rabba 15.

Five things brought about the redemption of the Israelites from Egypt: (i) The sufferings of the people; (2) their repentance; (3) the merits of their ancestors; (4) the expiration of the time fixed for their captivity; (5) the mercy of their God. These same causes will operate towards the realization of Israel's Messianic hopes and lead to the last redemption through Messiah. â Deut. Rabba 2.

There will be a great difference between the Egyptian and the last redemption. ' When you were delivered from Egypt," says God to Israel, ' you had to depart in haste; at the last deliverance you shall not go in haste nor by flight, (Isa. 52. 12). At the Egyptian deliverance I, in my manifestation, went before you (Exod. 13. 21). At the last deliverance ' the Lord will go before you and the God of Israel will be your reward." (Isa. 52. 12).â Exod. Rabba ig.

' All your former redemptions," God says to Israel, have been accomplished through the instrumentality of men, and were, consequently, not lasting in their effect. You were delivered from Egypt through Moses and Aaron; you were rescued out of the hands of Sisera by Deborah and Barak; from the power of Midian you were saved by Shamgar. I myself will be your last and your everlasting Redeemer."â Tanchuma Achray.

Great chariots, precious stones and other valuable gifts will the nations bring to Messiah. This means that the nations will bring Israel as a present to Messiah. â Midr. Song of Songs 4.

Just as Juilali, though not the eldest, hail always precedence of Reuben and the other tribes (as is to be seen in various parts of the Bible â Numbers 2. 3, 2. 9, 7. 12; Judges i. 2, 20. 18), so he will have precedence in announcing the coming of Messiah, as foretold by the prophet Nahum (i. 15).â Numb. Rabba 2.

To Judah were revealed all the great men and what will happen to them from the time of Jacob till the coming of Messiah.â Numb. Rabba 13,

The perpetual light in the Mishkan was typical of the light of King Messiah.â Levit. Rabba 31.

All the gifts which Jacob felt himself constrainedâ out of fearâ to present to Esau, will be restored to Israel at the advent of Messiah.â Gen. Rabba 75.

Moses, the first redeemer, rode on an ass, gave the Israelites manna for food, and brought up the water. So also shall Messiah be seen riding on an ass (Zech. 9), shall bring down manna from on high (Ps. 70. 16), and cause the rivers of Judah to flow with water (Joel 4. 18). â Midr. Eccles. i.

' The envy of Ephraim shall depart and the adversaries of Judah shall be cut off' (Isa. 11. 13). That means that amongst the Jews themselves, at the time of Messiah, there will be perfect peace and harmony.â Tanchuma Vayeegash.

There is no redemption without faith.â Tanchuma Beshallach.

Three things Israel despised, viz., the kingdom of heaven, the kingdom of the house of David, and the Temple, and God withholds His blessings from them till they mend their ways in these things. That they will do so the prophet Hosea (3. 5) tells us. ' Afterwards shall the children of Israel return and seek their God ' means that they will again accept the kingdom of heaven, ' and David their king' obviously means the formerly rejected House of David, ' and shall fear the Eternal and his goodness' refers to the Temple.â Midr. Samuel 13.

Messiah will be asked which place He selects as His residence. His reply will be, ' Need you ask Me? Surely Zion, my holy mountain."â Midr. Samuel 19.

Amongst the various names of Messiah, who was born on the day on which the Temple was destroyed, is that of " hi D;; p DH D (Menachem ben Amiel).â Numb. Rabba 13.

The proper name of Messiah is IJplii 'n (the Lord our righteousness).â Midr. Lament, i.

It is neither desirable nor consistent with the teachings of Judaism, or with present day sentiment, to make attacks or adverse reflections on any rehgious creed. But, while disclaiming any desire to provoke theological controversy, or to accentuate religious differences, I should like to append a few observations to this collection of excerpts from the Midrash on the subject of Messiah.

What impels me to do this is the existence of organizations for the conversion of the Jews to Christianity, and the possibihty of attempts being made to make capital out of some of the Rabbinic passages which I have cited.

It has been my privilege to come into contact with many Christian clergymen, both in England and in the Cape Colony, during more than forty years, and I have reason to know, and am glad to acknowledge, that there could not be a body of men more learned and pious, and more free from religious rancour and intolerance. My own experience has abundantly proved that it is possible for sincere Jews and Christians to associate on terms of friendship and mutual respect, and that no friction need arise from their differences of opinion on certain matters. But, at the same time, these differences do exist; and if a Jew refuses to adopt Christianity on the strength of arguments drawn from Jewish writings, he must be prepared to justify his attitude. I will therefore touch very briefly on one or two of the arguments brought forward in support of the belief in Jesus as the Messiah.

The prophetic utterances which Christians quote as foreshadowing the coming of Messiah are quoted re- )catedly by the Rabbis, and, in my opinion, have been largely borrowed by Christians from that source. These prophecies cannot be assumed without further proof to refer to the founder of Christianity.

I do not wish to go into the question whether the term ' Messiah' means an epoch of time or a personal Messiahâ a matter on which Jews are by no means unanimous.

But it must be apparent to every thinking and unbiassed mind that not one of the prophetic utterances and predictions or of the Midrashic sayings can apply to the founder of Christianity any more than to the other numerous claimants to the Messianic dignity who have appeared from time to time. Jesus of Nazareth, no less than the other claimants, utterly failed to answer to the description of the Messiah in the prophets, and to accomplish the work which the prophets predicted.

One has but to glance at the present condition of the worldâ not the heathen, but the Christian worldâ after more than nineteen hundred years from the supposed advent of the Messiah; one has but to obsen'e how anxious, for instance, nations are to convert their Krupp guns into ploughshares and their machine guns into pruning hooks. One has but, amongst very many other things, to consider the peace on earth which now exists throughout the world! I would also remind those who see in the name 1jpi2 'H as applied to Messiah, a convincing proof of the divinity of Jesus, that Jerusalem is also called â i: pi: i 'H (Jer. 33. 16). In a similar way, the altar which Moses erectedâ in commemoration of his victory over Amalekâ he dignified by naming it D2 TT (Exod. 17. 15).

And there is, in my humble opinion, amongst other arguments, one argument against the belief in Jesus as the Messiah, which is unanswerable.

The Messiah, according to all who believe in a personal Messiah, Jews and Christians alike, is to be a descendant of David. Now, according to Christianity, Jesus, the sonâ though not the only sonâ of Mary, was the offspring of immaculate conception, and had no earthly father from whom to take his pedigree. Even assuming that (as some of my Christian friends assert, but without proof) Mary was a descendant of David, that would not make Jesus a descendant, because pedigrees are reckoned from the father's, and not the mother's, side. God being the Father of Jesus, and God not being a descendant of King David, it follows that Jesus, His alleged son, cannot be King David's descendant.

In support of my argument I may state that in the first four chapters of Numbers, the words DlirrbIi D'? Dnij D' 2'7 ' After their families by the house of their fathers," occur more than twenty times. There is not in the whole range of Holy Writ an instance where we find a phrase repeated so many times in so short a space.

And this tends to show Moses' anxiety to impress us with the fact that descent is to be reckoned on the father's side. On his father's side Jesus is not a scion of David, and consequently he cannot be the Messiah.

It is forbidden to inquire what existed before creation, as Moses distinctly tells us (Deut. 4. 32): ' Ask now of the days that are past which were before thee, since the day God created man upon earth." Thus the scope of inquiry is limited to the time since the Creation.â Gen. Rabba i.

The unity of God is at once set before us in the history of creation, where we are told He, not they, created.â Gen. Rabba i.

The Torah was to God, when He created the world, what the plan is to an architect when he erects a building.â Gen. Rabba i.

The ' l ' being the first letter of the Hebrew Alphabet, demurred at her place being usurped by the letter 2, which is second to her, at the creation; the history of which commences with the latter instead of with the former. She was, however, quite satisfied when told that in the history of giving the Decalogue, she w ould be placed at the beginning in the word 02M, for the world has only been created on account of the Torah, which, indeed, e. xisted anterior to creation; and had the Creator not foreseen that Israel would consent to receive and diffuse the Torah, creation would not have taken place.â Gen. Rabba i.

There is a difference of opinion as to the day on which angels were created; one authority decides for the second day, on the ground that they are mentioned in connexion with water (Ps. 104. 3, 4), which was created on that day; while another, arguing from the fact that they are said to fly (Isa. 6.), assigns their creation to the fifth day, on which au other flying things were created. But all authorities are agreed that they did not exist on the iirst day of creation, so that sceptics cannot say that they were helpers in the work of creation. â Gen. Rabba i.

The title of an earthly king precedes his name, for instance, Emperor Augustus, etc. Not so was the will of the King of kings; He is only known as God after creating heaven and earth. Thus it is not said D n' 'i'i-)a (God created), but Q Tlbik i l2. ' In the beginning created God heavens and earth '; He is not mentioned as God before He created.â Gen. Rabba i.

Even the new heavens and earth, spoken of by the Prophet Isaiah (65. 17), were created in the six days of creation.â Gen. Rabba i.

When any divergence is found in the Scriptures, it must not be thought that it is by mere accident, for it is done advisedly. Thus, for instance, we invariably find Abraham, Isaac and Jacob; but once, as an exception, Jacob is mentioned before the other Patriarchs (Levit. 26. 42). Again, whilst Moses has always precedence over Aaron, in one instance we find Aaron's name placed before that of Moses (Exod. 6. 26). This is also the case with Joshua and Caleb; whilst the former normally precedes the name of Caleb, there is one exception (Numb. 14. 30).

This is to show us that these men were equally beloved by God. The same is the case with the love and honour due to parents; whilst the father is as a rule mentioned first in this connexion, once (in Levit. 19. 3) the mother is mentioned before the father. This is also intended to indicate that children owe the same love and honour to the mother as to the father.â Gen. Rabba i.

The man that gloats over another man's disgrace and thinks himself raised in dignity by it, is unworthy of future bhss.â Gen. Rabba i.

Light is mentioned five times in the opening chapter of the Bible. This i)oints to the five books of Moses. ' God said let there be light ' refers to the book of Genesis, which enlightens us as to how creation was carried out. The words ' And there was light ' bear reference to the book of Exodus, which contains the history of the transition of Israel from darkness to light. ' And God saw the light that it was good ': this alludes to the book of Leviticus, which contains numerous statutes. ' And God divided between the light and between the darkness ': this refers to the book of Numbers, divided as that book is between the history of those who came out of Egypt and that of those who w ere on their way to possess the promised land. ' And God called the light day ': this bears reference to the book of Deuteronomy, which is not only a rehearsal of the four earlier books, but contains Moses' eloquent dying charge to Israel and many laws not mentioned in the preceding books.â Gen. Rabba 3.

' And the earth was without form and void." There seems to be some reason for the earth's despondency, as though she was aware of her lot beforehand. This may be illustrated by the following parable: A king acquired two servants on precisely the same conditions, but made a distinction in their treatment. Regarding the one, he decreed that she should be fed and maintained at the expense of the king. For the other, he decided that she must maintain herself by her. own labour. In the same way, the earth was sad because she saw that the heavens and the earth were equally and at the same time called into being by the same ' let there be ' or will of God, and yet the heavenly bodies feast on and are maintained by Divine Glory; whilst earthly bodies, unless they labour and produce their own sustenance, are not sustained. Or, again, it is as though the king decreed that the one servant should be a constant dweller in his palace, whilst the other should be a fugitive and a wanderer; or gave to the one perpetuity or eternity, and to the other, death. Thus, the earth knowingâ as though by inspirationâ God's words spoken afterwards to Adam (Gen. 3. 17): ' Cursed is the ground for thy sake," put on mourning, and thus was ' without form and void."â Gen. Rabba 2.

In the words ' and there was evening and there was morning one day," the ' one day ' referred to is the Day of Atonementâ the day of expiation.â Gen. Rabba 2.

There seems to be a covenant made with the waters that whenever the heat is excessive and there is scarcely a breath of air moving on land, there is always some breeze, however slight, on the waters.â Gen. Rabba 2.

God knew beforehand that the world would contain both righteous and wicked men, and there is an allusion to this in the story of creation. The earth without form," means the wicked, and the words ' and there was light ' refers to the righteous.â Gen. Rabba 3.

Other worlds were created and destroyed ere this present one was decided on as a permanent one.â Gen. Rabba 3.

Rain is produced by the condensed effusion of the upper firmament.â Gen. Rabba 4.

' How is it," asked an inquisitive matron of Rabbi Jose, ' that your Scriptures crown every day of creation with the words: " And God saw that it was'good," but the second day is deprived of this phrase?" The Rabbi sought to satisfy her by pointing out that at the end of the creation it is said: ' And God saw all that He had made, and it was exceedingly good," so that the second day shares in this commendation. ' But," insisted the matron, ' there is still an unequal division, since every day has an additional sixth part of the praise, whilst the second day has only the sixth part without the whole one, which the others liave for themselves." The sage then mentioned the opinion of Rabbi Samuel, that the reason for the omission is to be found in the fact that the work begun on the second day was not finished before the following (the third) day; hence we find the expression ' it was good ' twice on that day. â Gen. Rabba 4.

Three were accused: Adam, Eve and the Serpent; but four were sentenced, viz., the earth, as well as those three. The earth received her sentence as the element out of which rebellious and fallen man was formed.â Gen. Rabba 5.

The waters of the various seas are apparently the same, but the different taste of the fish coming from the various seas seems to contradict this.â Gen. Rabba 5.

God made a condition with Nature at the Creation, that the sea should divide to let the Israelites pass through it at the Exodus, and that Nature should alter her course when emergency should arise.â Gen. Rabba 5.

When iron was found, the trees began to tremble, but the iron reassured them: ' Let no handle made from you enter into anything made from me, and I shall be powerless to injure you."â Gen. Rabba 5.

The following are God's presents, or free gifts, to the world: The Torah (Exod. 31. 18), Light (Gen. i. 17), Rain (Levit. 26. 4), Peace (Levit. 26. 6), Salvation (Ps. 18. 36), Mercy (Ps. 106. 46). Some add also the knowledge of navigation.â Gen. Rabba 6.

When creation was all but ended, the world with all its grandeur and splendour stood out in its glorious beauty. There was but one thing wanting to consummate the marvellous work called into existence by the mere ' let there be," and that was a creature with thought and understanding able to behold, reflect and marvel on this great handiwork of God, who now sat on His Divine Throne surrounded by hosts of angels and seraphim singing hymns before Him.

Then God said, ' Let us make man in our likeness, and let there be a creature not only the product of earth, but also gifted with heavenly, spiritual elements, which will bestow on him reason, intellect and understanding." Truth then appeared, falling before God's throne, and in all humility exclaimed: ' Deign, O God, to refrain from calling into being a creature who is beset with the vice of lying, who will tread truth under his feet." Peace came forth to support thispetition. 'Wherefore, 0 Lord, shall this creature appear on earth, a creature so full of strife and contention, to disturb the peace and harmony of Thy creation? He will carry the flame of quarrel and ill-will in his trail; he will bring about war and destruction in his eagerness for gain and conquest."

Whilst they were pleading against the creation of man, there was heard, arising from another part of the heavens, the soft voice of Charity: ' Sovereign of the Universe," the voice exclaimed, in all its mildness, ' vouchsafe Thou to create a being in Thy likeness, for it will be a noble creature striving to imitate Thy attributes by its actions. I see man now in Spirit, that being with God's breath in his nostrils, seeking to perform his great mission, to do his noble work. I see him now in spirit, approaching the humble hut, seeking out those who are distressed and wretched to comfort them, drying the tears of the afflicted and despondent, raising up them that are bowed down in spirit, reaching his helping hand to those who are in need of help, speaking peace to the heart of the widow, and giving shelter to the fatherless. Such a creature cannot fail to be a glory to His Maker." The Creator approved of the pleadings of Charity, called man into being, and cast Truth down to the earth to flourish there; as the Psalmist says (Ps. 85. 12): ' Truth shall spring out of the earth; and righteousness shall look down from heaven to abide with man '; and He dignified Truth by making her His own seal.â Gen. Rabba 8.

The sun alone without the moon would have sufficed for all his purpose, but if he were alone, the primitive people might have had some plausible excuse for worshipping him. So the moon was added, and there is less reason for deifying either.â Gen. Rabba 6.

The progeny of man is reckoned from his father's and not from his mother's family.â Gen. Rabba 7.

' Let us make man." God may be said to address the spiritual and the material elements thus: ' Till now all creatures have been of matter only; now I will create a being who shall consist of both matter and spirit."â Gen. Rabba 8.

' In our form, in our likeness." ' Hitherto there was but one such creature; I have now added to him another who was taken from him. They shall both be in our form and likeness; there shall be no man without a woman and no woman without a man, and no man and woman together without God." Thus in the words VVi Wik ' man and woman ') there is the word H', (God).â Gen. Rabba 8.

If they are unworthy the from the word Wi and the n from nwi is taken away, and thus n God, departs and there are left the words Wik") li'N " fire and fire."

Adam was created with two bodies, one of which was cut away from him and formed Eve.â Gen. Rabba 8.

If man had been created out of spiritual elements only there could be no death for him, in the event of his fall. If, on the other hand, he had been created out of matter only, there could be no future bliss for him. Hence he was formed out of matter and spirit. If he lives the earthly, i. e. the animal life only, he dies like all matter; if he lives a spiritual life, he obtains the spiritual future bliss.â Gen. Rabba 8.

Michael and Gabriel acted as ' best men ' at the nuptials of Adam and Eve. God joined them in wedlock, and pronounced the mnrriage benediction on them. â Gen. Rabba 8.

Rabbi Meier wrote a rtTljl 13D (scroll) for his own use, on the margin of which he wrote, in connexion with the words: ' And God saw that it was good," ' This means death, which is the passing from life transitory to life everlasting."â Gen. Rabba 9.

God knows our thoughts before they are formed.â Gen. Rabba 9.

There is a limit to everything except to the greatness and depth of the Torah.â Gen. Rabba 10.

After destroying Jerusalem and the Temple, plundering all its valuables and doing much what he hked, Titus became intoxicated with his success and indulged in gross blasphemy. ' It is all very well," he said, for the God of the Jews to conquer kings of the desert, but I attacked Him in His very palace and prevailed against Him." When he was on his return voyage to Rome, with the booty robbed from the Temple, a great tempest arose on the sea and threatened him with shipwreck. He again had recourse to blasphemy: ' The God of the Jews," said he, ' seems to have dominion over the waters; the generation of Noah He destroyed by water, Pharaoh and the Egyptians He drowned in the waters, and over me He had no power until I gave Him the chance by using the elements over which He possesses this subtle power." Suddenly a perfect calm set in, the sea became quite smooth, and Titus prosecuted his voyage without let or hindrance. Arrived in Rome with the golden vessels of the Temple, he was given a great reception, and a large number of distinguished men went to meet him.

After resting from his fatigue, he appeared again before a distinguished assembly, and was offered wine; but whilst he was partaking of it a microbe, so minute that it was imperceptible, found its way into his glass, and soon began to cause him intense pain in the head. In the course of a short time the insect grew, and with it grew the pain in Titus' head, till it was decided to have recourse to an operation, to open his skull, in orderâ as the Romans saidâ to see what the God of the Jews employed as punishment for Titus. An insect of the size of a pigeon and of the weight of nearly two pounds was found in Titus' brain. Rabbi Eleazer, son of Rabbi Jose, who was then in Rome, saw with his outi eyes the insect when taken out of Titus' skuu.â Gen. Rabba 10.

Even flies, parasites and microbes have their purpose to fulfil, and there is nothing superfluous in creation.â Gen. Rabba 10.

The river Sambation casts up stones all the days of the week, but desists from doing so on Sabbathâ indeed, on Friday after midday, when it becomes quite calm, as a proof of the day which is really the Sabbath.â Gen. Rabba ii.

Rabbi Judah Hanasa invited his friend Antoninus to dine with him on the Sabbath day, when all the viands were served cold. After a time the Rabbi again had the pleasure of his friend's company at dinner on a week-day, when warm food was served. Antoninus, however, expressed his preference for the food he had enjoj'ed at his friend's table on the Sabbath, though it was cold. ' Ah," said the sage, ' there is something missing to-day which we cannot procure." ' But," replied Antoninus, ' surely my means can procure anything? ' ' No," answered the Rabbi, ' your means cannot procure the Sabbath; it is the Sabbath that gives the zest to the food."â Gen. Rabba 11.

The merciful Creator did not overlook the wild goat or the coney, but provided for them a refuge and a protecting shelter. It follows that he created all that is necessary for man.â Gen. Rabba 12.

The light, when first created, would have enabled man to see from one corner of the earth to the other; but the wicked men of the generation of Enos, the flood, and the Tower caused that light to be withdrawn from this world, and it is preserved for the righteous in a higher sphere.â Gen. Rabba 12.

The nose is the most important feature in man's face, so much so, that there is no legal identification of man, in Jewish law, without the identification of the nose.â Gen. Rabba 12.

All the rivers go into the sea and the sea is not full, because the waters of the sea are again absorbed, and this causes the mist which rises from the earth. When the clouds have absorbed the mist, the moisture becomes condensed, and loses its salty substance before it comes down again on earth in the shape of rain.â Gen. Rabba

The Hebrew word for ' forming ' is, in connexion with the formation of man, spelled exceptionally 1ii "1 with two "', which is not its proper spelling. This is to be taken as a hint that man was formed out of two elementsâ spirit and matter. This is also manifested in man's life. His material part has need of matter to sustain him, and of the other laws of nature; he grows, flourishes, decays and dies. But, on the other hand, he resembles spiritual beings by walking upright, by his power of speech and thought, and by being able in some degree to see behind him without need of turning his head round; which facility is given to man alone and not to the lower animals.â Gen. Rabba 14.

The appearance of Adam and Eve, when just formed, was like that of persons of twenty years of age.â Gen. Rabba 14.

Rabbi Jose b. Chlafta paid a visit of condolence to a man who had lost a dearly beloved son. He met there a man of sceptical ideas, who, observing the Rabbi's silence, asked him whether he had nothing to say to the mourner. ' We," said the good man, ' believe in a meeting again hereafter." ' Has our friend not sorrow enough," observed the sceptic, ' that you must needs add to it by offering him foolish words as comfort? Can a broken pitcher be made whole? ' he argued. ' Your owti Psalmist does not seem to think so when he says (Ps. 2. 8): " Thou shalt dash them to pieces like a potter's vessel." " And yet," answered the Rabbi, ' there is even a vessel made by human hands, or rather by blowing, viz. a vessel made from glass, which, when broken, can be made whole again by the same process, by blowing. And if such is the case with anything made by human skill, shall we doubt it where the Great Master blew into the nostrils His own breath? 'â Gen. Rabba 14.

The builder mixes a thick sand with a thinner one in the mortar, by which contrivance the latter becomes very strong and the building more substantial. In creating the first pair, something of this method was adopted. Adam was the strong and Eve the weaker. This mixture of the weak with the strong is beneficial to the liuman race.â Gen. Rabba 14.

Man was originally formed with a tail like the lower animals, but this was afterwards taken from him out of consideration for him.â Gen. Rabba 14.

God designed man for workâ work for his own sustenance; he who does not work shall not eat.â Gen. Rabba 14.

Perhaps in the proper order of things, Abraham should have been the first man created, not Adam. God, however, foresaw the fall of the first man, and if Abraham had been the first man and had fallen, there would have been no one after him to restore righteousness to the world; whereas after Adam's fall came Abraham, who established in the world the knowledge of God. As a builder puts the strongest beam in the centre of the building, so as to support the structure at both ends, so Abraham was the strong beam carrying the burden of the generations that existed before him and that came after him.â Gen. Rabba 14.

Here in this life we have the Spirit = the soul, blown into our nostrils; hence it goes from us at death.

In futurity the soul, when restored, will be given to us, as it is said in Ezek. 37. 14: a complete gift never to be returned.â Gen. Rabba 14.

The river Euphrates (n")E)) is the chief and choicest of all rivers.â Gen. Rabba 16.

The Greeks, amongst other insults which they heaped on Jews, had a satirical saying. The Jews should write on the horn of an oxâ alluding to the making of the golden calfâ that they are not the portion of the God of Israel.â Gen. Rabba 16.

Why," asked a matron of Rabbi Jose, ' did God steal a rib from Adam? ' ' Steal, did you say? ' replied the Sage. ' If one were to take away from your house an ounce of silver, and give you in return a pound of gold, that would not be stealing from you. ' ' But," persisted his friend, ' what need was there for secrecy? ' 'It was surely better, ' replied R. Jose, ' to present Eve to Adam when she was quite presentable, and when no traces of the effects of the operation were visible."â Gen. Rabba 17.

That woman exercises more influence over man than he possesses over woman was illustrated by a couple who were famous for their piety, but who were eventually divorced. The man married a woman of questionable habits, and soon copied her conduct and became hke his new wife, conspicuous for his evil deeds; whilst the divorced woman married a notorious sinner, and converted him into a pious man.â Gen. Rabba 17.

Woman is formed out of bone. Touch a bone and it emits sound; hence woman's voice is thinner than man's. Again, man is formed from earth, which is comparatively soft and melts when water comes over it; whilst woman, being formed from hard substance, is more stubborn and unbending.â Gen. Rabba 17.

Sleep is a sixtieth portion of death; a dream is the same proportion of prophecy and the Sabbath of the Future bliss,â Gen, Rabba 17.

Dreams, something like prophecy, are the offspring of imaginations and comparisons which we may form whilst awake.â Gen. Rabba 17.

Sleepiness and laziness in a man are the beginning of his misfortune.â Gen. Rabba 17.

Man in celibacy is in sublime ignorance of what is meant by the words good, help, J03', blessing, peace and expiation of sin. He is, in fact, not entitled to the dignified name of man.â Gen. Rabba 17.

Rabbi Jose, the Galilean, married his nieceâ his sister's daughterâ who proved an exceedingly bad wife, and took a delight in abusing him in the presence of his pupils, who urged him to divorce her. This he refused to do, pleading that he was not in position to make provision for her maintenance, without which it would not be just to cast her adrift. One day he brought home with him Rabbi Eleazar b. Azaria, to whom, as well as to her husband, she offered a frown as her greeting. Upon inquiry as to what repast there was to place before his guest, R. Jose received the reply that there was nothing but lentils. His sense of smell, however, told him that there was something more savoury, and looking into the simmering pot on the liob, he found its contents to be stuffed chickens. After a deal of persuasion the good woman was prevailed upon to place the tempting morsels before her liusband and his guest. Rabbi Eleazar, who, having overheard the answer which the woman first gave her husband, that there was nothing better than lentils, expressed his surprise that chickens were served. In order to screen his wife. Rabbi Jose made the remark that perhaps a miracle had hapj ened in honour of so distinguished a guest. The true character of the woman, however, reached the ears of Rabbi Eleazar, and he also learnt that it was owing to his friend's inability to provide for her maintenance that he was not divorced from her. The means to make provision for her were then soon found, and she was duly divorced from her husband.

Rabbi Jose had the good fortune to find a very much more desirable helpmate in his second wife, but no such good luck followed his divorced wife. She married the town watchman, who, after a lingering illness, was struck with total blindness, and he employed his wife to guide him through the streets for the purpose of begging. When they arrived at the street in which Rabbi Jose lived, the woman retraced her steps, but the man, though blind, knew every street, owing to his having been watchman of the town, and demanded his wife's motive for so persistently avoiding a certain street. She eventually had to divulge her reason, and this led to quarrels between the couple; the man saying that his wife deprived him of a source of income by avoiding the very street where he expected to find a decent revenue. The quarrels soon culminated in blows bestowed by the blind man upon his unhappy wife. This scandal made quite a stir in the small town, and did not escape the ears of Rabbi Jose, whose worldly affairs had vastly improved, and who, in fact, was now a man of affluence, possessing property in the little town. When he became aware of the sad plight his former wife was in, he placed one of his houses at the disposal of herself and her husband, and made them, in addition, a monetary allowance which placed them beyond the reach of want till the last day of their lives.â Gen. Rabba 17.

Woman attains discretion at an earlier age than man. â Gen. Rabba 18.

Woman was not formed from Adam's head, so that she might not be haughty; nor from his eye, so that she might not be too eager to look at everything; nor from his ear, so that she might not hear too keenly and be an eavesdropper; nor from his mouth, so that she might not be a chatterer; nor from his heart, lest she should become jealous; nor yet not from his hand, so that she might not be afflicted with kleptomania; nor from his foot, lest she should have a tendency to run about. She was made from Adam's rib, a hidden, modest part of his body, so that she too might be modest, not fond of show, but rather of seclusion. But woman bafiles God's design and purpose.

She is haughty and walks with outstretched neck (Isa. 3.16), and wanton eyes (Isa. 3. 6). She is given to eavesdropping (Gen. 18. 10). She chatters slander (Numb. 12. II), and is of a jealous disposition (Gen. 30. i). She is afflicted with kleptomania (Gen. 31. ig), and is fond of running about (Gen. 34. i). In addition to these vices women are gluttonous (Gen. 3. 6), lazy (Gen. 18. 6) and bad tempered (Gen. 16. 5).â Gen. Rabba 18.

When the Jews returned from Babylon, their wives had become brown, and almost black, during the years of captivity, and a large number of men divorced their wives. The divorced women probably married black men, which would, to some extent, account for the existence of black Jews.â Gen. Rabba 18.

The higher the position the greater is the fall, and this applies to the serpent, who not only was the chief of all animals, but walked upright like man, and when it fell it sank into the reptile species.â Gen. Rabba 19.

The delight of the Shechinah is to dwell here amongst men. Adam's fall caused it to retire from earth to the first heaven. Cain drove it, by his misdeeds, further into the second, the generation of Enos further still, and the generation of the flood again to the fourth. The generation of the Tower, the Sodomites and the Egyptians of Abraham's time finally drove the Shechinah into the seventh heaven.

Then arose Abraham, who induced the Divine Glory to descend one degree nearer. So also did Isaac, Jacob, Levi, Kehos, Amram and Moses, so that the Shechinah was once more brought down to dwell with man.â Gen. Rabba 19.

Like the desire of a woman for her husband is the desire of Satan for men of Cain's stamp.â Gen. Rabba 20.

' Dust thou art and unto dust shalt thou return." The grave is the only thing which every man has honestly acquired and can honestly claim.â Gen. Rabba 20.

To protect Cain from being killed, a dog was given him, who accompanied him and protected him against all comers.â Gen. Rabba 22.

When Cain went abroad, after killing Abel, he met his father Adam, who expressed his surprise at Cain's life being spared. The son explained that he owed his life to the act of repentance, and to his pleading that his sin was greater than he could bear. Adam thus received a hint of his error in not having fallen back upon repentance instead of putting the blame on Eve. He there and then composed a hymn, now known as the Ninety-second Psalm, which, in the course of time, became lost or forgotten. Moses, however, found it and used it, and it became known as the prayer of Moses, the man of God.â Gen. Rabba 22.

Do not befriend an evil man and no evil will overtake you.â Gen. Rabba 22.

The i in ")2i evil inclination, at first behaves like a guest, but eventually becomes master. He makes not only the open streets, but the palace also, the centre of his traffic; wherever he observes a vain or proud person, or any traces of vice in a man, he says, ' He is mine."â Gen. Rabba 22.

The evil enticer (or i "in "iii) is as cunning as the famous dogs of Rome, who feign sleep when they see the baker with the basket of bread approaching the palace, and are thus able to snatch the loaves from the incautious carrier. He pretends at first great mildness, the gentleness of a woman, but soon shows the boldness of a strong man; he begs admittance like an outcast.

lat eventually becomes master of the situation.â Gen. Kabba 22.

' Sin lieth at the door ' (Gen. 4. 7). Happy is the man who can rise above the sin that lieth in waiting for him.â Gen. Rabba 22.

Cain was a twin, for with him was born a girl; and Abel was one of three, for with him came two girls.â â Gen. Rabba 22.

Three men craved for things of earth, and none of them made a success of his occupation. Cain was a tiller of the ground; we know his sad history. Noah attempted to become a husbandman, and he became a drunkard. Uzziah became a leper (2 Chron. 26. 10-20).â Gen. Rabba 22.

In the early time of creation, in the time of Lemech, a medicine was known, the taking of which prevented a woman's conception.â Gen. Rabba 23.

The deluge in the time of Noah was by no means the only flood with which this earth was visited. The first flood did its w ork of destruction as far as Jaffe, and the one of Noah's days extended to Barbary.â Gen. Rabba 23.

Naamah, daughter of Lemech and sister totubalcain, was Noah's wife.â Gen. Rabba 23.

It is an error to think that Cain was stronger than Abel, for the contrary was the case, and in the quarrel that arose Cain would have fared worse had he not appealed to Abel for compassion and then attacked him unawares and killed him.â Gen. Rabba 26.

Man should look upon the birth of a daughter as a blessing from the Lord.â Gen. Rabba 26.

For seven days the Lord mourned (or deplored) the necessity of destroying His creatures by the deluge. â Gen. Rabba 27.

God will wipe away tears from off all faces (Isa. 25. 8). This means from the faces of non-Jews as well as Jews. â Gen. Rabba 26.

Rabbi Judah Hanasa was an exceedingly meek man, who always tried to put the virtues of others above his own. He used to say: I am prepared to do anything reasonable that any man may ask me to do. Though the chief of the Rabbis of his time he rose when he saw Rav Hunnaâ much his inferior in learning, piety and positionâ explaining that heâ Rav Hunnaâ was a scion of the tribe of Judah on his father's side, whereas he himself was only from that of Benjamin, and that only on his mother's side.â Gen. Rabba 33.

Mercy and compassion are the great virtues which bring with them their own rewards, for they are recompensed with mercy and lovingkindness from the Mercy-seat of God. There was once a great drought in Palestine which afflicted its inhabitants long and severely. Rabbi Tanchuma proclaimed a fast day once, twice and thrice without propitiating the heavens to send down the much needed rain. He then assembled the people for prayer.

Before the congregation engaged in prayer, the good man intended to address his flock; but a report was brought to him that a certain man had been seen giving a woman some money within the precincts of the House of Assembly, an act which, under all the circumstances, could not but excite suspicion. The Rabbi had the man brought before him and asked him in what relationship he stood with the person to whom he was seen to have given money outside. ' She is my divorced wife," answered the man simply. ' And how is it," insisted the Rabbi, ' that you are on cordial terms with her and continue to give her money? ' 'I am on no friendly footing with her; as for giving her money, she is in want, and that is a sufficient reason for my relieving her distress," replied the man. ' Her want obscured all other considerations and the peculiarity of our relationship." The Rabbi was much affected by the man's generous nature and kindliness, and preached his sermon on charity and brotherly love, a sermon worthy of the distinguished sage, showing that those virtues stand on an eminently higher level and are more efficacious than fasting and chastising of the body, and asking his audience to imitate ' the man in the street," who set them such a good example. The good man then lifted up his heart in prayer, in which the congregation joined, and invoked the Throne of Mercy on behalf of a people imbued with mercy and compassion. The service was barely brought to a close when copious showers came down to refresh the parched ground and replenish the empty water tanks, and the people were once more happy.â Gen. Rabba 33.

The very punishments with which God visits His erring children are often turned into blessings. When the deluge was sent on a sinning world all the fountains of the great deep were opened (Gen. 7.11), but when the deluge ceased not all the fountains were stopped (Gen. 8. 2). Those containing the mineral waters with their healing properties were left open for the great benefit of man. â Gen. Rabba 33.

The difference between the solar and the lunar year is that the former is eleven days longer than the latter.â Gen. Rabba 33.

The period covering the second hal f of Tishri, the whole of Cheshvon and the first half of Kislev is the season for sowing. The second half of Kislev, the whole of Tebeth and first half of Shvat is winter. The second half of Shvat, the whole of Adar and first half of Nisson is spring. The second half of Nisson, the whole of lyar and first half of Sivon is harvest time, according to climate. The second half of Sivon, the whole of Tammuz and fust half of Ab is summer, and the second half of Ab, the whole of Ellul and first half of Tishri is autumn.â Gen. Rabba 34.

The wicked make no resistance, but abandon themselves to their evil inclination.â Gen. Rabba 34.

Noah began by being righteous in his generation, but fell back and became a man of earth (Gen. 9. 20). Moses, on the other hand, began his career as an Egyptian (Exod. 2. 19), but developed into a man of God.â Gen. Rabba 36.

By Japhet, Gomer and Magog Africa is meant, and by Tiros Persia.â Gen. Rabba 37.

The sexes of both man and the lower animals were meant to be separated in the ark during the deluge. This is clear from the way in which they entered the ark: first Noah and his three sons went in, and then their wives separately (Gen. 7. 7). But when they came out of the ark after the flood, God commanded Noah, ' Go out of the ark, thou and thy wife, thy sons and their wives ' (Gen. 8. 16), thus putting the sexes together again. Ham among the human beings, and the dog among the lower animals, disregarded this injunction and did not separate from the opposite sex in the ark. The dog received a certain punishment, and Ham became a black man; just as when a man has the audacity to coin the king's currency in the king's own palace his face is blackened as a punishment and his issue is declared counterfeit.â Gen. Rabba 37.

Artaban sent Rabbi Judah Hanasa as a present a pearl of great value, and when he asked the Rabbi a present of equal value in return, the sage sent him a parchment (Ephesian letters). Artaban thought it unworthy, since his own gift was of such priceless value. Rabbi Judah replied that not only was his present precious above all the possessions of both, but it had immeasurable advantage over the valuable pearl, as care must be taken of the pearl, whilst his amulet would take care of its possessor.â Gen. Rabba 35.

We are not allowed to say any portion of Holy Writ by heart, but must always read it from the Scroll. Thus 1 See Rapoport's Erech Millin as to Artaban.

CxeNESIS RABBA ' ' when Rabbi Meier was once in Asia on Purim, and was unable to find a copy of the book of Esther, he wrote the book out from memory (as he knew it by heart), and then made another copy from which he read to the congregation.â Gen. Rabba 36.

If a man has entertained you only with lentils, do you entertain him with flesh. If one shows you small favours, bestow on him great ones when an opportunity occurs.â Gen. Rabba 38.

There is not an evil which fails to bring benefit to some one.â Gen. Rabba 38.

Terah, the father of Abraham and Haran, was a dealer in images as well as a worshipper of them. Once when he was away he gave Abraham his stock of graven images to sell in his absence. In the course of the day an elderly man came to make a purchase. Abraham asked him his age, and the man gave it as between fifty and sixty years. Abraham taunted him with want of sound sense in calling the work of another man's hand, produced perhaps in a few hours, his god; the man laid the words of Abraham to heart and gave up idol worship. Again a woman came with a handful of fine flour to offer to Terah's idols, which were now in charge of Abraham. He took a stick and broke all the images except the largest one, in the hand of which he placed the stick which had worked this wholesale destmction. When his father returned and saw the havoc committed on his ' gods ' and property he demanded an explanation from his son whom he had left in charge. Abraham mockingly explained that when an offering of fine flour was brought to these divinities they quarrelled with each other as to who should be the recipient, when at last the biggest of them, being angry at the altercation, took up a stick to chastise the offenders, and in so doing broke them all up. Terah, so far from being satisfied with this explanation, understood it as a piece of mockery, and when he learnt also of the customers whom Abraham had lost him during his management he became very incensed, and drove Abraham out of his house and handed him over to Nimrod. Nimrod suggested to Abraham that since he had refused to worship his father's idols because of their want of power, he should worship fire, which is very powerful. Abraham pointed out that water has power over fire. ' Well," said Nimrod, ' let us declare water god." ' But," replied Abraham, ' the clouds absorb the water; and even they are dispersed by the wind." ' Then let us declare the wind our god." ' Bear in mind," continued Abraham, ' that man is stronger than wind, and can resist it and stand against it."

Nimrod, becoming weary of arguing with Abraham, decided to cast him before his godâ fireâ and challenged Abraham's deliverance by the God of Abraham, but God saved him out of the fiery furnace. Haran too was challenged to declare his god, but halted between two opinions, and delayed his answer until he saw the result of Abraham's fate. When he saw the latter saved he declared himself on the side of Abraham's God, thinking that he too, having now become an adherent of that God, would be saved by the same miracle. But since his faith was not real, but depended on a miracle, he perished in the fire, into which like Abraham he was cast by Nimrod, This is hinted in the words (Gen. 11. 28): ' And Haran died before his father Terah in the land of his nativity, in Ur of the Chaldees."â Gen. Rabba 38.

Abraham, Joshua, David and Mordecai issued their own coinage. The coins of Abraham had the figure of an old man and an old woman on the face of the coin, and those of a youth and a maiden on the obverse, signifying that after Abraham and Sarah had grown old their youth was renewed and they begat a son.

Those which Joshua issued bore the figure of an ox, and on the obverse that of a unicorn, alluding to the words (Deut. 33.17) ' His glory is like the firstling of his bullock, and his horns are like the horns of unicorns '; for Joshua was descended from Joseph, concerning whom those words were uttered. The coins which David issued had a shepherd's staff and satchel on the face, and a tower on the obverse, in allusion to his having been raised to the throne from the sheepcote. Mordecai's coins bore sackcloth and ashes on the face, and a crown of gold on the obverse, these symbols being a ' multum in parvo ' of his career.â Gen. Rabba 39.

What has now become a popular expression, viz. ' The man in the street," is a phrase used in the Midrash. â Gen. Rabba 41

The pure of heart are God's friends.â Gen. Rabba 41.

Lot enjoyed four great benefits in accompanying Abraham. He became rich, became the possessor of property, was rescued from 36 kings who pursued him, and was sav ed with his family at the destruction of Sodom and Gomorrah. Yet Amnion and Moab (Lot's descendants) inflicted four great sorrows upon Abraham's descendants, to whom they owed their very existence. They hired Balaam to curse. Eglon king of Moab gathered the children of Ammon and subjected the Israelites to his yoke 18 years. The war which Ammon and Moab waged against Israel, as recorded in 2nd Chronicles, and the destruction of Jerusalem and the Temple, and all its attending sorrows, are lamented by Jeremiah in the Book of Lamentations. Therefore there came four prophets to prophesy the downfall of these two ungrateful nations, viz., Isaiah (see the 15th chapter of his book), Jeremiah (in his 49th chapter), Ezekiel, who prophesies against Ammon in the 25th chapter of his book, and Zephaniah, who proj hesies that the fate of Ammon and Moab will be like that of Sodom and Gomorrah.â Gen. Rabba 41.

Once a man, twice a child.â Gen. Rabba 42.

Nations in Abraham's time desired to proclaim him their prince, their king, and even their god, but he indignantly dechned, and took that very opportunity to point out to them that there is but one Great King, one Great God.â Gen. Rabba 42.

Being aware that wine carries misfortune in its trail, as we find for instance in the case of Noah and Aaron's sons, one might indulge in the hope of finding a pleasant exception in the wine that Melchizedek brought out to Abraham. But not so, for immediately after this act of mere courtesy Abraham had to face unpleasant tidings when he was told that his offspring would be slaves and afflicted for four hundred years in a land not their own. â Gen. Rabba 43.

Hagar was the daughter of the Pharaoh who captured Sarah, and on restoring her to Abraham he presented Sarah with Hagar as her maid.â Gen. Rabba 45.

If a man calls you an ass, the best way is to take no notice of it; but if you are called so by two or more persons take the bit into your own mouth.â Gen. Rabba 45.

Do not depart, whether from a great or an insignificant individual, without leave-taking and parting greetings. â Gen. Rabba 47.

If you are in Rome do as the Romans do. Moses, when he spent forty days and forty nights in heaven, where there is neither eating nor drinking, neither ate nor drank. On the other hand, when the angels visited Abraham, they partookâ or pretended to partakeâ of the meat and drink which was prepared for them.â Gen. Rabba 48.

The names of the Hebrew months, as at present used, and the names of angels, were brought with them by the Jews on their return from the Babylonish captivity.â Gen. Rabba 48.

Angels have no back to their necks, and cannot turn their heads round.â Gen. Rabba 49.

One angel cannot perform two duties at a time, nor are two angels sent to perform one and the same duty.â Gen. Rabba 50.

The feeble prayer which a sick person can offer himself is infinitely better than all the prayers offered for him by others.â Gen. Rabba 53.

Every one is (morally) blind until his eyes are opened for him from above,â Gen. Rabba 53.

Man's fatherly compassion does not extend beyond his grandchildren.â Gen. Rabba 54.

Have no compunction to admonish where admonition is called for; it will produce not animosity, but eventually love and peace.â Gen. Rabba 54.

Job was born when the Jews went down to Egypt; he married Dinah, Jacob's daughter, and he died when the Israelites left Egypt.â Gen. Rabba 57.

Job probably never existed, and if he did exist, the events recorded concerning him never took place. The whole narrative is intended as a moral lesson.â Gen. Rabba 57.

Rabbi Meier came to a place where he found a family (a people?) remarkable for dying young. They asked him to pray for them, but he advised them to be of a charitable disposition in order to prolong life.â Gen. Rabba 59.

Abraham was the blessed of the Eternal, and he was the blessing of mankind (Gen. 12. 3). Moses was the miracle and miracle worker of the Israelites, and God was his own miracle (Exod. 13-15.) ' And Moses built an altar and called the name of it 'â 02 'H- ' The Lord my miracle' (also ' the Lord my banner '). David was Israel's shepherd (i Chron. 11.), and God was David's shepherd (Ps. 23.). Jerusalem was the light of the world (Isa. 60.), and God is its light (Isa. 60.).â Gen. Rabba 59.

When Rebecca left her parents' house they blessed her, and prayed that she might be the mother of millions of people (Gen. 24. 60). Yet she was barren till she herself and Isaac supplicated the Lord. Hence we see that it makes a difference who offers prayers.â Gen. Rabba 60.

All the numerous disciples of Rabbi Akiba hastened their own death by their vices of envy and unchari-tableness; but his last seven pupils took warning by the fate of their predecessors, and they prospered. These are the seven pupils: Rabbi Meier. R. Jose, R. Simeon, R. Eleazar b. Chanania, R. Jochanan the Sandal-maker, and R. Eleazar b. Jacob.â Gen. Rabba 61.

Man is in duty bound to look to his son's religious education until he attains the age of thirteen, and then to offer thanks to God for having relieved him of his responsibility.â Gen. Rabba 63.

When pronouncing his blessing upon Jacob, Isaac said, ' The voice is Jacob's voice, but the hands are the hands of Esau." Thus Isaac's blessings fixed upon each of his sons what should be his power. Jacob's power and function should be his voice =prayer, and Esau's might was to be in his hands. So long then as Jacob exercises his power or function, that of prayer, he need have no fear of the hands of Esau, of the persecutions of those amongst whom his lot may be cast.â Gen. Rabba

The garments which Esau put on when he went hunting, were originally Adam's; they had on them figures of various animals, and hunting was thereby facilitated, as the animals on seeing the garments came running towards the wearer. Nimrod coveted these garments, and resolved to kill Esau in order to possess himself of them. Esau, being aware of his constant danger, says when selling his birthright to Jacob, ' Behold I am on the point to die."â Gen. Rabba 63 and 65.

When the pig pauses from his gluttony and lies down to rest he stretches out his foot to show his cloven hoof, and pretends that he belongs to the clean kind of animals. â Gen. Rabba 65.

A person afflicted with total blindness eats more than one blessed with the sense of sight: sight having more of satiating than appetising effect.â Gen. Rabba 65.

All members of man's body were given him for use, yet over some he has no power of restraint. His eyes sometimes see what he would rather not see, his ears often hear against his will, and his nose smells occasionally what he would rather dispense with.â Gen. Rabba 67.

Italy is a fat land, i. e. a fertile country.â Gen. Rabba 67.

Dreams neither injure nor benefit: they are vain.â Gen. Rabba 68.

Matches are made in heaven.â Gen. Rabba 68.

In three different places of Holy Writ are we told that heaven appoints the wife of a man: in Gen. 24. 50, Judges 14. 4, and in Prov. 19. 14.â Gen. Rabba 68.

Just as two knives are both sharpened by being rubbed one against the other, so scholars improve and increase in knowledge when in touch with one another.â Gen. Rabba 6g.

The portion of the Temple called n t: n'X the Drawing-court, was so called because the people drew thence the Holy Spirit.â Gen. Rabba 70.

Rabbi Meier was asked by a sceptic how he could justify the conduct of Jacob, who, having vowed (Gen. 28.-22.) to give to God a tithe of all He might bestow upon him, yet, out of the twelve tribes with which he was blessed, consecrated one tribe only to the service of God, which represented only the tithe of ten. The Rabbi replied: ' Out of the twelve tribes there were to be deducted the firstborn, who were themselves consecrated to God, and no tithe had to be given out of them.â Gen. Rabba 70.

Were it not for the patience and endurance which Rabbi Joshua manifested towards Onkeles, he would have slipped back into his former heathenismâ Gen. Rabba 70.

With the birth of a child a woman escapes blame for household accidents which would otherwise be charged to her. If anything is wasted or broken, there is no longer any inquiry as to who has done this; it is taken for granted that the child did it.â Gen. Rabba y-.

The ten tribes are on the other side of the river Sam-bation, and the Jews at present scattered over the earth are those of Judah and Benjamin.â Gen. Rabba 73.

The blessings that Isaac bestowed upon Jacob were endorsed from heaven (Gen. 27. 28, 29): ' God give thee of the dew of heaven, and the fatness of the earth, and plenty of corn and wine. Let people serve thee, and nations bow down to thee: be lord over thy brethren, and let thy mother's sons bow down to thee." Micah (5. 6) says ' the remnant of Jacob shall be as the dew from the Lord." (Isaiah 30.-23.) ' Then shall ye sow the ground, and it shall be fat and plenteous." The same prophet (49. 23):' And kings shall be thy nursing fathers and their queens thy nursing mothers." And in Deut. 26. 19, ' And to make thee above all nations."â Gen. Rabba 75.

Frequently does David, in his prayers, use the phrase ' Arise, O God ' (in Psalms 3, 7, 9,10,17). We do not find a direct response to this prayer; but when he uses this prayer in connexion with oppression of the poor, the answer he receives is, ' Now I will arise, saith the Lord' (Ps. 12. 5).â Gen. Rabba 75.

The fact that we awake from sleep is some evidence for the resurrection.â Gen. Rabba 78.

Man in distress pledges himself to good deeds; man in prosperity forgets his good resolutions.â Gen. Rabba 81.

The righteous require no monuments; their lives and their teachings are their monuments.â Gen. Rabba 82.

We are told that Abraham took his wife Sarah, and the souls they had gotten in Haran, and they went forth into the land of Canaan. By this is meant the souls that they had brought away from idolatry and brought to the knowledge of the living God.â Gen. Rabba 84.

Man should be on his guard not to fall in love with his wife's sister.â Gen. Rabba 85.

Before the first captivity of Israel took place (the Egyptian captivity) the ancestor of their last redeemer (Perez) was already born.â Gen. Rabba 85.

Slaves do not, as a rule, bring blessings on their master's house, but Joseph's master's house was blessed because of Joseph. Slaves are not remarkable for being scrupulous, but Joseph gathered in the silver in Egypt for his king. Slaves are not distinguished for their chastity and modesty, but Joseph would not listen to a sinful suggestion.â Gen. Rabba 86.

Potiphar showed the subtlety for which the Egyptians were famous where their own interest was concerned. He boasted to his friends that as a rule a white man has a Cushite, a coloured man, for his slave, whilst he, a Cushite, contrived to obtain a youth of the white race for a slave. Hence it became a saying in Egypt," The slaves sold (i. e. the Ishmaelites who sold Joseph); the slave bought (alluding to Potiphar, Pharaoh's servant); and the freeman has become the slave of both."â Gen. Rabba 86.

A certain matron discussing Joseph with' Rabbi Jose maintained that the Biblical version of the incident with Potiphar's wife is not the correct one, but is intended to screen Joseph, whose virtues are vastly exaggerated. Rabbi Jos6 replied that Holy Writ is no respecter of persons, and records the history of those of whom it speaks just as it happened, the vices as well as the virtues. He cited Reuben's and Judah's transgressions, which are detailed without any attempt to screen them.â Gen. Rabba 87.

It was obviously to Joseph's advantage that the chief butlerâ though he did not wish to benefit Josephâ had not mentioned Joseph's name to Pharaoh until all the astrologers had failed to interpret Pharaoh's dream to his satisfaction. Otherwise, if Joseph had been called before them, it might have been thought that they were able to interpret the dream.â Gen. Rabba 89.

In your intercourse with the world it is well to bear in mind that there are thousands of men whose characteristic is lying, and woe to those that trust them.â Gen. Rabba 8g.

The heathen stands by his god. (Gen. 41. i.) The Jewish God stands by his people. (Gen. 28. 13.)â Gen. Rabba 89.

A dream towards morning is likely to be fulfilled.â Gen. Rabba 89.

During the twenty-two years that Joseph was separated from his brethren neither he nor they had tasted wine; hence they were somewhat overcome by drinking wine at the banquet to which he invited them in Egypt.â Gen. Rabba 92.

By the law of God even a slave, when his master knocked out his eye or tooth, had to be set free because of the pain he had suffered. Surely it cannot be worse with God's own children; when they undergo hardship, sorrow, and trouble in this life, their pain will surely purify them from the dross of iniquity, and they will inherit futurity.â Gen. Rabba 92.

Man when reproached with his misdeeds becomes confused and confounded. Balaam, when reproached by the humblest of animals and asked ' What have I done unto thee, that thou hast smitten me these three times? Am not I thine ass, upon which thou hast ridden ever since I was thine unto this day? Was I ever wont to do so unto thee? ' was constrained to reply ' Nay." Joseph, telling his brethren who he was, said," I am Joseph, your brother, whom you sold to Egypt." And his brethren, ten great, proud, and mighty men, could not answer him, for they were confounded in his presence (Gen 45.3). ' How then, 0 man, will it be with me ' (so do thou ask thyself),"when I stand before God's tribunal and a record of my conduct, during my life, is placed before me!"â Gen. Rabba 93.

To rebel against the king is to rebel against the King of Kings.â Gen. Rabba 94.

At the approach of the death of Moses the two silver trumpets which he had made for the purpose of calling the people together (Num. 10. 2) were hidden, so that no one else should use them.â Gen. Rabba 96.

A book of pedigrees was found in Jerusalem, wherein it was stated that Hillel was a descendant of King David. â Gen. Rabba 98.

The effects of the blessing bestowed upon Judah by his father are to be seen even at the present time. Jacob said (Gen. 49. 8), ' Judah, thou art he whom thy brethren shall praise." If an Israelite describes his race, he says, ' I am a Jew, i. e. a Judaite," he does not describe himself as a Reul:)enite or a Simconite.â Gen. Rabba 98.

Slander is compared to an arrow, not to any other handy weapon, such as a sword, etc., because like an arrow it kills at a distance. It can be uttered in Rome and have its baneful effect in Syria.â Gen. Rabba 98.

Amongst a number of great men who all reached the same age are Moses, Hillel, Rabbi Johanan b. Zakkai, and Rabbi Akiba. Moses' years were divided into three equal portions, viz., forty years in Pharaoh's palace, forty years in Midian, and forty years as leader of the Israelites in the wilderness.

Rabbi Jochanan too had his forty years of trade, forty years of study, and forty years of serving his people. Rabbi Akiba was forty years an ignoramus, forty years he gave himself to study, and for forty years he served his community.â Gen. Rabba 100.

King David was a descendant of Miriam.â Exod. Rabba i.

Jethro, who was originally a priest of Midianite idolatry, renounced his idols, and with them his priestly position. For this he was boycotted and excommunicated by his former compatriots; no one was to perform any work for him or his; or, indeed, to have any intercourse with them. His daughters, who were therefore compelled to look after their father's flock, were persecuted by the shepherds. Moses, from a sense of chivalry, seeing women do the work which generally was done by the stronger sex, and. yet being harassed by them, offered the women his assistance.â Exod. Rabba i.

It would be a serious error to say that Moses murdered the Egyptian. In slaying him he was the executioner of a man who, even by the laws of the Egyptiansâ who observed what are known as the seven commandments of the sons of Noah, one of which was prohibition of murderâ deserved death. According to a tradition, this Egyptian ravished the wife of an Israelite, and to escape accusation by her husband he killed him, and thus incurred death.â Exod. Rabba i.

He who lifts up his hand in a threatening manner against a fellow-man, though he may not actually strike him, is designated a wicked man.â Exod. Rabba i.

When Pharaoh's daughter indicated to her maidens, who accompanied her to the river, her intention of saving the weeping child (Moses), her maidens expressed their disapproval, arguing that it would be bad enough for any of the king's subjects to disregard his decree, but in the king's own daughter such a want of loyalty would be highly reprehensible. Their argumentsâ lest they should have the effect desired by themâ were cut short by the angel Gabriel, who struck them all down except one, so that the dignity of the princess should not be outraged by not having even one maid to attend on her. Hence, at the opening of the narrative we find maidens attending her, but when she rescued the child she sent her maiden, not maidens. â Exod. Rabba.

Moses, before he left Egypt, succeeded in securing for the Israelites the observance of rest on the Sabbath, by pointing out to Pharaoh the necessityâ in his own interestâ of granting his slaves one day every week freedom from labour, and thereby invigorating them for the renewal of labour after their rest.â Exod. Rabba i.

In calling his two sons by the names of Gershom and Eliezer, Moses, like Joseph and other righteous men, intended to have the fact of God's hclj) constantly before him. Since his sons would be with him, and he would often address them or call them by name, he would remember his gratitude to God.â Exod. Rabba i.

Amongst Pharaoh's advisers or counsellors were Balaam, Job, and Jethro. Balaam advocated the persecution of the Israehtes; as a retribution, he fell by the sword. Job was silent, and would not advise either way, and he had his punishment for this act of unfriendliness. Jethro would not countenance any suggestion of persecution, and was rewarded by having his family raised to greatness (i Chron. 2.).â Exod. Rabba i.

' The new king ' who arose in Egypt is not to be taken literally, for it was the same Pharaoh who had elevated Joseph. But when the Egyptians suggested the enslaving of the Israelites he protested, pointing out that the people were saved from starvation by an Israelite. This so displeased the Egyptians that they dethroned him; and being for three months deprived of his throne, go THE MIDRASH he at last gave in, and ' did not know Joseph," that is, the benefits conferred by him on the land. Thereupon he was reinstated. Hence the expression, ' a new king who knew not Joseph': when he pretended to know nothing of Joseph and his benefits, then his kingdom was renewed.â Exod. Rabba i.

There is more than appears on the surface in the words (Exod. i. 5), ' For Joseph was in Egypt." It is intended to convey to us the noble character of this pattern of righteousness; to tell us that all the time he was in Egypt, during all his vicissitudes whether as a slave or as a ruler, there was no change in his character or in his humility and piety.â Exod. Rabba i.

' He that spareth his rod hateth his son," as the wise king tells us (Prov. 13. 24). Yet we are aware that a father would be very indignant with any one who should beat his son. But we have examples before us of the pernicious result of indulging one's son and putting no restraint upon him. The reward of such treatment is not love and affection, but rather estrangement between parent and child, where a timely and judicious chastisement would have averted it. Take the case of Ishmael, of whom it is traditionally said that he did very much in accordance with his own sweet will, that he actually had his own idols brought into Abraham's house when he was but a lad of fifteen years. His father's forbearance had only the effect that Ishmael so indulged in his evil propensities that eventually he was driven out of his father's house, without provision being made for his maintenance, a thing which can only be accounted forâ with a tender-hearted man like Abrahamâ by the fact that the lad had, by his evil ways, actually incurred his father's hatred. Other instances we have, like Isaac and his son Esau, or David and his son Absalom.

Further, King Solomon adds, ' but he that loveth him chasteneth him betimes.' This may well be applied to God's dealings with his son (Israel). ' I have loved you," says God to Israel, and this very love brought affliction with it.â Exod. Kabba i.

There is no place without God's presence. Even in the bush He was present, and this was the lesson of God's omnipresence that Moses learnt when he was called out of the bush.â Exod. Rabba 2.

Moses, when tending Jethro's flock in the wilderness, proved himself a tender shepherd. He was not above carrying a little lamb, becoming footsore in its search for water, on his shoulder back to the flock. God said, ' This tender shepherd of man's flock shall be the shepherd of my own flock."â Exod. Rabba 2.

Moses, leading Jethro's flock into the wilderness, was typical of his leading God's flock in the wilderness. Sheltering, feeding, and getting drink for the sheep were the forerunners of his obtaining for Israel the sheltering protection of the pillars of fire and cloud, and a supply of manna, quails, and water in the wilderness. â Exod. Rabba 2.

The burning bush was typical of the indestructibility of Israel. Just as the bush, though continually burning, was not consumed, so would the fire of Egyptian persecution and oppression of other nations be unable to consume Israel.â Exod. Rabba 2.

Moses wanted to know God's name, and God tells him, ' I am that I am '; that is to say, ' I am calledâ or to 1)6 calledâ in accordance with my work in this world." When I judge mankind I am D" '? Elohim, that being the title or designation for judgment. When I war with the wicked I am known as jmhi2ii Zevooth. When I execute judgment for the sins of man I am known as nti '? El Shadai, and when I am visiting the world with mercy I am "J1 or mn Adonoi, the Eternal.â Exod. Rabba 3.

Moses' assertion, ' Behold they will not believe me nor hearken unto my voice; for they will say, the Lord hath not appeared unto thee ' (Exod. 4. i) was an ungenerous remark on his part, unworthy of him, as it was prejudging the people adversely. This seems to be borne out by what follows. God asked him what he had in his hand, and the answer was ' a rod," an appropriate instrument with which he deserved to be punished for his harshness. Then the rod turned into a serpent, pointing out to him that he had adopted something of the vices of the reptile, which slandered God himself to Adam and Eve (Gen. 3. 5).â Exod. Rabba 3.

There was no false modesty in Moses' hesitation to accept the most important mission, that of dehvering the Israelites from Egyptian bondage. Judging from past events he felt that this mission was too vast and too important for him. When God wanted to save one individualâ he reasonedâ and that individual Lot, he sent one of his angels for the purpose. Even to save Ishmael angels were employed. Measured by that standard, Who am I, to be the deliverer of this great multitude? 'â Exod. Rabba 3.

The matron whom we find so often arguing with Rabbi Jose observed one day to that sage, ' My god is surely greater than yours. When your God appeared to Moses in the bush, Moses merely covered his face, whilst when my god (the serpent) made its appearance he could not stand his ground at all, but had to run away out of fear." ' Not so," returned the Rabbi," for in order to be out of the power of your god it sufficed for Moses to step a few paces back, but whither could he have fled from the presence of Him who filleth the earth?"â Exod. Rabba 3.

There was a secret sign handed down to the Israelites in Egypt, a legacy left by Jacob, who entrusted it to Joseph, and he again to his brother Asher, who handed it down to his daughter Serach. She was blessed with longevity, and was living when Moses made his appearance before Pharaoh. The tradition was that the one who appeared in Egypt as the messenger of God with the tidings of their redemption would use the word ips ' visiting," that God visited them and saw what was done to them in Egypt. Thus they would know and believe that he was really sent by their God. Hence we find that when Moses used the words ' llp3 lp3," and not until then, the people believed that the Lord looked upon their affliction, they bowed their heads and worshipped. (Exod. 4. 31.)â Exod. Rablxi 5.

That one should not be wise above what is written is well demonstrated in the life of King Solomon. The Torah says that the king whom the Israelites should set over them should not multi ily horses to himself, nor wives, in order that he might not cause the people to return to Egypt, and that his heart might not turn away (Deut. 17. 16, 17). ' Then," argued Solomon, ' since the reason for the paucity of wives and horses is given, I am sure that I can stand proof against these; I can multiply horses and wives and shall not turn away and will not cause my people to return to Egypt." Unfortunately he was not )roof against the prohibitions, as it is recorded against him (in i Kings 2.1-7). And one can also see the wisdom of the Torah in withholding any reason for many commandments it enjoins.â Exod. Rabba 6.

How beautiful was that simple life and faith of the Patriarchs and their submission to the Divine will. To Abraham God said, ' Lift up thine eyes and look from the place where thou art, northwards, southwards, eastwards, and westwards; for all the land which thou seest to thee I will give it and to thy seed for ever." Yet when he needed a sepulchre for his beloved Sarah he could get none until he bought it from Ephron; but he murmured not. Isaac, too, was told, ' Sojourn in this land, and I will be with thee, and will bless thee, and unto thy seed I will give all these countries." But when he dug for water the herdmen of Gerar disputed with his herdmen for the water which they found, and he was obliged to seek another place, and do over again the work which had been expended in vain in Gerar. Then again Jacob was told the land upon which he lay should be given to him and to his seed for ever, etc. When, however, he wanted to pitch his tent in the city of Shechem in the land of Canaan he had to purchase a ' parcel of the field ' upon which his tent was spread for a hundred pieces of money. There was no murmuring on the part of these smiple and holy men, who knew well that God would carry out his promises to them in his own good time.â Exod. Rabba 6.

There is not a word in Holy Writ without its purpose. In the statement that ' Aaron took him Elishaba the daughter of Aminadab, sister of Nachshon, to wife," the addition of the brother's name is apparently superfluous. But in truth its purpose is to caution the would-be Benedick to inquire of the character and disposition of the brothers of her whom he intends to marry, since most sons take after the character and disposition of their mother's brothers.â Exod. Rabba 7.

When Moses was performing the miracles in Egypt to convince the Egyptians that he was the messenger of God, Pharaoh simply ridiculed him and asked him ironically, ' Art thou bringing straw to Eprayne (where there was plenty)? Art thou not aware that the Egyptians are past masters in magic? People usually take their wares to places where they are scarce. Here children of four or five years of age can work this sort of conjuring." And he actually had some children brought out of school, and they and Pharaoh's wife performed similar works to those of Moses. ' Is he a wise man," continued Pharaoh, ' who carries muria (a sort of salt) to Spain or fish to Acco? ' Moses refrained from controversy, but merely replied, ' Where there is the market of greenstuff there I take my greenstuff."â Exod. Rabba 9.

When praying on behalf of Pharaoh to remove the

See Dr. Sach's Beitrdge zur Sprach iind Alterthumsforschidig aus jiidischen Quellen, 2nd vol., page 3, for the word Muria.

plague of hail from him, JMoses went out of the town to do so (Exod. Q. 20), because he would not pray in the midst of the idols and abominations that polluted the place and rendered it unfit for prayer to the throne of mercy. He went into the open, pure air of God to pray to God. â Exod. Rabba 12.

Even from such hardened sinners as Pharaoh and the Egyptians God did not withhold the opportunity of mending their ways. Before a plague visited them Moses was charged to warn them of its coming, to-morrow, if they remained ol)durate.â Exod. Rabba 13.

Behold God as a pleader as well as an accuser. Whilst He complains of a sinful nation (Isa. i. 4) He pleads, ' Open ye the gates that a righteous nation may enter' (Isa. 26. 2). Again, designating Israel as a people laden with iniquity, He yet condescends to say, ' Thy people are all righteous ' (Isa. 60. 21). Though declaring them to be children that are corrupted, He calls them ' children taught of the Lord ' (Isa. 54.13). Whilst they are 'aseed of evildoers," He says, their. seed shall be known amongst the heathen ' (Isa. 61. 9). Again they are told, ' When you make many prayers I will not hear." Yet He assures us (Isa. 65. 24) ' Before they call I will answer." Wliilst declaring that our new moons and our feasts his soul hateth. He invites us to come and prostrate our selves before Him on new moons and sabbaths.â Exod. Rabba 15.

The rite of proclaiming and sanctifying the month at the appearance of the new moon is traced back to the time of the Exodus, when Nisson was placed at the head of the months. The ceremony was of the same importance as are dates in legal documents and in evidence, and the month only began when it had been proclaimed by the representative of the community.â Exod. Rabba 15.

Water, air, and fire were created before the world; the water begat darkness, the fire begat light, the ni").

spirit or air, begat wisdom, and with these the world is always governed, viz. wind, fire, wisdom, light, darkness and water.â Exod. Rabba 15.

For the purpose of effecting Israel's redemption God did not disdain to appear in a place where there were images of idols or other impurities.â Exod. Rabba

The kingdom of Greece was a terror to the world, but Mattathias the priest, with faith and not with weapons, boldly met the terror and defeated it.â Exod. Rabba 15.

Who is she that looketh forth as the morning, fair as the woman? ' (Song, 6.10). She is no other than Esther, who like the morning star was the light brought to Israel in the dark days of Media. ' Clear as the sun and terrible as an army with banners ' (Song, 6. 10): these were no other than Mattathias the High Priest and his sons, who like an army with their banners stood up against the evil power of Greece, from which every power fled as one flees from the strength of the mid-day sun. Their army and their banners were faith in their God; they were stimulated by the words of the prophet (Joel 4. 6-10), ' The children of Judah and the children of Jerusalem have ye sold unto the Grecians. Beat your ploughshares into swords and your pruning-hooks into spears; let the weak say, I am strong."â Exod. Rabba 15.

Certain commandments were given to Israelites exclusively; and these are mostly known by the word DD"? (to you). The observance of the Passover in the month of Nisson (Exod. 12): Not to make graven images (Levit. 26): Tobe just in judgment (Hosea5.): Righteousness and charity (Deut. 24.): To be merciful and compassionate (Deut. 13.): Sabbatical years and Jubilees (Levit. 25.): and various others (Deut. 11.), tithes, concerning the Firstborn (Deut. 14.), Sacrifices (Exod. 20.), Fringes (Num. 15.), Festivals (Levit. 23.), Atonement Day, etc. On the other hand there are special gifts, viz.: God's blessings (Levit. 25. and Numb. 6.), Palestine (Levit. 25.), the Torah (Prov. 3.), and Light (Isa. 60.). â Exod. Rabba 15.

The reconstruction of the calendar, as far as the months are concerned, Nisson having taken the place of Tishri, as the head of the months, at the Exodus, was but in proper keeping with things. A king proclaimed the day of the birth of his son as a holiday; the son was taken captive and enslaved, but eventually set free. The day of his freedom was henceforth ordered to be observed as the holiday, instead of the day of his birth. Thus God distinguished the month when his son, Israel, was set free from thraldom, and crowned it as henceforth the first or head of the months.â Exod. Rabba 15.

There is a remedy for every sin, viz. prayer and repentance; but there are three grievous sins for which there seems to be no expiation, and these are murder, idolatry and adultery. If therefore one says to you, Let us go and murder, and we shall escape punishment," beware of what was said even in the early days of the world's existence, before the Torah was given: ' He that sheds man's blood, through man his blood shall be shed." If you are enticed to commit adultery and are perhaps persuaded that you can atone for it, flee from the very thought. The two laws, the one appertaining to the Nazirite and the one concerning a woman suspected of misconduct, are advisedly placed side by side because of their affinity to each other. The Nazirite, for instance, who takes upon himself to abstain from wine, is told that he is not permitted to partake of the very fruit that produces intoxicants, so that the good resolution may not be frustrated, which would probably be the case were he to indulge in the tasting of the grape. Remember that a woman also is mentioned as a fruitful vine, so that a woman's and your own conduct should be like that prescribed for the Nazirite. Do not say, I will guard myself against so great an offence as actual adultery, but there can be no harm in say, kissing, embracing, or caressing and fondling my neighbour's wife. Bear in mind that the Nazirite's resolution not to partake of wine was supplemented by the prohibition of partaking of the fruit that produces wine. ' Can a man take fire in his bosom," says the wise king, ' and his clothes not be burnt? Can one go upon hot coals and his feet not be scorched? So he that goeth to his neighbour's wife; whosoever toucheth her shall not be innocent' (Prov. 6,). If again you are persuaded to commit the very grievous sin of idolatry, let these serious words ever be before you: ' He that sacrificeth unto any god, save unto the Eternal only, he shall be utterly destroyed ' (Exod. 22. 20). And not only are we prohibited the worship of a strange god, but all accessories of such worship are forbidden, even for the purpose of medicine, such as using some of the incense for a medicine, or any of the groves for any purpose whatsoever. We are told, ' And there shall cleave nought of the cursed thing to thine hand ' (Deut. 13. 17); ' Neither shaft thou bring an abomination into thine house, lest thou be a cursed thing like it' (Deut. 7. 26).â Exod. Rabba 16.

There is in heaven an accuser and a defender of man; the name of the former is Semoel and that of the latter Michael.â Exod. Rabba 18.

Onkeles, who became a convert to Judaism, complained to the Rabbis that God's love for converts only went to the extent of giving them bread and raiment (Deut. 10.18): ' You have now joined the house of Israel," replied one rabbi, ' and you should bear in mind that Israel (Jacob) asked the Lord only to give him bread to eat and raiment to put on, and therefore you might be contented with the promise to give you spontaneously what Israel had to petition for." ' More than this," added another of the wise men, ' the bread and raiment mentioned are not to be taken in their literal sense only, for since you have entered the folds of God's people you are not precluded from eating the shcwbread and having for your raiment the priestly garments."â Exod. Rabba 19.

God may be regarded as saying to would-be proselytes: ' Perhaps you may hesitate to come within my fold because I have put a stigma on you by enacting, in connexion with the Passover lamb, ' No stranger shall eat thereof." Inquire then of the Gibeonites who were received within the pale of the Israelites by practising fraud and because they feared earthly evil; yet I punished Saul and his household because they did not deal kindly with the Gibeonites 2 Saml. 21.). If I valued the Gibeonites' conversion, how much more will I be pleased with those who seek to come under the banner of my law, not out of bodily fear but from motives of the higher life."â Exod. Rabba 19.

When, at the Exodus, Moses was anxious to take up Joseph's bones for interment in Palestine, Serach the daughter of Asher was still living, and she pointed out the spot of Joseph's sepulchre.â Exod. Rabba 20.

Honour the physician so long as you do not require his skill.â Exod. Rabba 21.

David advisedly calls one of his Psalms (Psalm 90.) ' A prayer of Moses, the man of God," and another Psalm (Psalm 102.) he names ' A prayer of the afflicted," to convey to us the truth that the prayer of the greatest and of the most humble of men, that of the richest and that of the poorest, of the slave and of the master, are equal before God.â Exod. Rabba 21.

Prayers should be said in common, master and man, mistress and maid, rich and poor together, for all are equal before God.â Exod. Rabba 21.

By Isaac's blessings Esau became the possessor of the power of the hand, and he made good use of it. When the Israelites intended passing his country he warned them of his handy sword (Num. 20.). Not less does Jacob (i. e. Israel) appreciate his power of the voice, i. e. prayer. There will come a time when each will take the full benefit of the power possessed by him. Esau's is predicted in the thirty-fourth chapter of Isaiah, and that of Israel in the thirty-third chapter of Jeremiah.â Exod. Rabba 21.

The approach of Pharaoh on the shores of the Red Sea was worth a hundred fast days and a hundred formal or ordinary prayers. It caused the Israelites to lift up their hearts and eyes in trust and sincerity to their Heavenly Father, to whom they prayed and to whom they looked for help.â Exod. Rabba 21.

If your hands are stained by dishonesty, your prayers will be polluted and impure, and an offence to Him to whom you direct them. Do not pray at all before you have your hands purified from every dishonest act.â Exod. Rabba 22.

With all their professed faith, in Egypt, there was no real faith in the Israelites until they saw God's wonders on the Red Sea. Prompted by that faith they were enabled to compose and sing the exquisite song of praise. â Exod. Rabba 23.

The song of praise that Israel offered on the Red Sea was pleasing to God as an outburst of real gratitude. There had indeed been no such praise offered to God since creation. Adam, formed out of dust and put above all creation, omitted to praise the Creator for the dignity conferred on him. Even Abraham, rescued from the fiery furnace and made conqueror of the kings he pursued, or Isaac when dehvered by the message of God from the knife, or Jacob when he resisted the attacking angel, withstood the enmity of Esau and the men of Shechem, not one was prompted to offer hymns to God for his protecting power and deliverance. It was left to the poor enslaved and oppressed Israelites, rescued from thraldom, to sing that exquisite h3ann to the glory of their God.â Exod. Rabba 23.

EXODUS RABBA loI

Through their faith the Israehtes on the Red Sea became j)ossessed of the Holy Spirit.â Exod. Rabba 23.

Man is the proudest of God's creatures, the eagle is the haughtiest amongst the birds, the ox amongst the cattle, and the lion amongst the beasts of the field. Hence it was the image of these four which Ezekiel saw in his vision on the throne of God.â Exod. Rabba 23.

So persistent were the Israelites in their desire to return to Egypt, that Moses had to use force, after persuasive language had failed, to make them continue their journey Their arguments were that God's object in bringing them out of Egypt was fivefold (i) to give them the Egyptians' goods, to which they were entitled as wages for their work; (2) to lead them through the Red Sea; (3) to shelter them with his cloud of glory. (4) to avenge them on the Egyptians; (5) to enable them to sing hymns of praise to Him. Now that all these things were accomplished, the Egyptians drowned, and not sufficient left in Egypt to force them again to slavery, their best step would be, they thought, to return to a country where, free from slavery, they could enjoy life infinitely better than in the wilderness that faced them, where there was no bread and no water, not to mention the fish and the onions of Egypt. But Moses pointed out to them that there was a great debt which they had not yet discharged. ' Ye shall serve God upon this mountain' (Exod. 3. 12), which was, in fact, the token beforehand of God's being with Moses and his mission to Pharaoh.â Exod. Rabba 24.

' He made his people go forth like sheep and guided them in the wilderness like a flock ' (Ps. 78. 52). ' Like sheep 'â like the sheej) of Jethro which Moses led to the wilderness; so he led the Israelites through the wilderness, for as sheep are not brought into the dwelling-house, and there is no fixed fund out of which to maintain them, so was it with Israel; they had no buildings wherein to dwell, they had to pick up their food in the open. Not however like sheep destined for slaughter, for they are God's holy flock; he who touches that which is holy unto the Lord incurs guilt, and he who touches Israel, God's firstborn, shall offend; evil shall come upon them, says the prophet (Jer. 2.). â Exod. Rabba 24.

That Saturday is the Sabbath proclaimed on Sinai was fully demonstrated to the Israelites in the wilderness. When, contrary to God's ordinance, they went out on that day to gather manna and found none, Moses told them ' See," â he did not say ' Know ' but See â that God has given you the Sabbath, pointing out to them visibly the Sabbath day.â Exod. Rabba 25.

The observance of the Sabbath proclaimed on Sinai by an Israelite outweighs all other commandments. And from the point of view that the Sabbath was established as a token between God and his people (Exod. 31. 13) one is justified in saying that it is not right and proper for a non-Jew to observe that Sabbath; it is the expression of a relation so intimate that the intrusion of a stranger would be resented.â Exod. Rabba 25.

The ways of the Lord are inscrutable; it is vain for mortal man to define how his work is done. If you wish to find out whence punishments or blessings come, you will be confounded in the attempt. The fire and brimstone brought upon Sodom and Gomorrah came from heaven (Gen. 19.). You may perhaps conclude that punishment only comes thence, but you will then find the beneficial dew coming from heaven (Micah 5). The Egyptians received their plagues from heaven, and the retribution of the Ammonites came down from heaven (Joshua 10.); Sisera was fought against from heaven (Judg. 5.). On the other hand goodness and blessings came from heaven (Deut. 28.). Bread seems to come from earth only (Ps. 104.), but it comes from heaven also (Exod. 16.). Water came from earth (Numb. 21.), and you will find water from heaven (Deut. II.).

The same confusion will meet you if you try to find the position or attitude of angels. You may conclude that they fly (Isa. 6. 6), but behold they stand (Isa. 6. 2). You find them sitting (Judg. 6.), and you find them walking too (Zech. 3). You conclude, in one instance, that they appear in the figure of a woman (Zech. 5.), but they are men (Gen. 18.), and they are also wind and fire (Ps. 104.â Exod. Rabba 25.

Because of his love, God did not disdain to do the work proper to a servant for the Israelites in the wilderness. He held a light for them through their wanderings there. He washed them, clothed them, and shod them (Ezkl. 16.). He carried them and watched over them when asleep (Ps. 121.).â Exod. Rabba 25.

Every prophecy, afterwards uttered by various prophets, was handed over on Sinai at the time of the giving of the Decalogue, but was to be kept unproclaimed until each prophet had received the charge of proclaiming his respective prophecy.â Exod. Rabba 28.

' I am the first and I am the last, and beside Me there is no God ' (Isa. 43. 6) I am the first, I have no father; I am the last, I have no brother. Beside inle there is no God; I have no son.â Exod. Rabba 29.

Nature was silent and at rest when the Decalogue was proclaimed on Sinai. No animal made a sound, no fowl flew, the very angels kept silent, and desisted from praises before God. The billows of the sea became calm and at rest, and no creature uttered a sound whilst the words were uttered by the living God saying, ' I am the Lord thy God."â Exod. Rabba 29.

When Onkeles intimated to his uncle Hadrian his intention of becoming a convert to Judaism, the uncle ridiculed his nephew's taste for attaching himself to a people of such low estate and so despised. He asked Onkeles to tell him what prompted him to such a folly. Onkeles' reply was, ' The Jew, the most insignificant, and may be the most despised amongst men as he now is, knows more about God and the creation than any man amongst the other peoples, and the Torah contains nothing but Truth." The uncle then permitted his nephew to dive into the study of the Torah, but forbade him circumcision, which however Onkeles underwent.â Exod. Rabba 30.

Poverty is man's greatest affliction.â Exod. Rabba 31.

Moses offered his life for Israel and for the Torah, therefore these were designated as his. In Isaiah (63. 11) we are told, ' Moses and his people," and in Malachi (3. 4) ' Remember the law of Moses my servant."â Exod. Rabba 30.

Rabbis Gamaliel, Joshua, Eleazar b. Azaria and Akiba were preachers in Rome.â Exod. Rabba 30.

Repentance makes virtues almost of the very vices of the penitent sinner.â Exod. Rabba 31.

Riches, might, and worldly wisdom are not only not always a blessing to their possessors, but may be the very causes of their destruction. Korah and Haman had their fall brought about by their riches. Goliath paid with his life the penalty of his might, and Balaam's wisdom was his destruction.â Exod. Rabba 31.

The poor are styled ' God's own."â Exod. Rabba 31.

He who lives by usury in this world shall not live in the world to come.â Exod. Rabba 31.

' Behold I send an angel before thee, to keep thee in the way, and to bring thee into the place which I have prepared, etc' (Exod. 23. 20-22). ' Up to the time of the grievous sin of the people," says God to Moses, ' I myself was leading them (Exod. 12.). By their making and worshipping the golden calf they have forfeited that high privilege and tender care. I will now send you an angelâ or messengerâ to lead you in the way. Beware not to rebel against him, for my name is in him; he comes by my authority; what he tells you he says in my name." A similar expression is used in connexion with Moses himself, when God says (Exod. 19. 9), ' Behold 1 come unto thee in a thick cloud that the people may hear when I speak with thee, and may believe in thee for ever," which obviously does not mean that they should believe in Moses as a deity, but they should believe that he (Moses) speaks as God's messenger.

Further, regarding the words that the angel shall not forgive their sins if they rebel against him, the meaning is that he has no such power as forgiving sin. Moreover, the words, 2 l n bi may mean ' Thou shalt not change him: not change him for God because he has taken up the leadership in the wilderness, instead of God who led you hitherto, and therefore worship him and pray to him for the forgiveness of sin. I alone forgive iniquity and pass away sin.â Exod. Rabba 32.

When Moses was charged with the erection of the Mishkan he inwardly wondered that God who filleth the worlds above and below should require a residence made for Him. But the Lord said to him, ' Israel is my flock (Ezkl. 34.), 'and I am their shepherd ' (Ps. 80.): make a hut for the shepherd whither he shall come to tend them. â Exod. Rabba 33.

In giving his Torah to Israel, God is like a king who gives his only daughter in marriage, and makes it a condition with her husband that there shall always be a room kept for him in their house. If we wish to have the Torah, we must have God also. This is the meaning of the words ' Make Me a sanctuary that I may dwell therein."â Exod. Rabba 33.

My light, the Torah, says God to man, is in thy hand; but thy light, the soul, is in my hand. Take care of my light, so that I may take care of thy light.â Exod. Rabba 37.

Gold is one of the things for the non-existence of which man would probably be all the better. It was originally called into existence for the service of the Mishkan and of the Temple.â Exod. Rabba 37.

God requires but earnest prayer and a penitent heart.

Israel was redeemed from Egypt in answer to prayer. Joshua became a conqueror because of his prayer; in the days of the judges help was obtained by prayer; Samuel's help for his people was granted in reply to prayer.â Exod. Rabba 38.

It was but proper that Aaron the holy (Ps. 106.) should enter the holy place (Exod. 15.) to make atonement before the Most Holy (Levit. ig.) for a holy people (Levit. 19.). â Exod. Rabba 38.

The poor amongst Israel plead before the Lord, saying, ' If one of our rich transgresses, he can bring a sacrifice for his accidental sin and it is atoned (Levit. 4. 22); but what are we, who have no means to purchase sacrifices, to do in order to expiate our sins? ' In reply they are told to have regard to the words of the Psalmist and the prophets.

The Psalmist says (Ps. 26. 6, 7), ' I will wash my hands in innocency," and lest you should think that he alludes to the bringing of bullocks and goats he hastens to add, ' So will I encompass thine altar, that I may cause to be heard the voice of thanksgiving and tell all thy wondrous work."

And the prophet Hosea tells you (Hosea 14. 3), ' Take with you words and return to the Lord." Words, words of earnest prayer and not sacrifice, do I require.â Exod. Rabba 38.

The tribe of Judah was the elite of the Israelites, that of Dan the plebeian. For the erection of the Mishkan God called for Bezaleel from the tribe of Judah, and commanded that Aholiab, from the tribe of Dan, should be placed with him; they jointly should do the work (Exod. 31. 1-6), to demonstrate that all, the one of high estate and the one of low estate, are alike before God. â Exod. Rabba 40.

The Tablets of the commandments were called Tablets of Stones, because the punishment for violating the commandments was death by stoning.â Exod. Rabba 41.

Israel is the most arrogant among nations, like the dog amongst beasts and the cock amongst fowls.â Exod. Kabba 42.

Moses, in pleading for the Israehtes against their projected destruction for making the golden calf, had recourse to all sorts of excuses in order to avert the threatened punishment. ' When appearing on Mount Sinai and proclaiming Thyself as the only God," he pleaded. Thou didst say, ' I am the Lord thy God," not in the plural, ' Your God," so that this ignorant people, just set free from slaver5 may perchance have taken this proclamation as strictly applying to me only." The using of this argument seems to have been a fact because, whilst at the giving of the commandments the singular 1'

'7 ' thy God," is used, thereafter the word DD ':'. ' Your God," is used. Moreover, ' Moses said, ' this golden calf may be thy coadjutor, O God. Thou causest the sun to shine: the golden calf will take over some of the workings of nature, and may cause the rain to descend. Thou wilt send down the dew, and the golden calf will cause the herb to grow." Moses received the merited rebuke from God, who said," Thou also hast become an idolater; is there any power in that idol which the people have made themselves as a god? is it anything but inanimate matter? ' ' Why then," Moses said, ' shouldst Thou bo angry with thy people who have made this worthless, powerless thing? ' Further Moses argued and pleaded ' Why does thine anger grow against the people whom Thou hast brought out from Egypt? They have been slaves of the Egyptians, a people who worshipped animals as their gods; and can it be wondered at that they imitated their masters? A man once got for his son a trade which brought him into contact with a set of men of questionable repute, whose habits he soon adopted. The father became incensci to such an extent that he threatened his son's destruction; but a friend pleaded for the son by pointing out to the father that he, by the force of circumstances, had somewhat contributed to the evil habits of his son, by having put him into a trade which brought him into the company of evildoers. The Israelites are but like children prone to adopt the ways and manners of their elders, and if they are now destroyed there will be no chance for them to develop the better and higher life, to redeem the evil they have done, and to live by the law which Thou hast proclaimed." Moses prevailed with his prayer. And yet we see distinctly that not until Moses made mention of the Patriarchs was the reply ' And the Lord repented of the evil which He thought to do to His people ' given. Just as a vine, to which Israel is likened (Ps. 80. 9), requires dead branches to support and prop the living ones, so Israel requires his departed ancestors' merits for his support. Thus Solomon says (Eccl. 9.) 'And I praise the dead which died long ago'; and so Moses, perceiving that his pleadings and prayers of forty days' duration (Deut. 9, 18-25) were left unanswered, made mention of the Patriarchs, and then his prayer was answered. There was yet another reason for Moses' mention of the three Patriarchs in his intercession for the Israelites. ' If death," he said, is total annihilation, and there is now nothing of Abraham, Isaac, and Jacob, I have no plea for the sinning people; but if they â the Patriarchsâ live in another, better and higher sphere, what of the promise made to them to multiply their offspring like the stars of the heavens? ' Finally Moses mentioned that God was prepared to spare Sodom and Gomorrah if there could be found ten righteous men; and he agreed to produce the number demanded to save a sinning community, i. e. Aaron, Eliezer, Ithamar, Phineas, Joshua, Caleb and himself, but there were still three lacking to make up the Ten. Then Moses inquired of God again whether the righteous who depart from this world live in another world, and he received a reply in the affirmative. ' Remember then," he prayed, ' the Patriarchs, Abraham, Isaac, and Jacob, who with the seven names mentioned will make up the ten righteous; for whose sake vouchsafe to save thy people."â Exod. Rabba 43 and 44.

If thou hast done any meritorious act, do not ask at once for the reward thereof; if you receive it not, your offspring after you will receive it. What would have become of us if our Patriarchs had asked for and received the reward of their merits whilst they lived?â Exod. Rabba 44.

Moses considered the breaking of the Tablets preferable to delivering them to the people, after they had made the golden calf. He was like a man commissioned by a king to convey the marriage contract to his future bride, who learns on his way that the would-be bride has rendered herself guilty of a serious indiscretion. He decidesâ in the woman's own interestâ not to proceed further with the nuptial contract, but to tear it up, as she will thus still be unmarried and her guilt less serious than if she were guilty of her misdeed after she had received her marriage lines. â Exod. Rabba 43 and 46.

When God first called Moses, not being then an expert proj)het, he was addressed in a voice similar to that of his own father, and he thought that his father had come to him from Egypt. God then told him that it was not his earthly father who called him, but the God of his father. Then, we find, Moses hid his face, which he did not do when first called by his name; not in fact until he heard the words, ' I am the God of thy fathers."â Exod. Rabba 45.

It is prohibited to preach out of manuscript. Sermons are to be delivered without the help of any writing before the preacher.â Exod. Rabba 47.

If you want a vine to flourish it should be replanted on another soil. God replanted his vineâ Israelâ from no THE MIDRASH

Egypt to Palestine, and it became famous.â Exod. Rabba 44.

There were two ships: the one left the harbour, and the other entered it. The spectators expressed their joy over the ship that was leaving, but took hardly any notice of the incoming one. Amongst the spectators was a man of sound sense, who pointed out to the crowd that their joy was misplaced, inasmuch as there should be more joy at a ship safely returned from its voyage than for the ship whose fate no one could foretell. This is what King Solomon meant when he said that the day of death is better than the day of one's birth, since no one can foretell the career of the newly-born child, whilst if a man goes hence with a good record behind him such death is better than a new birth.â Exod. Rabba 48.

And they brought earrings, rings, tablets and jewels of gold ' (Exod. 35. 22). We have here five different articles of gold, in accordance with the law laid down (Exod. 21.): if one defrauds with a bullock, he shall pay five-fold. They had committed a sin with the gold in making the golden calf, and they brought to the sanctuary the five-fold penalty.â Exod. Rabba 48.

Why was the Mishkan called ' the Tabernacle of Testimony' (Exod. 38. 23)? Because it testified to the fact that Israel gained forgiveness and was received again into God's favour. A king had a beloved wife, but she had forfeited his love by her conduct and was sent away; and the public concluded that the couple had parted for ever. After a lapse of time the king reinstated his first love, but the populace were still dubious about the reconciliation. When however she was seen in the king's palace adorned with all the charms befitting a queen, the happy relations between the king and his consort could no longer be doubted. So when the Shechinah vouchsafed to dwell in the Mishkan, it was a glorious demonstration that the Lord was reconciled with his people.â Exod. Rabba 51.

A pupil of Rabbi Simeon b. Joshua went abroad and returned with wealth. When the other pupils came to know of it, they too clamoured to go abroad. The Rabbi bade them follow him, and he brought them to a valley where he pulled out a quantity of gold coins, saying, ' If it is gold you want, here it is; take it. Remember, however, that not every one can have a double reward. Perchance if you have this gold, which may procure you pleasures on earth, you are likely to have no reward hereafter, where the righteous can rely on receiving it."â Exod. Rabba 52.

The great characteristic of Mosesâ humilityâ pervades his life throughout. When he was first charged with the mission to Pharaoh his hesitation in accepting the charge was based upon self-abasement. ' Who am I," he says, ' that I should go to Pharaoh and that I should bring out Israel from Egypt? ' Any other man, having been selected by God Himself as the fit and proper person to be his own messenger, would surely have been induced to think more of himself; but not so Moses. Coming to the Red Sea, he again retires in his humility, not being bold enough to take the initiative until called upon by the Lord. And thou lift up thy rod, and stretch out thy hand over the sea and divide it, (Exod. 14). At the l r bni, the Tabernacle of the congregation, his deep humility again manifests itself; he does not venture to approach until the Lord calls him (Levit. I. i).â Levit. Rabba i.

If you are a man of distinction and entitled to a prominent seat at an assembly, seat yourself, nevertheless, two or three seats lower, for it is better to be told ' Go up," than to be asked to ' go down." Hillel was wont to say," If I condescend I am exalted, but if I am haughty I am degraded."â Levit. Rabba i.

Pharaoh's daughter married Caleb.â Levit. Rabba i.

The Torah sets us an example of refinement of speech. If allusion is made to an offering made by man, it is said (Levit. I. 2,) If any man of you bring an offering,' but if anything objectionable needs to be spoken ofâ such as lo )iosy â the expression is not ' if any one of you shall have leprosy," but ' if there shall happen to be a boil in any flesh." Further, when a blessing is pronounced it is given fully and distinctly, ' these shall stand up to bless the people ' (Deut, 27. 12); but when it is necessary to threaten with a curse, the words ' the people ' are omitted, and the phrase used is, ' they shall curse."â Levit. Rabba 2.

Better for you to have no more than two ' Zehubim ' (coins = about a shilling) as the means with which to gain a livelihood, than to be a man of large capital and employ it in usury.â Levit. Rabba 3.

If sincere converts to Judaism enter heaven, Antoninus will be at the head of them.â Levit. Rabba 3.

The proverb says," If you give out your money in usury you will lose what you gain as well as your original capital."â Levit. Rabba 3.

Whom will the Lord hold responsible after death for the unrighteous life on earth? The body as inanimate matter can surely not be affected by anything done to it. The soul has surelya very tangible plea in the fact that all misdeeds were committed by the body whilst alive, for which it (the soul) 'â 'ould not be held responsible. But it is as though the owner of a very valuable garden, being anxious for the preservation of his fruit, employed two men, one blind and the other lame, to watch his orchard.

Said the lame one to the blind, ' Would I could walk! I could feast on the wonderful and enticing fruit which I see all round about me." ' I," said the blind man, ' am strong enough in my legs, but unfortunately have not the sense of sight, and cannot even feast my eyes on the choice fruit of which you tell me. Supposing," suggested he to his lame comrade, ' you were to get on my back and pilot me to those wonderful trees which you see, I could with ease carry you there and you could pluck the coveted fruit for both of us." The suggestion wits adopted, and the garden was quickly despoiled.

When the owner visited his garden, he was shocked at the havoc committed on what to him was his most precious possession, and charged the two men with depredation.

Said the bhnd man, ' I surely cannot be guilty of the theft of a thing the existence and whereabouts of which I could not even see." ' Neither was I able," said the lame watchman, ' to lay my hand on any of the fruit, for you know that my legs refuse to carry me a step." The owner of the orchard was, however, able to demonstrate the method employed by the pair in robbing him of his precious fruit, by taking the lame man and putting him on the back of the blind watchman, and making the latter carry the former to the trees. Thus the Psalmist intimates (Ps. 50. 4), ' He will call to the heavens above and to the earth that He may judge his people': that is to say. He will unite man's heavenly element (the soul) with his earthly element (the body) again, and will fix the responsibility on the reunited whole.â Levit. Rabba 4.

' Your Torah tells you," argued a heathen with one of the Rabbis, ' to be guided by the majority. Why then do you decline to adopt the religion of the majority? ' ' Apart from the fact," replied the sage, ' that a large number is no argument in a matter of religion, and my Torah also tells me ' You shall not go after the multitude to do evil," I will ask you a question. ' Have you any children?" ' Yes, to my sorrow," replied the questioner, ' for they cause me sorrow with their religious views; whenever they come together there is contention between them as to the truth of their respective beliefs." ' Try then," retorted the Rabbi, ' to create unity and harmony regarding religion in your own family, rather than waste your efforts in trying to bring me to your views." When the questioner had gone the Rabbi's disciples said to him, ' It is well that the heathen left you with the lame argument you gave him; but what have you in reality to say as to the paucity of followers of our religion?"

' Esau's family," answered their teacher, ' is spoken of as consisting of so many souls, whilst the seventy members of Jacob's family are described as one soul, because the former had many gods, but the latter had au of them one and the same God. So that even if a majority were an argument in favour of religion, still, though we are apparently smaller in number, we are actually larger if we are not divided in our monotheism ' â Levit. Rabba 4.

Great and dignified names which have been given to Israel have also been bestowed on other nations, such as ' Congregation," ' mighty," ' wise," ' perfect," and ' righteous."â Levit. Rabba 5.

If a man is a witness, whether he has seen or otherwise knows of a thing, if he does not testify he shall bear his iniquity (Levit. 5. i). ' You, my people," says God to Israel, 'have both seen (Deut. 4. 35), and know (Deut. 5. 39) that I am God, and thus you are my proper witnesses (Isa. 43.10). If then you will not proclaim Me as God to all nations of the earth, you shall bear your iniquity."â Levit. Rabba 6.

A certain ruler there was, who when thieves and the recipients of their stolen goods were brought before him, invariably discharged the former and severely punished the latter.â Levit. Rabba 6.

If you sit in judgment and you find one of the litigants anxious to verify his statement by taking an oath, have suspicion against that individual.

There was a man named Bar Talmion with whom one deposited a sum of money for safe keeping. When the depositor called for his deposit Bar Talmion said, Surely I have placed in your own hands the amount you left with me. When they came before Rabbi Asse and his court Bar Talmion was anxious to verify his assertion on oath, and the two litigants accompanied by the Rabbi went to the synagogue to have the oath taken there. At the entrance of the sacred edifice Bar Talmion said to the plaintiff, " Just take this stick and hold it for me whilst I take the solemn oath." The stick being unusually heavy excited suspicion, and was broken to see the cause of its remarkable weight, when the coins deposited with the rascal fell out from the hollow made for the purpose of being a receptacle for the money; the perjurer having placed the stick in the hands of the plaintiff, thinking that by this subterfuge he could honestly swear that he had returned the money to the claimant's own hands.â Levit. Rabba 6.

Broken things are not admired, but God is pleased with a broken spirit and contrite heart.â Levit. Rabba 7.

God pairsâ in marriagesâ and appoints all destinies.â Levit. Rabba 8.

By the ordinance of sacrifices we are taught lessons of frugality. He who could afford it had to bring a bullock; if a man's means did not reach so far, then a sheep was as well accepted; and if that was beyond his means, a goat was accepted, or a dove if a goat was too costly; and the very poor who could afford neither of these could bring a handful of flour. This very inexpensive sacrifice could be brough tin two instalments (Levit. 6.).â Levit. Rabba 8.

All sacrifices, except thankofferings, will be abolished in future; and even should prayer be abolished, that portion thereof which comes under Praises will not be abolished.â Levit. Rabba 9.

All contention amongst the Israelites ceased when they stood at the foot of Sinai to receive the commandments, and owing to the peace and harmony that existed then amongst them they were fit and qualified to receive God's behests.â Levit. Rabba 9.

Amongst the heavenly bodies and beings there is no envy, jealousy, hatred or contention; yet it is said (Job 25. 2), ' He maketh peace in his high places." How much more, then, is peace needed amongst God's creatures in this lower sphere.â Levit. Rabba 9.

The creation of peace and goodwill amongst men towers above all other God's commandments. Take for instance that b2a'Jtiful commandment of restoring your enemy's lost cattle. One is not bidden to go and seek them, only if you meet them you are bound to restore them (Exod. 23). Or again the injunction regarding a birds' nest; you have not to seek this out, it is only when you happen to meet with one that your duty applies. But with regard to peace and goodwill we are distinctly asked to pursue it (Ps. 34.). We are to seek and establish it in our midst, and pursue and found it ever ' vhere else.â Levit. Rabba 9.

The )rophet Amos was a stutterer.â Levit. Rabba 10.

Where repentance effects half, prayer is wholly effective.â Levit. Rabba 10.

Without the young there would be no pupils, and without them there would be no scholars; and without them again there would be no want of the Torah, without which we would have no place of worship, no l lace of study; and without these God w'ould not vouchsafe his Shechinah amongst us.â Levit. Rabba 11.

King Solomon was very abstemious till he married Pharaoh's daughter; then he began to indulge in wine rather freely. On his marriage there was a double rejoicing, the one in honour of the Temple, and the other to celebrate his (forbidden) marriage. His new wife danced eighty rounds; and Solomon, who kept the keys of the Temple under his pillow, overslept himself four hours, and there could consequently be no service in the Temple the following morning. His mother administered to him a sharj) rebuke for this, reminding him of his father's great joy when the prophet Nathan foretold the birth of Solomon, and that his great joy was because of the Temple which his son was to build for the service of God, which he (Solomon) so shamefully neglected.â Levit. Rabba 12.

Alexander of Macedonia invariably rose when he saw Simeon the Righteous. Some of his ministers expressed their amazement that so proud a king should riseâ as they saidâ for a Jew. His explanation was that when he embarked on a war and had previous to his starting seen the image of this holy man he could reckon on victory.â Levit. Rabba 13.

The last Darius was the son of Esther.â Levit. Rabba 13.

God considered all the nations, and found Israel in the wilderness the most fit and proper to be the recipients of his Torah. Likewise Sinai was decided to be the most fitting spot for the purpose. Jerusalem was fixed upon as the best place for the Temple, and Palestine as the country for Israel.â Levit. Rabba 13.

A man is not consulted by his parents as to whether he wishes to be brought into this world. â Levit. Rabba 14.

Man is the last in creation and the first in responsibility. â Levit. Rabba 14.

A woman can only conceive either immediately before or a certain number of days after menstruation.â Levit. Rabba 14.

There was a limit to every prophet's inspiration. Beeri, the father of Hosea, only uttered a few words of prophecy, and as they were insufficient to be embodied in a book by themselves, they were incorporated within the book of Isaiah, viz. verses 19 and 20 of the 8th chapter of Isaiah.â Levit. Rabba 15.

Man's body should contain an equal portion of water and blood; if the blood increases and preponderates over the water, he becomes afflicted with leprosy.â Levit. Rabba 15.

It is very dangerous to be within four yards of a leper, and of his breath even within a hundred yards.â Levit. Rabba 16.

Schiller expresses the same idea.

Ninety-nine out of a hundred evils which overtake man can be traced to his own acts.â Levit. Rabba 16.

If your prayers are earnest, hope for the fulfilment of them.â Levit. Rabba 16.

The human tongue is not free, like some other members of the human body, but is confined in the mouth, and moreover is constantly in moisture: yet how many burns can it cause with its sharp edge and its fire. How much worse then would it have been, were that dangerous member of the human body possessed of more facilities.â Levit. Rabba 16.

If speech is silver, then silence is gold.â Levit. Rabba 16.

Sweet is the attainment of the evil inclination at the start, but bitter, very bitter in the end.â Levit. Rabba 16.

Antoninus asked Rabbi Judah Hanasi to pray for him. ' May you be protected against cold," said the wise man. Antoninus demurred, saying, ' Oh, an additional coat will do that for me." ' Then," exclaimed the Rabbi," may you be sheltered against heat and drought!" a wish that thoroughly pleased Antoninus.â Levit. Rabba 16.

At the approach of the Israelites to the promised land, the Girgashites offered no resistance, but were ready to vacate their country for the Israelites to take possession of it, in consideration of which compensation was granted them, viz. Africa was given to them, a country in every respect as good as the one they had given up. The Gibeonites formed a peaceful alliance with the Israelites, l)ut thirty-one of the princes and chieftains offered resistance and were conquered.â Levit. Rabba 17.

At first sight it would be difficult to understand why the message concerning leprosy in the land which the Israelites were to take possession of should be couched in language like that of a promise. ' When you come into the land of Canaan," says Holy Writ, ' I put the plague of leprosy in a house of the land of your possession ' (Levit. 14. 34). But when the Canaanites heard of Israel's approaching their borders, they hid their treasures in the secret places of their houses and in the fields; and when they vacated the country in haste their hidden treasures, which they had no time to take up, were left behind. When therefore the plague of leprosy was sent, the houses,â according to the law of Mosesâ had to be razed to the ground, and the hidden treasures were discovered and taken possession of by the Israelites. Joshua sent these tribes due notice of the approach of the Israelites to possess themselves of the land of promise, and offered them the opportunity of either leaving the country with all their movable property or offering resistance, in which event, in case of their defeat, they would forfeit their movables with their immovables.â Levit. Rabba 17.

The prophet Obadiah was an Edomite who embraced the Jewish faith.â Levit. Rabba 18.

God tells man, ' Behold, I am pure, my habitation is pure, my ministering angels are pure, and the spark of Myself (the soul) deposited with you is pure: take heed that you restore to Me that spark in the same state of purity as when it was given to you."â Levit. Rabba 18.

If man with all his knowledge and wisdom were to try his utmost to alter so little of nature or of creation as even to make the wing of the raven white, he would utterly fail in his efforts. Equally would they fail, if all nations of the world were to endeavour to annul one word of the Torah.â Levit. Rabba 19.

Nebuchadnezzar came to Jerusalem and took up his position at the side of Antisachia. The great Sanhedrin went out to him, asking the object of his coming. He demanded to have Jehoiakim delivered to him, or he would lay siege to the city. Jehoiakim pleaded hard against being delivered into the hands of Nebuchadnezzar, but was reminded of his shocking career of iniquity, of the gross and unspeakable misdeeds he was guilty of. He was given up to Nebuchadnezzar, who put him in irons, subjected him to a cruel death, and had the corpse exhibited in a wooden box in the shape of a donkey, throughout Judea. He then set Jechoniah, the son of Jehoiakim, on his father's throne, but when he returned to Babylon his people reproached him for his act of folly in having given the throne to the son of so inveterate an enemy and so notorious a sinner. Nebuchadnezzar then returned to Jerusalem and demanded the delivery of Jechoniah, with which demand the people complied. Before he was given over to Nebuchadnezzar he went with the keys of the Temple to the top of his house and threw the keys down, saying that he delivered them up to God? who would appoint a worthier man to take charge of them. He was carried to Babylon, and through the influence of Shealtiel and Nebuchadnezzar's wife (Shemirimith) he was treated with less rigour, and he was even subsequently allowed certain privileges. His son Zcrubbabel was born in Babylon, and the kingdom was restored to this good man. Jechoniah died penitent and at peace with his Maker.â Levit. Rabba 19. (See also Gen. Rabba 94.)

If you want to court derision, give your opinion on weighty matters in the presence of your teachers or your superiors.â Levit. Rabba 20.

Do not enter any house without some indication of your coming, such as knocking at the door: even in your own house you should not make your appearance suddenly or unexpectedly; something may be going on there which, however innocent, may cause you annoyance and may lead to a want of peace and harmony in your household. â Levit. Rabba 21.

The 27th Psalm contains the song of the Red Sea.â Levit. Rabba 21.

The high-priest with all his dignity and greatness was not to enter the Sanctuary in golden but in modest linen garments. It would be inconsistent that he who made atonement for the people should be attired in the very material (gold) with which they committed such grievous sin. Another reason for the humble attire was that the high-priest was to be impressed and to impress others with humility and not with pride.â Levit. Rabba 21.

There were but eighteen priests ministering in the first Temple, but they were skilful servants, and the Temple service was kept up for four hundred and ten years. Not so was it, unfortunately, in the second Temple, where over eighty priests officiated. With a few honourable exceptions, they were unworthy to serve on the altar of God. Some bought their position with money, and there were others amongst them who did not disdain to use witchcraft.â Levit. Rabba 21.

He who defrauds his fellow-manâ no matter how small an amountâ has it in him to go to the extent of taking life.â Levit. Rabba 22.

A king had a stupid son who was in the habit of eating all sorts of abominations when absent from his father's table. The king ordered that his son should be indulged in his fancy at hisâ the king's, ownâ table, considering this the best means of weaning his son of his objectionable habit. Thus the Israelites, when in Egypt, got into the habit of offering sacrifices to the Egyptian gods; they were therefore commanded to bring the sacrifices which they used to offer to demons (Levit. 17. 7) unto the Tabernacle of the Lord. â Levit. Rabba 22.

The present Rome is Edom.â Levit. Rabba 22.

Adultery can be committed with the eyes.â Levit. Rabba 23.

The nineteenth chapter of Leviticus contains the Ten Commandments.â Levit. Rabba 24.

The inhabitants of Canaan had vices similar to those of the Egyptians, as regards witchcraft and immorality. The Israelites, who had seen nothing but evil practices 1 See also laimonides' Moreh Nehitchini, cap. 3.

up to now, would be prone to concludeâ seeing the same vicious practices amongst the remaining nations of Canaanâ that these practices were common to mankind. Wherefore God tells them (Levit. i8. 2), ' After the doings of the land of Egypt wherein you dwelt shall ye not do, and after the doings of the land of Canaan wherein I bring you shall ye not do." As in Egypt, so will you be in Canaan, a rose amongst thorns.â Levit. Rabba 24.

Thy camp shall be holy ' (Deut. 23. 15). By this it is meant that we must be choice in speech.â Levit. Rabba

The Israelites were commanded to plant trees in Canaan when it came into their possession (Levit. 19. 23). Thus they were to occupy themselves in agriculture, and even imitate their God, who after calling the world into existence planted trees therein.â Levit. Rabba 25.

Adrianus (Hadrian) was passing on his way to Tiberias when he saw a very old man digging holes preparatory to planting trees. Addressing the old man, he said: ' I can understand you having worked in your younger days to provide food for yourself, but you seem to labour in vain at this work. You can surely not expect to eat of the fruits which the trees, that you intend planting, will bring forth? ' 'I," said the old man, ' must nevertheless do my duty as long as I am able to do it." ' How old are you? ' asked Adrianus. ' I am a hundred years old," replied the planter, and the God who granted me these long years may even vouchsafe me to eat of the fruit of these trees. But in any case I do not grudge the labour on them, and as it pleases the Lord so He may do with me." Promise me," said Adrianus, ' that if you should be alive when these trees bear figs you will apprise me of it." When the trees brought forth their fruit the old man loaded a basket full of figs, and made his way with the fruit to the king's palace. Arrived at the gate he was at first refused admission, but owing partly to his persist- ence and partly to his venerable appearance his wish for an audience was conveyed to the king, who granted it. On being asked his wish, he reminded the king that he was the old man whom his majesty had observed planting trees, and that he had expressed the wish to be acquainted with the fact if the old man should be alive when the trees bore fruit. ' Here," continued the old man, ' I have brought a basket full of the figs which I plucked from the trees your majesty saw me planting." So pleased was Adrianus with the incident that he accepted the fruit from the gray-haired man and ordered the basket, now empty, to be filled with coins.â Levit. Rabba 25.

The word "IDii' used for' cock' instead of the word 'pjjnn is Arabic.â Levit. Rabba 25.

Slander injures the slanderer, the victim, and the listener, and sad indeed may be its baneful effects. A man, it is related, was affianced to a woman afflicted with this dreadful vice, and in spite of the man's entreaties she could not or would not give up entirely the vicious practice. One day she told her affianced that his own father had made unbecoming advances to her, and suggested that, in order to satisfy himself of the truth of her statement, he should arrive at the house in the evening unexpectedly, and he would find his father making advances to her. Arriving at the house, he found his father in a kneeling posture before the woman, as he was begging of her, on his knees, to give up her slanderous habits and render herself worthy of being the wife of such a good young man as his beloved son was. The young man, however, remembering what his affianced had repeatedly stated, and seeing his father in a suspicious attitude, considered her story confirmed, and in a moment of rage killed his father. On the affair being investigated it was found that the murdered man was quite innocent. His son was put to death for the murder, and the woman suffered the same penalty, for being the chief cause of tlie whole tragedy. Thus wore three lives sacrificed through a lying and slanderous tongue.â Levit. Rabba 26.

There is a Rabbinical phrase not infrequently met with, viz. t m 2y:;' D "3Dn nai by mum bj ' He who wilfully transgresses the enactments of the sages deserves the bite of the serpent." The Midrash explains this peculiar expression as follows: One asks the serpent," Why are you so fond of hiding under fences? ' and its reply is, ' Because I broke down the first great fence of the world, the fence that existed between Adam and death." Now the enactments of the sages are Dm; i ' fences," set round about the law of God to guard it, and he who breaks through them deserves to meet with the one hidden under them who was the first to break them.â Levit. Rabba 26.

King Saul's conduct may well be compared to that of the king who decreed that all the cocks of the town should be destroyed, but the following day, having to undertake a journey and wishing to rise early, gave orders to procure him a cock to wake him at an early hour. Saul ordered all witches and wizards to be destroyed, and yet he was anxious to seek out a witch to learn from her the secrets of heaven.â Levit. Rabba 26.

God makes no choice of persecutors, but rather of the persecuted. Abel was the victim of Cain, Abel's offerings were accepted; Noah was persecuted by his contem-l-)oraries, Abraham by Nimrod, Isaac by the early Philistines, Jacob by Esau, Joseph by his brothers, Moses by Pharaoh, David by Saul, and Saul himself by the Philistines; and amongst all these the persecuted and not the persecutors were chosen by God. This does not apply to man only, but also to the lower animals. The ox is pursued by the lion, the sheep by the wolf, and not the pursuer, but the pursued, is chosen for God's altar.â Levit. Rabba 27.

Heathens were in the habit of taunting the Israelites with making the golden calf, a transgression which they said would never be forgiven them. As a mark, therefore, of having pardoned their sin,-God mentioned the ox at the head of sacrifices.â Levit. Rabba 27.

The trumpets jmsiti used in the Temple could be made from the horns of any animal, but might not be made from the horns of a cow, because that animal was connected with Israel's idolatry.â Levit. Rabba 27.

Israel had not to maintain the three leaders with whom God provided them in the wilderness, though it is invariably incumbent on any organized society to have to maintain their officers of state. Here on the contrary they were the means of sustaining the people: Moses brought down the manna, Miriam brought up the waters of the wells, and Aaron invoked the clouds of glory.â Levit. Rabba 27.

It cannot be doubted that those who instigated the Israelites to make the golden calf were of ' the mixed multitude," who fastened themselves on to the Israelites at the Exodus, and there is incontestable evidence of this in the words employed at the end of the pernicious work, for it is said (Exod. 32. 4) ' These are thy gods." Had the Israelites been the workers of this iniquity, they would have more appropriately said ' This is oiir god that brought us out," etc.â Levit. Rabba 27.

The number seven seems to be particularly selected and sanctified. Arovoth is the seventh name of heaven, and is especially favoured (Ps. 68. 5). " Tebel" is the seventh name by which this world is known, and that too has special mention (Ps. 96. 4). Enoch was in the seventh generation from Adam, and Moses was in the seventh generation from Abraham; David was the seventh son of Jesse, and Asa was the seventh king after Saul. Then the seventh day was sanctified as the Sabbath, the seventh year as the sabbatical year, and seven sabbatical years as the Jubilee; and almost the whole of the seventh month is devoted to solemn festivals.â Levit. Rabba 29.

The Temple required no light from the outer world, but had to diffuse light io the outer world. The formation of its windows indicated this fact.â Levit. Rabba 31.

There were some beautiful traits in the character of the Israelites in Egyjjt, by which alone they merited redemption. They did not change their names, such as Rufus instead of Reuben, Leon in lieu of Simeon, Listus in place of Joseph, or Alexander for Benjamin. Neither had they changed their language, but they retained the Hebrew tongue. They eschewed slander, and they were very chaste.â Levit. Rabba 32.

The merciful man," says King Solomon, ' doeth good to his own soul, but he that is cruel troubleth his own flesh ' (Prov. 11. 17). Solomon meant by this, the rich who disdain to invite their poor relatives to their festive tables.â Levit. Rabba 34.

The opening words of the forty-first Psalm, ' Happy is he that considereth the poor," were interpreted by the rabbis in various ways. It is maintained by one authority that the words fit him whose better propensities prevail over the evil ones; another has it that they allude to him who visits the sick; and yet another refers the words to the man who not only helps the poor, but considers the best way of really helping them without making them feel the sense of shame which receipt of charity may cause them. Thus Rabbi Jonah, to whose knowledge it came that a person, formerly in affluence, had met with reverses, approached the man with the words: ' I understand you have some expectations, and I shall therefore be glad to advance you some money with which you can make some profitable transactions, and then you can pay me back when you have no longer need for the money." The question of assisting the man having thus been opened in an inoffensive manner, he was only too glad of the proffered help, and was then told that there was no need to repay the money, as it was a gift.â Levit. Rabba 34.

Rabbi Tanchuma, son of R. Cheya, laid it down as a maxim that it is man's duty, when he becomes aware of any one having come down in the Vv orld, to consider the best means of helping him as quickly as possible. He himself would never purchase anything for his household without, at the same time, providing an equal quantity for the poor.â Levit. Rabba 34.

When the poor stand at your door, remember that their Maker stands at their right hand (Ps. 109), and consider it a high privilege for you to help them.â Levit. Rabba

It is man's duty to keep his body in a state of cleanliness, as well as to keep his soul in a state of purity. Hillel, when going to bathe, used to tell his pupils that he was going to do a godly deed. Once his pupils ventured to ask for an explanation. Have you not observed," said he to his disciples, ' how the caretakers in the theatres and other public places always wash the statues and keep them clean? If then such care is bestowed on inanimate sculptures, the works of man, it must surely be a holy duty scrupulously to clean the handiwork and masterpiece of God.â Levit. Rabba 34.

The works of the wicked are darkness (Isa. 29. 15), and their retribution is darkness (Ezkl. 31.): like a pot of earthenware whose cover is of the same material.â Numb. Rabba i.

The tribe of Levi took no part in the making of the golden calf, and moreover punished the offence of the others (Exod. 32.). They were therefore set apart for the service of God, and were not to be numbered in common with the rest of the people.â Numb. Rabba i.

The tribe of Levi then was not to be numbered with the people. A great king had many legions, a census of which was necessary, but amongst them was one legion known as the king's body-guard. His mandate therefore was to separate his own bodyguard from the ordinary legions and not to count them together, since these were exclusively for the service of the king. Thus the people were counted by themselves (Numb. 2. 33) and the Levites by themselves (Numb. 3. 14).â Numb. Rabba i.

If the Gentiles would only consider how beneficial the Temple of Jerusalem was to them they would have ornamented and guarded it. At the consecration of that Temple we find the following prayer offered by King Solomon: ' Moreover, a stranger that is not of thy people Israel, but cometh out of a far country for thy name's sake, when he shall come and pray towards this house, hear Thou in heaven thy dwelling place, and do according to all that the stranger calleth to Thee for, that all the people of the earth may know thy name, and fear Thee, as do thy people Israel' (i Kings 8. 41, 42).

Mark then that to the Israelites' prayer there is a condition attached for the granting thereof. For the prayer of Solomon proceeds: ' Then hear Thou from heaven thy dwelling-place, and forgive, and render unto every one, according unto all his ways, whose heart Thou knowest' (2 Chr. 6. 30). There is a condition or the fulfilment of the Israelites' prayer, but to the prayer of the stranger or non-Jew no condition is attached, and Solomon prays that the Lord may grant his prayer unconditionally.â Numb. Rabba i.

Potiphar, frequently observing Joseph moving his lips (in prayer), demanded one day an explanation of this (to him) strange conduct. When told by Joseph that he was praying to his God, he asked him to let him see that God. Joseph invited him outside, and told him to look up at the glaring sun, which, of course, Potiphar was unable to do. ' This," said Joseph, ' is one of my God's messengers. How can you then hope to look at the great Master when you are unable to look at one of his servants?"â Numb. Rabba i.

The world was like a wilderness before the Exodus and the giving of God's behests on Sinai.â Numb. Rabba 2.

The Israelites were the first to introduce national flags. â Numb. Rabba 2.

Since Israel was consecrated to the service of God and the Divine Glory was to dwell in the Mishkan which they erected, it was but proper that they should have also their banners. Each tribe had to have colours on its banner corresponding to the colours of the precious stones which were on Aaron's breastplate.

The banner of Reuben was red, and in the centre painted mandrake. That of Simeon was green, and in its centre it had the picture of Shechem. That of Levi had a tricolour, one stripe of white, one of black, and one of red, and in the centre it carried the picture of the Urim and Tumim. Judah's banner had the colour of the sky, and in the centre the picture of a Hon.

Issachar's banner was blackish, and had in the centre the picture of the sun and the moon. Zebulun had a whitish banner which carried the picture of a ship in the centre. Dan's banner had the colour of sapphire, and an image of a serpent in its centre. Gad's was a mixture of black and white, and carried the picture of a camp. Naphtali's had the peculiar colour of a pale reddish wine, and the picture in its centre was that of a hind. Asher's banner bore tlie colour of a precious stone, the ornament of a woman, and the picture of an olive-tree in the centre. The colour of Joseph's banner was of a deep black, and had the following pictures: Egypt, then an ox representing Ephraim, and a unicorn to represent Manassch. Benjamin's banner had some of the colours of each tribe, i. e. twelve different colours, and the picture of a wolf in the centre.â Numb. Rabba 2.

Moses was much perplexed in trying to arrange the positions which the tribes should take up with their banners, as he was anxious to avoid jealousy amongst them. If, thought he, I tell Reuben, for instance, to take his position in the east, he might say the south would suit him better, and so on. But he was spared the ordeal, for the tribes had it clearly arranged at their father's deathbed how they should take up their respective positions when they should go out to bury him.

When Jacob was dying, says Rabbi Chuma, son of Chananiah, he assembled his sons (Gen. 49.) and charged them to live a godly life and to take upon themselves the kingdom of heaven. Having finished this charge, he made arrangements with them concerning his burial. He would not have any of their children (who had Canaanite mothers) nor any of the Egyptians concern themselves with his funeral, but the sons should prepare everything and follow him to his grave in manner following: Judah, Issachar, and Zebulun should take uj) their i)o. sition on the east, Reuben, Simeon and Gad on the south, Asher and Naphtali on the north. Joseph should not carry the corpse (therefore his sons were permitted to do so), for he was a king and they must pay him deference. Levi should not carry the coffin, for he was destined to carry the Ark of God and to be separated for holiness. ' And," said Jacob, ' as I now arrange with you as to your respective positions at my burial, so shall it be arranged when the Lord causes his Shechinah to dwell in the midst of you in your journey with your flags."â Numb. Rabba 2.

Regarding the four winds of heaven, from the east Cometh out light for the world, therefore Judah who represents sovereignty, Issachar the pattern of learning, and Zel)ulun who represents navigation and commerce, dwelt with their flags on the east side, and were the leaders in the journey. The west sends forth snow, hail, heat and cold. From the south come beneficent dew and beneficent rains; and from the north comes darkness. On the south therefore was Reuben, who represents repentance, bringing forth God's mercy and compassion: he was accompanied by Gad, the type of a troop which he shall overcome; and Simeon was in their centre, because Simeon requires strength and mercy to be his shelter, and that is obtained by repentance. They â those three mentionedâ were second in the journey, showing that repentance is second to the Torah only. When those two )arties with their banners were arranged, the Levites came forth carrying the Mishkan. On the west thereof were i)laced Ephraim, Benjamin and Ma-nassch, being able to weather the snow and hail. Dan, the followers of Jeroboam, who darkened Israel with two golden calves which he erected, took his place on the north, and was joined by Asher who was to bear light to Dan's darkness, and by Naphtali who was blessed with plenty. These were the last in the journey with the banners.â Numb. Rabba 2.

Thus shall be thy seed ' (Gen. 15. 5) was the blessing of God unto Abraham. A traveller being a long time on his journey without finding any shelter, or any wholesome water, or a shady tree under which to take his rest, all at once beheld, at a short distance, a large tree. On near-ing it he found, to his delight, that not only had the tree extensive branches, affording him shade against the scorching sun, but the ground around it was very clean and fit for him to lie down to rest; its fruit was sweet and exceedingly palatable, and near it there flowed a brook of j ure wholesome water, of which he partook to his delight. Having appeased his hunger with the delicious fruit, quenched his thirst with the beautiful water, and rested his aching limbs, he now rose to proceed on his journey. Gazing up at the noble tree, he exclaimed, ' What shall I bless thee with? That thy branches shall be extensive? Such is already the case. That thy fruit shall be good and the water round about thee sweet and pure? That is already thy portion. I can only bless thee with this, that all the trees planted from thy seed may be as noble in every respect as thou art." Thus God said to Abraham: I cannot bless thee with faith, for that thou already hast, nor with peace, charity, or goodwill to man, for these virtues are already thine. ' Thus shall be thy seed' is the only blessing I can bestow on thee." â Numb. Rabba 2.

Israel is compared to sand (Gen. 22.). Just as sand, if it gets into food, destroys the teeth, so if you touch Israel you will bring down calamity upon you (Jer. 2.). Just as sand going through fire becomes converted from a dull substance to a clear glass, so Israel going through the fire of persecution comes out brighter and clearer. Moreover, other nations are comj ared to lime (Isa.33.12.) and Israel to sand. As one cannot build with lime unless it is mixed with sand, so the nations cannot exist or flourish without Israel in the midst of them.â Numb. Rabba 2.

The Israeutes are compared to stars, to dust, and to sand. There was a man who was efficient in three different handicrafts, a goldsmith, a potter, and a glass-blower. Those who respected him alluded to him as the goldsmith; those who were indifferent to him called him the glassblower; and those who had contempt for him named him ' the potter." Thus Moses who loved his flock calls them (Deut. i.) ' the stars of heaven '; Hosea, who was indifferent to them, speaks of them as ' the sand on the seashore '; and Balaam who was their enemy calls them ' the dust of Jacob."â Numb. Rabba 2.

The Israelites are declared to be holy unto the Lord (Jer. 2. 3). It is forbidden to touch holiness, therefore those who persecute them will not escape retribution.â Numb. Rabba 2.

Nisson was the most suitable month, neither too hot nor too cold, nor a rainy month; therefore it was selected for the Exodus.â Numb. Rabba 3,

No one under thirty years of age was eligible for the office of priest.â Numb. Rabba 3.

A child born after seven months of pregnancy can live, but not one of eight months.â Numb. Rabba 4.

The Ark was the most precious of all that the Mishkan contained.â Numb. Rabba 4.

People might have had some misconception as to the holiness of incense and the Ark, were they not specially mentioned as very holy.

Though incense is connected with the death of Nadab and Abihu and with the perishing of Korah and his associates, one must not conclude that its power was only for punishment, for it is mentioned also as having stayed the plague (Numb. 17.). The holy Ark too was the means through which a host of Philistines and the men of Beth-Shemesh were killed; but one must not forget the blessings which it also brought (2 Saml. 6. II, 12).â Numb. Rabba4.

Hungation (a heathen sage) called the attention of Rabbi Jochanan b. Zakkai to a discrepancy in the number of the Levites (Numb. 3.). Moses declares them to be 22,000, but when you count their number separately you find as follows: 7,500 8,600, and 6,200, making a total of 22,300. ' Hence," he said, ' it is clear that your Moses was dishonest, or he was ignorant of elementary arithmetic. ' God said," he proceeded, ' that the firstborn who outnumber the Levites (and consequently cannot find Levites to redeem them) should redeem themselves by giving each five shekels, and the whole amount received was to be given to Aaron and his sons. In reality there were more than sufficient Levites to redeem the whole of the firstborn, and there was no call for the latter to pay their shekels for redemption; but Moses, if he was able to count correctly, purposely gives the number of Levites as less than they actually were, in order that the (presumed) deficiency should cause a certain number of the firstborn to pay five shekels each, which were to find their way into the pockets of Moses brother and nephews."

The reply of R. Jochanan was: ' Moses was neither dishonest nor ignorant of elementary arithmetic, but you, though you are able to read, are unable to think or to understand. When he counted the Levites simply to ascertain their number, there certainly were 22,300, but when he ascertained how many there were for the purpose of redeeming or replacing the firstborn, 300 out of that number of Levites had to be excluded, inasmuch as they were (in addition to being Levites) also firstborn and could not redeem themselves, and could not be counted, in that capacity, as Levites." The answer satisfied Hungation.â Numb. Rabba 4.

He that serves on God's altar must be free from haughtiness and false pride. Eleazar, the son of Aaron, styled ' the chief over the chief of the Levites ' (Numb. 3. 32) did not disdain to carry a vessel with oil in his right hand, one with incense in his left, and the daily meat offerings hanging down from his girdle, and he would not allow any one else to carry them for him.â Numb. Rabba 4.

The infliction of stripes, given in the Torah, was not a severe punishment, and was moreover given in many instances in lieu of capital punishment, which the delinquent might have deserved besides. When the punishment had been inflicted, there was to be no further reproach attached to the punished individual, but he was to be received in the community as a brother (Deut. 25).â Numb. Rabba 5.

Pedigrees are reckoned after the father's, not after the mother's side.â Numb. Rabba 6.

Unless one makes marked progress in his study and acquires very considerable knowledge within five years, he had better give up further attempts.â Numb. Rabba 6.

The badger, the li nl, mentioned in Exod. 35. 23, was a unique creature with one horn in its forehead, and it was unknown whether it belonged to the clean animals or the beasts of the field until Moses used its skin for the Mishkan, when it was known to belong to the clean kind of animals. It ceased to exist after its use for the Mishkan.â Numb. Rabba 6.

The word M used for the priestly benediction has its origin in the word Dux, frequently found in the Mid-rash, meaning ' man of distinction '; and as this service was the function of the Priestsâ Ducheâ it took its name from the men performing it.â Numb. Rabba 7.

David in saying (Ps. 33.) ' The eyes of the Lord are over those who fear Him, who hope for his lovingkind-ness," alludes to the tribe of Levi, who had no share in the division of the seven nations and no earthly heritage, but are servants on the altar of God.â Numb. Rabba 5.

The malady of lejirosy was incurred by those who were guilty of either adultery, idolatry, murder, profaning God's name, profane language, haughtiness, robbery, lying, perjury, slander, or unduly intruding in another man's sphere.â Numb. Rabba 6.

WTien the king dies, long live the king. When the wise man dies it is not always an easy matter to replace him.â Numb. Rabba 6.

The nature of the work which the Israelites had to perform in Egypt maimed many of them, but when they stood at the foot of Sinai to receive the Decalogue all were cured; there was not one of them cither blind, deaf, lame, or with any other defect.â Numb. Rabba 7.

At the giving of the Ten Commandments the whole house of Israel, without distinction of tribes, were alike willing and ready to take upon themselves the burden of the Law. ' All the people together answered and said," etc. (Exod. 19.); but the whole of Israel soon after became unfaithful, and the one tribe only, that of Levi, kept steadfast to God's behests and proved themselves worthy of his service.â Numb. Rabba 7.

God bestowed three virtues on Israelites by which they may always be known. An Israelite is to be compassionate, merciful, and modest.â Numb. Rabba 8.

' God loveth the righteous' (Ps. 146.). This expression has special reference to those of the righteous who are not priests or Levites. Priests and Levites inherit their dignity, and are spoken of as ' a house," e. g." the house of Aaron' or ' the house of Levi," but righteousness is not hereditary; there is no ' house of righteousness '; it comes spontaneously to good and worthy men.â Numb. Rabba 8.

'The Lord prescrveth the strangers." The W"), the proselytes who embrace Judaism, are kept steadfast in their faith by God Himself, and are in every respect like a Jew born. Love is granted to Israel (Obad. i.): the same gift is bestowed on them (Deut. 10.). Songs are given to Israel (Isa. 61.), and also given to them (Isa. 56.). Preservation is promised to Israel (Ps. 121.), and preservation is promised to them.â Numb. Rabba 8.

Sincere converts to Judaism, who seek shelter under the wings of the Shechinah, and worship only the one Holy God, and Jews of a blameless character, pay by their lives a tribute of honour to God.â Numb. Rabba 8.

When the Gibeonites asked for Joshua's help (Josh. 10) he was disinclined to inconvenience his own people to afford assistance to what he termed ' these strangers, ' but he was reminded that he himself was the offspring of one who was an alien in Egypt, Joshua being a descendant of Joseph.â Numb. Rabba 8.

An Arabian prince complained to Rabbi Akiba against his wife, who being an Arabian woman gave birth to a perfectly white child. The Rabbi, who was always anxious to establish good and friendly relations amongst men, especially amongst those who should live in peace and in harmony, knowing the beams on the ceiling in the Arabian's house to be dazzling white, mentioned Jacob's contrivance of obtaining speckled sheep, and pointed out that the phenomenon of his child might be due to the extreme whiteness of his ceiling at which the princess gazed.â Numb. Rabba 9.

Of the many that go to sea most return, only a small percentage are lost. Also of those who plunge into the sea of matrimony most are happy, and only a small number are misalliances.â Numb. Rabba 9.

Most of the many misdeeds which man is liable to commit he can to some extent redeemâ such as theft, fraud, etc.; but adultery never. The man who seduces another man's wife is beyond redemption.â Numb. Rabba 9.

' Thy camp shall be holy ' (Deut. 23.). This is Moses' warning against adultery when going to war, as God would remove his presence from their midst if there were adulterers in their camp.â Numb. Rabba 9.

However the Israelites in Egypt may, by reason of their slavery, have gone astray, they kej)t themselves pure from sexual vice.â Numb. Rabba 9.

It is not judicious to lodge in the same house with any womanâ even with wife, daughter, or sisterâ if the relationship is not known to the people of the place; for the world is slanderously inclined.â Numb. Rabba 10.

He that sanctifies himself here will receive sanctifica-tion from on high.â Numb. Rabba 10.

In man's intellect there seem to be four degrees, and thus we find him losing his wits by four several degrees when indulging in strong drink. When a man drinks one-fourth more than is good for him, he loses one-fourth of his intellect; when he indulges in as much again, half of his faculties are for the time paralysed; after the third cup over and above what is good for him, he begins to speak incoherently, indeed he knows not what he says; and when he has indulged in the full four parts he is intellectually wrecked.â Numb. Rabba 10.

Where wine goes in, intellect comes out, as well as. secrets.â Numb. Rabba 10.

Israel will have her kingdom restored to her.â Numb. Rabba 10.

See what an excess of wine did in the world. Noah came out of the ark with his three sons, his wife and their wives, who composed the human family of the world; and a fourth of this he cursed in consequence of his indulgence.â Numb. Rabba 10.

Intoxicants lead to fornication.â Numb. Rabba 10.

Wine was giv en to a criminal sentenced to death, before the execution, to mitigate his sorrow.â Numb. Rabba 10.

' And I have separated you from other nations that you shall be mine ' (Levit. 20. 26). The Jew is indeed unique in many respects. In his ploughing, sowing, reaping, shearing and threshing, in his firstfruits and liquids he has laws which teach him charity and unselfishness. And in his very appearance, as to his hair, etc., and in his reckoning of time, in all this he is separated.â Numb, Rabba lo.

There is a different proceeding in picking out the bad from the good or vice versa. If one wishes to separate the bad from the good, one usually does it in one attempt; whilst if the good are picked out from the bad one is, as a rule, not satisfied with one attempt, for one is eager to find more and more of the-good, and so reverts to seeking out more, in the hope of finding what is worth selecting. Thus the Holy One, blessed be He! in selecting Israel from the heathen, is continually looking forward for more of other nations to be brought under the wings of the Shechinah.â Numb. Rabba lo.

Intemperance of the Ten Tribes was the cause of their captivity.â Numb. Rabba lo.

When the prophets went forth on their mission the Holy Spirit rested upon them, and awed their audience, and inspired them with respect for the prophets.â Numb. Rabba lo.

The laws concerning the Nazirite are placed near the priestly blessings because he who debars himself from partaking of strong drink may look forward for the blessings of grace and peace which the priests pronounce.â Numb. Rabba ii.

It would seem strange that although God told Abraham, ' In thee shall all the families of the earth be blessed ' (Gen. 12. 8), yet we do not find Abraham blessing his own sons. But in his pure and simple faith Abraham left this to God himself, arguing that one son of his (Ishmael) might perhaps be unworthy of God's blessings. ' I am but flesh and blood 'â or dust and ashesâ as he was wont to say, and cannot decide so weighty a matter; when I am gone hence let the Lord do what seemeth good in his eyes." And after the death of Abraham we find that the Lord blessed his son Isaac (Gen.

25. 11), and this blessing Isaac bestowed on Jacob, and the latter on his sons.â Numb. Rabba 11.

It is the priest's function to bless the people in the name of the Lord, and the Lord blesses the priests.â Numb. Rabba 11.

Consider the great value of peace. Peace was the reward Abraham received for his faith and righteousness (Gen. 15). It was all that Jacob prayed for (Gen. 28). The reward of Aaron was a covenant of peace (Mai. 2.); the same was the reward of Phineas (Numb. 25. 12). The Torah could receive no higher dignity than that all its paths are peace (Prov.3.). Jerusalem is comforted with peace (Isa. 32.). On the other hand, when Ammon and Moab incurred retribution they were to be deprived of peace

(Deut. 23.). When Israel receives the priestly benediction, it is that of peace.â Numb. Rabba 11.

In pronouncing the priestly benediction, the Cohanim are to place themselves before the Ark with the whole congregation fronting them. The blessing can have no effect on any one behind them. The Cohanim are to form their hands in the shape of a window. The first part of the benediction, ' The Lord bless and keep thee ' refers to childhood, which requires keeping (care). The second portion, Give thee grace, ' refers to manhood, to intercourse with the world, and the last part, ' Grant thee peace, ' to declining years.â Numb. Rabba ii.

The truth of the Torah is a weapon to its possessor.â Numb. Rabba 12.

The ninety-first Psalm was composed by Moses.â Numb. Rabba 12.

If any one tells you that there is no such thing as resurrection, refer him to what one of God's servants (Elijah) (lid (i Kings 17.). If one says God does not receive the penitent, show him the case of Manasseh (2 Chr. 33.). If a man asserts that one who is known as a barren woman will never bear children, remind him of Hannah (i Sam. 2.). If you are told God does not deliver from the waters, cite Moses (Exod. 2.); if that He does not save from fire or wild beasts, mention Daniel (Dan. 3. and 6.); if that He does not heal leprosy, remind him of Naaman.â Numb. Rabba 14.

It is prohibited to add to the canon of the Bible, consisting of i Znhil Dnti'J twenty-four books.â Numb. Rabba 14.

There were many features in the life of Joseph remarkably similar to those of his father. Jacob's mother was for a time barren; so was Joseph's. Jacob's mother had two sons only; so had Joseph's mother. Jacob's brother sought his life; so did Joseph s brothers. Again, each went from Palestine to a foreign land, each had children born in a foreign country, the fathers-in-law of each were blessed for the sake of their sons-in-law; both Jacob and Joseph went to Egypt; each made his brothers swear to keep the promise made to him, each was embalmed, the bones of each were taken away from Egypt, etc. Hence the Scripture has it, ' These are the generations of Jacob," and follows at once with Joseph instead of with Reuben, who was the eldest.â Numb. Rabba 14.

' I have made thee a god to Pharaoh," said the Lord to Moses: a god to Pharaoh, but not a god.â Numb. Rabba 14.

' No man shall see me and live," said God (Exod. 33.). Not in this earthly life, but in the higher life.â Numb. Rabba 14.

God, notwithstanding the various injunctions concerning light (Exod. 27., Levit. 24., and Numb. 15.), requires no light from man. There is no darkness with Him (Ps. 139. and Danl. 2.).â Numb. Rabba 15.

Man's eyes have white and black in them; but the power of sight, the lens supplying light, is the black.â Numb. Rabba 15.

The respect and honour due to one's teacher, and indeed to learned men in general, includes the following: not to stand or sit in the place he has temporarily vacated, not to contradict anything he says, not to interrupt him whilst he speaks; to put any question you may have to put to him with marked respect, and to reply to anything he asks of you without frivolity.â Numb. Rabba 15.

Man's eyes and his heart prompt him to sin.â Numb. Rabba 17.

Four sorts of men may be termed wicked men: one who threatens personal violence, one who borrows and refuses to pay, he who is abusive to another and has no remorse when his temper has cooled down, and he who causes strife and ill-feeling amongst his fellows.â Numb. Rabba 18.

Aaron's staff (Numb. 17. 23) was the one Judah had (Gen. 38. 18), and this same staf was afterwards in possession of every king of Israel until the destruction of the Temple, when it was lost; but it will be restored to the hands of King Messiah.â Numb. Rabba 18.

When the Jews in the wilderness were bitten by the serpent, and they confessed their sin, they were at once forgiven. This illustrates the efficacy of repentance, and teaches us moreover the wholesome lesson not to tyrannize over one who has offended but expressed regret for it.â Numb. Rabba 19.

So great was King Solomon's wisdom that by merely looking at any one he could tell whether that person had a fatal disease. When he once sent to the king of Egypt for skilful masons to build the Temple, Pharaoh selected a number of sick men and sent them to Solomon. When Solomon saw them he detected a fatal disease in every one of them. He supplied the men with shrouds and sent them back to Pharaoh with a letter stating that he concluded that there were no shrouds in Egypt for the men Pharaoh sent, so he had furnished them with the necessary apparel and sent them back. They died shortly after.â Numb. Rabba 19.

If you have not acquired knowledge, what can you claim to be possessed of? If you have knowledge, what do you lack?â Numb. Rabba 19.

He who refuses to accept an apology from one who has offended him is wicked.â Numb. Rabba 19.

Let not the nations of the earth say that God has favoured Israel and neglected them, for whatever benefit He bestowed on Israel was given also to other nations. Solomon was a great king of Israel; so was Nebuchadnezzar a great king. David was wealthy; so was Haman. Moses was very great, and so was Balaam. But let us see what use the men of Israel made of their gifts, and how those of the other nations abused their gifts.

Solomon employed his wisdom to build that great Temple which was the admiration of mankind, to compose hymns of praise to God, to write books of moral lessons and instruction for the world; Nebuchadnezzar used his gifts for debauchery, revelry, and oppression. David used his wealth to the glory of the Giver; Haman offered his wealth to have a nation destroyed. Moses, the meek and the good, only lived for the good of others, and stood always in the breach between a sinning people and an offended God; Balaam was in feverish haste and anxiety to curse a people without having received the slightest provocation.

Further, all Hebrew prophets were concerned about the welfare of other nations as well as of Israel. Jeremiah bewailed the calamity of Moab (Jer. 48.); Ezekiel laments the sorrows of Tyrus (Ezkl. 27.); and Isaiah is full of grief for the reverses of other nations. God had granted his Holy Spirit to non-Israelites, but they were found wanting.â Numb. Rabba 20.

The angel who stood in the way of Balaam with a sword in his hands could have effected his purpose without a drawn sword. Do we not find that the angel of the Lord slew in one night Sennacherib and his army without any weapon? (Isa. 37.). But he showed Balaam howper-verse he was, in that he sought to reverse the order of things. Isaac's blessing to Jacob was that his power should be with his mouth (prayer), and to Esau he gave the power of the sword; whereas now Balaam was going to assume the power of Jacob: so the angel showed him his legal and rightful weapon, the sword; he showed him also the weapon by which he was to lose his life.â Numb. Rabba 20.

In the matter of Zelophehad's daughters, there arises first the question why, out of all the difficult matters that Moses had to decide and adjust, this one should have so perplexed him that he submitted it to God. Again, as soon as he received the judgment which he was to:)ro-nounce, we find him praying for the appointment of his successor, whilst he was yet, so to say, in the midst of his work. The fact is that Zelophehad's daughters had, as was the custom, in the first instance put the matter of complaint before the princes of ten, then before those of fifty; and when they hesitated to pronounce judgment it was referred to those of a hundred, who referred them to Moses. Moses, in his meekness, seeing that it had been before the several courts, none of which would give its decision, thought it would be arrogance on his part to consent tacitly to be a higher authority than the several princes wlio had had the matter before them, and so he submitted it to God. Seeing by the decision of the Most High that children, including daughters in the absence of sons, had to inherit their fathers' estates, and knowing that his sons were unqualified for his estate, viz. the leadership of the Israelites, he prayed now for a successor to himself, and the Lord told him that his mantle would fall on Joshua, his faithful disciple.â Numb. Rabba 21.

He who causes his fellow-man to sin is worse than he who seeks a man's life. The Egyptians pursued the Israelites with the sword (Exod.15.), Edom threatened them with the sword (Numb. 20.): yet the Israelites were told not to despise an Egyptian or an Edomite (Deut. 23.). But Ammon and Moab, who prompted the Israehtes to sin, were excluded from coming into the fold of Israel, even unto the tenth generation (Deut. 26.). Further, the Israelites were told, when going out to war, to offer peace first when approaching a town; but not so with the Midianites, whom they were commanded to attack and smite.â Numb. Rabba 21.

Moses declared (Exod. 4.) that he was not a man of words, but observe his eloquence in the book of Deuteronomy; an eloquence acquired since he gained possession of the Torah.â Deut. Rabba i.

The rebukes which the Israelites received from Moses would seem to have been more appropriately given by Balaam, and Balaam's blessings would, it seems, have been more fittingly uttered by Moses. But the admonition, if it had come from Balaam, would have had no effect upon the Israelites, who would naturally have concluded that they were the result of his animosity. If, again, Moses had spoken those blessings and words of j-jraise, others would have belittled them as emanating from the warm friendshij) of the warm-hearted Moses. But Moses' rebukes could not have failed to be laid to heart by the Israelites, coming from such a tried friend; and Balaam's blessings could by no means be construed by others as arising from partiality to the chosen people.â Deut. Rabba i.

The proper qualification of a n (judge) is the possession of the following virtues: he must be an able man, Godfearing, a man of truth, free from covetousness, a wise man, a man of understanding, and known amongst his people. If no such man can be found for the position, then one not the happy possessor of all the qualities enumerated may be chosen.â Deut. Rabba i.

God has a seal, and his seal is truth.â Deut. Rabba i.

A community rejecting the leadership of the great and selecting as its leaders insignificant individuals can only be compared to the serpent which decided to creep along tail foremost, in consequence of which it was hurt by thorns, burnt by fire, and injured by water; a community should not be led by one man only. Moses himself confessed his inability to lead single-handed.â Deut. Rabba i.

In futurity the righteous will stand on a higher level than angels.â Deut. Rabba i.

If sorrows overtake you, receive them with fortitude and resignation.â Deut. Rabba i.

In reply to his disciples who asked how far honouring of parents should go. Rabbi Eliezer the Great related to them that a man named Douma, whose mother's mind was demented so that she took a delight in grossly insulting him in public, had invariably only these words to answer her: ' Enough, mother." This same man was the possessor of some valuable precious stones, some of which men from Ashkelon came to purchase of him, to replace some which had fallen out and been lost from the priest's breastplate.

When he looked for the box containing the precious stones, he found that his father lying down in sleep had his feet on the little box. He declined to disturb his father's sleep, and would not bring out the jewels to show to the would-be purchasers. They, thinking that a big price would induce him to part with the stones, and knowing them to suit the purpose for which they wanted them, offered him a much larger price than was their value. Whilst they were arguing the father woke up; and when the men wanted to pay the son the increased price spontaneously offered, he refused to accept more than the original price, on the ground that the increase of the money offered was due to their belief that he would not part with the jewels for the figure they first named, whereas in reality he would not show them the stones because by so doing he would have had to disturb his father, and he wanted no payment for fihal duty.â Dent. Rabba i.

Tlierc were several incidents which brought about the redemption from Egypt, (i) There was the Israchtcs' distress (Exod. 2. 23). (2) They su ii)hcated God, which means repentance on their part. (3) There was the covenant with their fathers, which God remembered. (4) There was God's compassion. (5) The end of their captivity had arrived.

And the same will be the reasons of the last redemption, (i) Because of the sorrow Israel will find himself in; (2) because of repentance; (3) God's mercy; (4) He will remember the covenant of the Patriarchs; etc., etc.â Deut. Rabba 2.

The word ' prayer ' is a very wide term, and may mean prayer properly so called, or beseeching, crying, sighing, pleading, supplication, or petition. It can also be applied to adoration, praise and exaltation. It requires discrimination in its use. Thus we find that Job, the most righteous amongst non-Jewish prophets, had not employed the best phrases in its exercise. The words he used are: ' I would order my cause before Him and fill my mouth with argument ' (Job 23. 4).

Contrast this with the manner of prayer adopted by Moses and Isaiah. The former tells his people, ' I besought the Lord ' (Deut. 3. 23). Isaiah commenced his prayer with the words ' O Lord, be gracious unto us; we have waited for Thee '(Isa. 33. 2).

There is no time fixed when one can say he expects his )rayer to be answered; we have indeed no claim on God's mercy, and must leave the answering of our l rayers to God's own good time. Moses, for instance, was answered after praying for forty days (Deut. 9. 25). Daniel's prayer was heard after twenty days (Dan. 10. 3). Jonah was answered after the lapse of three days (Jon. 2.), Elijah in one day (i Kings 18. 37). David, on occasions, received answers to his prayers as soon as he prayed (Ps. 69. 14); and there is an answering to prayer even before the petition is sent up heavenwards (Isa. 65. 24).â Deut. Rabba 2.

Moses could not understand why his craving to enter the land of promise, to lay his bones there, should not be satisfied, since Joseph had his wish granted and had his bones taken up and buried in Palestine. He was supplied with a tangible reason. Joseph, he was told, in all his vicissitudes never denied his race or his country, but on the contrary seems to have felt a pride in calling himself a Hebrew; so that it was but fitting that he should have his sepulchre in the land of which he was so proud. With Moses it was different. He posed as an Egyptianâ Jethro's daughters mentioned him as an ' Egyptian man," and thereby he forfeited his right to have his resting-place in a country which he did not acknowledge.â Deut. Rabba 2.

Consider the immeasurable distance from us of what we know as God's dwelling-place, the heavens; yet how near He is to us when we call upon Him.â Deut. Rabba 2.

' What is the meaning," R. Samuel, son of Nachman, was asked, ' of David praying to God to hear him in an acceptable time? ' ' The gates of prayer," replied the Rabbi, ' may sometimes be closed, in contradistinction of the gates of repentance, which are 7iever closed."â Deut. Rabba 2.

' There seems to be more than one Creator," said a sceptic to Rabbi Samuel. ' Is it not written " In the beginning Elohim (the plural) created heaven and earth " Further, "Let us make man in our likeness." ' ' Do you find it said," returned the sage, ' they created, or are we told they saw or they said, or that man was formed in their image? In each instance you find the singular, and the ' Elohim ' is applied to Him in whom is combined all power and all might."â Deut. Rabba 2.

People are prone to imitate their superiors and their teachers, hence the great and serious responsibihty of rehgious teachers as to their conduct. There can be no greater injury to rehgion than that its teachers should disregard its teachings.â Deut. Rabba 2.

' I have created some things in pairs," says God," such as lieaven and earth, the sun and the moon, Adam and Eve, male and female in all animals, this life and the future life; but I am One." He that proclaims the absolute unity of God proclaims the kingdom of heavea â Deut. Rabba 2.

In vain have you acquired knowledge if you do not impart knowledge to others.â Deut. Rabba 2.

God filleth the world, and the human soul filleth the human body. God supports the world, and the soul supports the body. God is unique in the world, the soul is unique in the body. God neither sleepeth nor slum-bereth; the soul neither sleepeth nor slumbereth. God is pure, the soul is pure. God seeth and cannot be seen; the soul seeth and cannot be seen. Let the soul, which so far possesses the attributes of the Lord, praise and worship the Lord.â Deut. Rabba 2.

Let no man be deterred from repenting by knowing the great depth of his sin. Let him bear in mind that he does not come to a stranger but to his Heavenly Father.â Deut. Rabba 2.

When the Rabbis Eliazar, Joshua, and Gamaliel lived in Rome, a mandate went forth that no Jew. should be suffered to live after the lapse of thirty days after the decree. Amongst the ministers of state was one devotedly attached to the Jews and Judaism (in secret). He informed Rabbi Gamahel of the decision before it was made public, at the same time telling the Rabbi of his confidence that the great God of Israel would frustrate this evil decree. Returning home from his private interview with Rabbi Gamaliel, he informed his wife (who also was devoted to Jews and Judaism) of the decision arrived at concerning the destruction of the

Jews, which was to be carried out in a few days. As there was no other way out of the difficulty she advised her husband to commit suicide by means of poison, which, at that time, it was the practice of the Romans to carry in the hollow of their signet rings for use in case of emergency. This advice was based on the fact that amongst the Romans, when the fixed time for the carrying out of a decree had elapsed, the decree was no longer in force; and as it was also customary to observe thirty days of mourning for the death of any statesman, during which time no steps could be taken for the carrying out of a newly enacted law, the law would through the death of the statesman and the subsequent mourning become, at all events for a time, inoperative if not entirely obsolete. This advice the statesman followed: he sucked out the poison concealed in the hollow of his ring, thirty days of mourning were proclaimed and observed, the decree lapsed and was not enacted. On further inquiry by the Rabbis it was found that the late statesman had secretly undergone circumcision and had been (in secret) a devout convert to Judaism.â Deut, Rabba 2.

The phrase which we have in our ritual, ' Blessed be his name, whose glorious kingdom is for ever and ever," Moses brought down from heaven, where he heard these words from the angels when worshipping the Lord. We therefore utter this praise silently, being unworthy to use the praise which angels employ in their worship of God. On the Day of Atonement, however, when we shut the door to the outer world, when we strive after holiness, when indeed it is with us a day on which we are meant to be one with God, then we are like angels, and we are permitted to proclaim these words aloud.â Deut. Rabba 2.

Marriage conventions and agreements are not to be arranged without the consent of both parties to the contract, and the man is to pay the costs.â Deut. Rabba 3.

Sabbath observance outweighs all other commandments.â Deut. Rabba 3.

As patterns of honesty we have Rabbi Pinchas b. Joeer and Rabbi Simeon b. Shotoch. With the former, when lie lived in a certain town in the north, two men deposited two bushels of barley and left the place. As they did not return for some time, and he feared that the barley would spoil, he used it for sowing, sold all the crops that grew from it, and put away the proceeds of the sale. When the men returned, after a considerable time, he handed them quite a little fortune, the proceeds of the grain they had left with him. R. Simeon b. Shotoch bought a camel of an Ishmaelite. It was the custom of the Ishmaelites to hang a strap studded with precious stones round the necks of their camels, and in this instance the Ishmaelite forgot to remove the strap before handing over the camel to the purchaser.

When his pupils saw the trinkets on the camel's neck, they greatly rejoiced at their master's good fortune, of which he did not seem to be aware. They received a deserved rebuke from the good man, who said, ' I bought the camel and not the jewels; they belong to the Ishmaelite, and to him they shall be restored."â Deut. Rabba 3.

The Torah and righteousness are held in the right hand of the Lord. ' From his right hand went a fiery law for them ' (Deut. 33. 2). ' Thy right hand is full of righteousness ' (Ps. 48. 11).â Deut. Rabba 5.

Having clamoured for a king, the Jews learnt to their cost the great advantage of Theocracy. Saul caused many of them to fall by the sword of the Philistines (i Sam . 4.). Through David's act many of them j-erished by the plague (2 Saml. 24.). Ahab caused drought to visit them (i Kings 17). Zedekiah brought about the destruction of the Temple. When they saw tlie baneful effects of human administration, they supplicated for God's reign as before (Isa. 33.), and the Lord promised to be again their king (Zech. 14.).â Deut. Rabba 5.

Justice is one of the supports of God's throne.â Deut. Rabba 5.

When no justice is done here below, it will be executed from above.â Deut. Rabba 5.

To do justice and righteousness is more acceptable to God than sacrifices (Prov. 21. 3). Sacrifices were in vogue only whilst the Temple was in existence, but justice and righteousness must exist with and without the Temple. Sacrifices atoned only for sins committed in error, not for presumptuous sin: justice and righteousness atone for all sins.â Deut. Rabba 5.

All men alike, both those who know the living God and those who know Him not, lose their Jives, one may say, when they sleep; but God in his goodness restores their lives to all alike.â Deut. Rabba 5.

When Nathan the prophet brought to David the message that he was not to build God's house, he prayed for his own speedy death, so that the building of God's house might be expedited, but God said that he should live out his allotted time (2 Saml. 7.), because righteousness and justice, which David practised, were more acceptable to God than the building of the Temple and the offering of sacrifices.â Deut. Rabba 5.

The great Rabbi Meier, renowned for his learning and eloquence, was in the habit of holding discourses on Friday evenings previous to Divine service. These discourses commanded very large audiences, containing as they did a word in season for all classes of the community. The rich were exhorted to charity and compassion, the poor to hope and courage, employers to mildness and forbearance, and employees to fidelity and obedience. Parents carried away advice as to the training of their children. Teachers were impressed with the necessity of patience and endurance; and pupils were exhorted to obedience and diligence. Wivesâ for whose benefit especially the discourses were heldâ were taught the duties which are essential to make husbands and homes happy.

Amongst the women in the audience was one who had the misfortune to have a jealous husband. As soon as the sermon was over she hastened home, only to find the house in darkness and her husband ablaze with wrath, demanding to know where she had been. ' As you are aware, my dear husband," the wife replied," I, like others, appreciate so much the sermons and advice of the good and wise Rabbi, that, when able to do so, I like to hear him, and always feel that I carry away some useful lesson." This little speech only intensified the foolish man's anger. You shall not step over the threshold of my house," he cried, ' without going to your beloved Rabbi and passing your hand over his face, or performing some other foolish act." The poor woman at first looked upon this ridiculous order as a foolish whim which would soon pass. Unfortunately the fool persisted in his folly, and the affair became known in the town, and could hardly have escaped the ears of Rabbi Meier himself. The neighbours prevailed upon the poor woman to comply with her husband's wish. When however she appeared with her neighbour before the Rabbi, her courage failed her, but the sage, pleading weak eyesight, a remedy for which it was alleged would be the passing of a handover the eyes, induced the woman to do this, and then told her to go home and tell her husband of her compliance with his wish. To his pupils, to whom the Rabbi's conduct seemed strange, he explained that the good end of making peace between man and wife had justified this harmless subterfuge, since otherwise there would have been no peace for the poor woman.â Deut. Rabba 5.

Be not spiteful or revengeful, and do not harbour any wrong which you may have suffered at any one's hands. In spite of all the wtongs and sorrows the Egyptians have inflicted on Israel, God does not allow us to abhor an Egyptian.â Deut. Rabba 5.

Slander no one, whether brother or not your brother, a Jew or non-Jew.â Deut. Rabba 6.

The greater your talent the greater your responsibility. â Deut. Rabba 7.

' You are my sons," says God, ' when you accept My behests."â Deut. Rabba 7.

Do not pray in the porch of the synagogue, but in the synagogue itself. The synagogue requires no r W2-â Deut. Rabba 7.

Although the study of the Torah is so earnestly demanded, yet it would seem preferable for one to remain in ignorance of it than to acquire knowledge thereof and set its teachings at naught. If a king had two gardeners, one an expert in his craft who raised beautiful trees only to hew them down, and the other less skilled but also less destructive, he would surely punish the former rather than the latter.â Deut. Rabba 7.

God says to Israel, ' You are called my children, but you must take my law as your guide of life." It is as though a prince should ask his father to make it known throughout his kingdom that he is the king's son. The father tells him: ' Clothe yourself in purple and put on your coronet; then all will know that you are my son."â Deut. Rabba 7.

Joseph's bones, which were brought up from Egypt, were buried by the children of Israel in Shechem (Jos. 24. 32) because they sold him in Shechem (Gen. 27.). When thieves have stolen a cask of wine, the owner might well say to them: You have stolen the wine, the least you can do is to take back the empty cask to the place whence you took it.â Deut. Rabba 8.

The Torah is not in heaven, nor with those who occupy their time in studying the heavenly bodies.â Deut. Rabba 8.

Rabbi Samuel was a great astronomer, but devoted only his spare moments to the study of astronomy.â Deut. Rabba 8.

By saying that the Torah is not in heaven, Moses meant to convey that there is no other Torah to come thence to supersede this Torah, and there is no other man to come and bring another Torah from heaven.â Deut. Rabba 8.

If you are anxious not to forget the subject you study, then it is necessary to pass what you read through your hps, not merely to read the subject up. If you do not utter the words you read you will forget them.â Deut. Rabba 8.

Remember that whatever evil it may be possible to avert or delay, there is no such possibility with death. Death is no respecter of persons, against it there is no appieal, and after it there is no remedy, nor can you suggest a substitute such as your slave, nor can you plead for delay, saying that you are not quite ready to meet it, nor can you create anything to protect you from it.â Deut. Rabba 9.

One of the reasons why Moses called upon heaven and earth as witnesses (Deut. 33.) is that by them the Torah was given (Deut. 4.).â Deut. Rabba 10.

Moses had more than one reason for addressing the heavens and the earth and calling them as witnesses. In the first place it should not be forgotten that Moses, whilst only a man, was a heavenly as well as an earthly man. He was no stranger to heaven, and if he had addressed himself to the earth only he would have been like one who, being made governor of a dominion, should address one part of the country under his charge and ignore the other. But there is a weightier reason, inasmuch as the heavens and the earth will not be indifferent spectators at Israel's redemption, but will sing and shout and break forth in singing (Isa. 44. 33). Another important point: they were adjuncts at the giving of the Decalogue. Moreover, Israel had l:)ecn compared to the stars of heaven and to the dust of the earth.â Deut. Rabba 10.

Moses, probably on account of his anxiety lest after his death the Israehtes should go astray (Deut. 31. 29), prayed for everlasting life on earth. God said He could not gratify his wish, since in order to inherit the bliss of the future life he must give up earthly life.â Deut. Rabba 11.

The name of the angel who exercises in heaven the function of the usher of the court is Achazriel; the one who holds the position of secretary is Zagzuel, the chief of the Satanic ones is Smoel, and those fallen ones who became corrupted on seeing the beautiful daughters of man (Gen. 6. 2) are Uzoh and Azael.â Deut. Rabba II.

Moses was greater than every one. Adam, the first man created in the image of God, one might be inclined to consider above Moses; but one has to remember how he used his dignified position: one could almost apply to him the words of the Psalmist, ' Man that is in honour and understandeth not is like the beasts that perish ' (Ps. 49. 20). Then Noah might perhaps put in a claim, for he was saved by the Lord from the destructive flood. But remember that, though righteous enough to save himself, he could not save his generation of evil-doers; whereas Moses was able by his prayer to save hundreds of thousands of workers of iniquity from destruction. They might be compared to the captains of two sinking ships, one of whom manages to save himself, while the ship and all on it go to the bottom of the sea; whereas the other saves his ship and all on it. Abraham has, at first sight, a good claim to tower above Moses, at all events in regard to hospitable disposition; but such is not the case in reality: for what Abraham was able to obtain and bestow in a settled place Moses obtained and supplied to the great multitude in the wilderness. Isaac, on account of his submission to be sacrificed, might perhaps be thought greater than Moses, but not if we bear in mind how willingly Moses offered to be annihilated himself rather than the flock he loved.

Even physically Moses was superior, for whilst Isaac became blind in his old age, of Moses, at one hundred and twenty years of age, we are told that his eye was not dim nor his natural forces abated.

But then there is Jacob, who wrestled with an angel and prevailed over him; surely he is greater than Moses. But do not overlook the fact that Jacob contended with the angel where he was a stranger and Jacob was at home, whereas Moses went into the very home of the angels. There was never a man who possessed, like Moses, at one and the same time, such great and good qualities. He was a wise legislator, a great statesman, a skilful leader, a devout patriot, a tender friend, a pious priest, a most brilliant, and at the same time a very meek, man.

Whether we consider his great meekness, his wisdom, his prudence, his chivalry, his forgiving spirit, his unselfishness, his freedom from envy, his gentleness of disposition, or the sweetness of his nature, he was above every one, and the one man qualified to bless Israel.â Dcut. Rabba ii.

Heaven and earth wept at the death of Moses.â Deut. Rabba ii.

In no instance is it permitted to hear the evidence of a witness in the absence of the htigants.â Mid. Ruth i.

' The words of God were scarce," etc. (i Samla.). That generation was known as a generation of hypocrites: they pretended to adhere to the rehgion of their fathers, but worshipped idols in secret, and the Holy Spirit did not rest upon them.â Ruth Rabba.

Woe to the generation whose judges need judging. Learning can suffer no greater blow than when those who possess knowledge of the Torah and learning in general disregard the teaching which the Torah imparts. Take, for example, one who eloquently enlarges on the words, ' Thou shalt not wrest judgment, thou shalt not respect persons nor accept a bribe' (Deut. i6.), or ' You shall not afflict a widow or a fatherless child' (Exod. 22.), and yet is known to disregard any or all of these grand teachings. Can one imagine a greater blow to the Torah? To such men may well be applied the words of the prophet Hosea, ' Their mother hath become a harlot'â the Torah, which is a mother to its possessors.â Mid. Ruth I.

The following are the proper appellations for a corrupt judge:â Unrighteous, Perverter, Abomination, and Banned.â Mid. Ruth i.

There were two obscure prophets whose prophecy was not made known, as only prophecy which was of any utility at the time or in the immediate future was published or recorded; but the prophecy of the prophets mentioned will be made known at a future time.â Mid. Ruth 2.

MIDRASH RUTH T i

Moses, who always stood in the breach, has been compared to a shepherd who, when bringing home his flock for the night, finds the fence around their resting-place fallen in and has only time to put it up again on three sides, leaving on one side easy access to the wolf. This good shepherd placed himself on the open side, for the protection of his flock from the wolf and the lion.â Mid. Ruth 2.

Death is every one's portion, but it is not given to every man to leave a good reputation behind him. No one feels the death of a man like his wife, or of a woman like her husband.â Mid. Ruth 2.

A great and good man sheds lustre on the place in which he happens to live.â Mid. Ruth 2.

A would-be convert to Judaism should not at once be admitted into the fold, but should be mildly dissuaded from the step he intends taking. If he persists, and is steadfast in his desire, he is to be admitted.â Mid. Ruth 2.

What Boaz meant by telling Ruth ' Hearest thou not, my daughter? Go not to glean in another field ' (Ruth 2. 8) was to caution her against tainting her religion with the beliefs of any other. Having now become a Jewess she was to bear in mind the command which the Israelites heard and promised to keep, ' Thou shalt have no other gods beside Me."â Mid. Ruth 2.

Ten priests and prophets descended from Rahab, upon whom rested the Holy Spirit, because she sent the spies away for three days, knowing that they would be safe after that. The following are the priests and prophets: Jeremiah, Hilkiah, Sariah, Machsia, Hanomel, Salom, Baruch, Neriah, Ezekiel and Booza.â Mid. Ruth 2.

In this life it may be given to an obscure individual to become famous, or to a distinguished man to sink into obscurity; but there are no such changes in the life to come; as you enter it so you remain; the great cannot become small, nor the small great. The grandson of Rabbi Joshua was once in a trance for tliree days. When he awoke his father asked him where he had been and what he had seen. He said he had been in a world of great confusion, where he saw a large number of men, some of whom he recognized as coming from this world. Here they had held most dignified and honoured positions, but there he found them amongst the most despised and contemptible. When Rabbi Jochanan and Resh Lakish called to inquire how the sick lad was progressing, the father related to them what his son said he had seen. Resh Lakish, noticing some incredulity on the part of the father, said, ' Surely we have Scripture warrant for the lad's vision: " Thus said the Lord God, remove the diadem and take off the crown, this shall not be the same; exalt him that is low and abase him that is high " ' (Ezkl. 21. 26). Rabbi Jochanan fully endorsed the view of his friend, and was pleased with the Scripture quotation.â Mid. Ruth 3.

In this life misdeeds may be redeemed, and a good life may at the eleventh hour be rendered worthless by backslidings in old age; but in the world to come there is finality, there is no retracting and no improving. There are some who associate here with those who lead a life of vice, and when they all come before the tribunal of God, one is put amongst the righteous and another is given a place amongst the ungodly. On beholding this he is inclined to think there is partiality in God's judgment; for did not his friend, who is now in the company of the good, follow together with him the narrow track, and did they not alike indulge their vicious inclinations? Let such a man understand and know that his associate in vice and wickedness at last repented and made every effort to redeem his past. Then he will say, ' So will I do now to get myself out of this bad company." Then let him also understand that the world which he has now entered is"! like the sea, and the one whence he came like the dry land. He who goes to sea must fit himself out for the voyage whilst on land; for what he omits to take with him he will be unable to supply himself with at sea.â Mid. Ruth 3.

Said Hadrian to one of the Rabbis, ' I am better than Moses, your teacher, because I am alive and he is dead; and you are aware that your King Solomon said, A living dog is better than a dead lion." ' Could you prohibit anything, say the kindling of light or fire for only three days? ' asked the Rabbi. ' Certainly," replied Hadrian. In the evening Hadrian and Rabbi Joshua went up to tlie top of the house to sit down in the cool of the night, when the latter, observing smoke coming out of one of the chimneys of a house, asked his friend how it was that his prohibition was disregarded. Hadrian replied that in the house whence the smoke came there lived a man of distinction, who being unwell probably found it desirable to have a fire lit in his house. ' And yet," retorted the Rabbi, ' You consider yourself superior to Moses, although whilst you are living your lawâ which would only entail inconvenience for a day or soâ is at once set at nought; whereas the law of Moses, who said we must not kindle a fire on the Sabbath day,â which means fifty-two days in each yearâ is strictly observed by rich and poor though he is dead."â Mid. Ruth 3.

' Lord, make me to know mine end," prayed David (Ps. 39.), i. e. ' Tell me exactly when I shall die." ' That," said God, ' is a thing hidden from all men." Then may I know," persisted David, ' the measure of my days what it is." To which he received the answer: ' Threescore and ten years." He was further told that he would die on a Sabbath day. David, who had an objection to being kept above ground longer than was absolutely necessary, asked again that he might die on a Friday, so that he could come to his resting-place on the day of his death, which would be impossible were he to die on the Sabbath day. This wish of his to die a day earlier was not granted; and the reason given was that, as he was the sweet singer of Israel, God would prefer the hymns and prayers offered by him to the thousand burnt offerings which his son and successor would offer.â Mid. Ruth 3.

The earth has wings (Isa. 24.), the sun has wings (Mai. 3.), the cherubim have wings (i Kings 8.), and the seraphim have wings (Isa. 6.); but the righteous and those who are compassionate and merciful are sheltered under none of these wings, but under the wings of the Most High God.â Mid. Ruth 5.

It is a great and good thing for a man to have the blessings of a good man.â Mid. Ruth 6.

One of the characteristics of the righteous is that their aye is aye, and their nay is nay.â Mid. Ruth 7.

Do not sit down in the presence of one who is greater than you unless he invites you to do so.â Mid. Ruth 7.

Whilst expounding in the college of Tiberias on some texts of Holy Writ, Rabbi Meier was informed that his former great master, Elisha b. Abuya, was riding on horseback notwithstanding that it was the Sabbath day. Rabbi Meier went out to see his master, and was asked by the latter upon what text he was preaching. R. Meier told him, on the words ' The Lord blessed the latter end of Job more than his beginning ' (Job 42.). He was further questioned as to what interpretation he put on the text, and replied that the meaning was that Job was richer than he formerly was. Elisha criticised his pupil's version, and said it was not the one that Rabbi Akiba taught. He had maintained that Job's blessings consisted in his having repented of the reflections on God's judgment which he had expressed in former days. Having thus broken the ice. Rabbi Meier, after further discussions of other Scriptural texts, ventured to suggest to his great teacher the necessity of repentance, of imitating Job, and bringing down upon himself the blessings of Job's latter days. ' For me," observed Elisha, ' there is no hope; I am beyond the possibility of receiving pardon for my misdeeds. ' In further conversation he mentioned, amongst other things, the anomahcs he had observed in the course of his hfe, that those who hve in defiance of God's laws enjoy their hves and perfect immunity from punishment, whilst on the contrary those who scrupulously carry them out bring about their own destruction. ' Thus, for instance," he continued," I have seen a man commit the double sin of climbing up a tree on the Sabbath day and robbing a nest of the dam and her young, and climbing down, without any mishap to himself; whilst on another occasion I sawâ not on a Sabbath dayâ a man who found a birds' nest, and scrupulously observed the Scriptural injunction, and sent the dam away and took the young ones; but no sooner had he climbed down than he was bitten by a snake, and thus perished in the very act for which God promised long life. I therefore denounced all belief in futurity or in reward and punishment. Moreover," he went on, ' one Sabbath day, when it was also the Day of Atonement, I rode on horseback past a synagogue, and I distinctly heard an echo exclaiming: " The words of the prophet Malachi, Return unto Me and I will return unto you" apply to every one except to Elisha ben Abuya, who rebelled against God, and not for lack of better knowledge."

Some time after this Rabbi Meier visited his old master, s ho was lying on a bed of sickness. Said Elisha to his pupil, ' To what extent can a man indulge in sin and still hope to be received by God if he re )ents? ' Rabbi Meier quoted the words of the Psalmist: ' Thou turnest man back to dust, and saycst. Return ye children of men ; when he ob. served his old master shed tears. When Elisha, not long after this, died, the good man rejoiced, saying that he had reason to hope that his old master repented before his death. In the course of instructing his pupils. R. Meier was asked by some of them, ' If you were to pray for one's salvation, for whom would you pray first? ' He answered, ' For my father, and then for my teacher." When they expressed their surprise he explained to them that in the event of danger to the Torah, i. e. of the scroll being burned, the scroll is to be rescued together with the ark in which it is encased. Thus he was sure that Elishaâ in whom was the Torahâ would be saved for the sake of the Torah that was within him. When after the death of Elisha his daughters required pecuniary assistance, they applied to Rabbi Judah Hanasi. His first impulse was to decline their request, thinking of the words of the Psalmist, ' Let there be none to extend mercy unto him, neither let there be any to favour his fatherless children' (Ps. 109.). The daughters, noticing R. Judah's hesitation to help them, anticipated him by saying," We cannot plead our father's piety, but only his great learning." In the course of conversation the Rabbi detected great godliness in Elisha's daughters, and had provision made for them. He added, ' If this is the offspring of one who acquired the knowledge of the Torah without at the same time being blessed with the spirit of piety, how much better must it be in the case of one who makes the study of the Torah his life's aim for the sake of his Heavenly Father."â Mid. Ruth

Elisha b. Abuya used to make it his duty to call at infant schools and endeavour by his idle talk to divert the children's attention from religious instruction and direct them to frivolous matters.â Mid. Song of Songs i.

Scrupulousness causes cleanliness, which again leads to purity, and purity brings holiness, holiness meekness, and this prompts a fear of sin, a fear of sin begets saint-liness, and saintliness brings the Holy Spirit.â Mid. Songs I.

Moses, Aaron and Miriam died by having their souls drawn out by God's kiss. â Mid. Songs i.

The nations of the world are not justified in thinking that, because Israel is rebellious, God will change them for another nation. It is as though a black maid should expect her master to divorce his wife and marry her, because her mistress's hand had turned black.â Mid. Songs I.

' I am black but comely ' (Songs i. 5). So says the house of Israel: I am, to my knowledge, black, yet my God considers me comely. I am truly black with my deeds, but I am comely if the acts of my Patriarchs are accounted to me. And in Egypt I was at times black and at times comely. The same may be said about me concerning my i)osition at the Red Sea; there too I was l)oth black and comely. Black, as the Psalmist says: ' Our fathers understood not thy wonders in Egypt, they remembered not the multitude of thy mercies, but provoked at the sea, even the Red Sea ' (Ps. 106.). But I was ' Sec also March Nebuchim, vol. 3, cap. 51.

comely at the Red Sea when I said, ' He is my God, and I will prepare Him an habitation ' (Exod. 15.).

The same may be said regarding myself in Marah, when the people murmured against Moses saying, ' What shall we drink?" (Exod. 15.); but we were yet comely when Moses cried unto the Lord, who showed him a tree to sweeten the water for us. Or in Rephidim, when in consequence of our rebellion the place was named Massa and Meriba; yet we may be called even there comely, when Moses built an altar and called it Adonoi Nissi. We were black in Horeb, where the golden calf was made, but are we not comely even there when we say, ' All that the Lord hath said we will do and be obedient'? (Exod. 24.). We were black in the wilderness: ' How oft did they provoke in the wilderness? ' (Ps. y8.), and yet I am not devoid of comeliness there, if we see that the cloud covered the Tabernacle on the day the Mishkan was reared up (Numb. 9.). Further, I am surely black in the history of the spies when they brought up an evil report (Numb. 13.), but there is my comeliness in Joshua and Caleb. I am verily black in Shittim (Numb. 25.), yet there is my comeliness in Phineas. If I am made black by Achan (Joshua 7.) I am made comely by Joshua. The kings of Israel rendered me black, but the kings of Judah rendered me comely. And though I am a mixture of blackness and comeliness through all these enumerated events and conditions of things, I am perfectly comely in my prophets.â Mid. Songs i.

What wisdom considers to be her very crown, meekness looks upon as her mere sandal.â Mid. Songs i.

Do not look upon a parable or simile lightly, for some difficult passages of Scripture may be explained through them; just as one may find anything lost in a dark place by the aid of a candle.â Mid. Songs i.

The consecratory Psalm (30.) was actually Solomon's composition, although it bears David's name.â Mid. Songs I.

The Torah has been compared to wine, water, oil, and honey and milk. Just as we find water all over the earth's surface, so do we find the Torah; water will never cease from this globe, neither will God's laws cease. Water comes from the heavens, and the Torah came from heaven. There is a noise when water descends, and the Torah descended amidst thunders. Water quickens the thirsty soul; so does the Torah quicken him who is thirsty for knowledge. Water cleanses impurities, and God's laws do the same. Water coming down by drops can form a river; so if a man acquires Torah bit by bit he may eventually become a great scholar. Water, unless one is thirsty, cannot be drunk with any degree of pleasure; in the same way, unless one has a craving for the Torah, its study, if enforced, will become a burden. Water runs from high places and seeks the lower portions of the earth; so the Torah will not remain with the haughty man, but rather seeks out the lowly. Water is not kept in golden or silver vessels, but is best kept in earthenware; so the Torah will not be retained except by him who is meek of spirit. A man of distinction will not think it beneath his dignity to ask for water from the meanest individual, neither is any one too great to despise instruction from the most insignificant person. One may drown in water if one cannot swim; so, unless one possesses a thorough knowledge of the Torah and all its meanings, one may be drowned in it. But it may be said that water gets stale if kept for a time in a vessel, and that the same should apply to the Torah. Remember therefore that it is also likened to wine, which improves with age. Again, water leaves no trace on him who tastes it and the same, it might be said, must be the case with the Torah. But here again we must remember the comjiarison of the Torah to wine. Just as wine has a visilile effect on one who drinks it, so the studious man is at once known wiien one looks at him. Water does not rejoice the heart, and it might be concluded that the same is true of the Torah; hence it is likened to wine, since each rejoices the heart. Yet wine is sometimes injurious; not so the Torah, which is compared with oil. As oil is capable of anointing any part of the human body, so is the Torah an anointment to its possessor. But oil again has a bitter taste before it is purified; is this, then, equally true of the Torah? No; for the Torah is compared to milk and honey, each of which has an agreeable taste, while when blended they have healing properties as well as sweetness.â Mid. Songs i.

Israel is compared to oil. As berries do not yield their oil except when they are crushed, so Israel will not show his greatness except under the stress of persecution. As oil will not mix with other liquids, so Israel will not assimilate with other nations. Oil does not effervesce; so Israel is modest in speech. If a drop of water is put into a vessel full of oil, a drop of oil will fall out; so if an atom of levity is put into the heart of a wise man, an atom of his knowledge will be lost. Oil brings light; so Israel is the light of the world (Isa. 60.). Oil has no echo, neither has Israel in this world.â Mid. Songs i.

Any one who brings another under the wings of the Shechinah may be said to have created him. So it was said concerning Abraham and Sarah, ' The souls they have made in Haran ' (Gen. 12.) because of the souls they had rescued from idolatry and brought to the knowledge of God.â Mid. Songs i.

The Israelites were asked what security they could offer that the Torah about to be intrusted to them would be strictly observed by them. All proffered security, such as the Patriarchs, was rejected; but when they mentioned their children as security these were accepted. Therefore the prophet is charged to tell them, ' Thou hast forgotten tlie Torah of thy God, so will I also forget thy children ' (Hosea 4.).â Mid. Songs i.

From the point of view of religious observance one may say that poverty becomes the Jew; in poverty he is an observant Jew. Rabbi Akiba used to say, Poverty becomes a Jew as a red bridle becomes a white horse.â Mid. Songs i.

King Solomon's mind may well be compared to a hidden treasure, of the existence of which no one was aware until an expert pointed out the spot and its contents. His was a most brilliant mind, lying dormant till it was inspired from above, and then he became a veritable light to the Torah in his exposition, by prose, poetry, and simile, of many of its obscure passages.â Midrash Songs I.

Israel is justified in pleading for God's special protection, since concurrently with God's work on their behalf the light of the knowledge of God is brought about. The redemption from Egv'pt had the effect that such as Jethro, Rahab, and others were brought under the wings of the Shechinah. The miracles wrought on behalf of Hananiah, Mishael, and Azariah also caused a large number of proselytes to Judaism.â Mid. Songs i.

Rabbi Simeon b. Jochuah made it a point to cement affection between man and wife. A man came to him once from Sidon and asked him to grant him a divorce from his wife, as his ten years of conjugal bliss had brought him no offspring. The wise Rabbi, who read impulsiveness in the man's character, told him to go home and make a sort of a feast in commemoration of the coming event. ' I see no reason," he said, why a divorce should not be celebrated in some way, similar to the tying of the marriage knot." The man, in expectation of his approaching freedom, was right glad of the opportunity of making merry, and gave a banquet; and being in good spirits he said to his wife: ' See, I am prepared to give you the most valuable thing in my house to take with you if you offer no obstacle to our divorce, and will return to your father's house." When, after the banquet, he fell into a deep slumber, she got her servants to carry him to her father's house, whither she went her- self. On awakening and finding himself in the house of the man with whom he was about to sever his relationship, he asked his wife who was by his side the meaning of all this. ' I have done nothing against your expressed wish," said his spouse: ' it was only last evening that you offered me the most precious thing in your house." The man was very much touched by this manifestation of true affection on the part of his wife, and when they appeared again before the Rabbi the following day, the sly sage could not conceal a smile as he asked the man what he could do for him. ' My wife and I have come to ask your prayers on our behalf, so that the Lord may grant us an heir or heirs." The good man prayed to God to grant their desire, if in his wisdom it seemed good for them, and the couple did not remain childless for very many days.â Mid. Songs i.

Ben Azai was in a deep study, and to those who passed him it seemed as if he was sitting in the midst of a flame. They told Rabbi Akiba of it, who went to him and asked him. whether he was studying any mystery. ' Not at all," said Ben Azai. ' I was looking up the Pentateuch, the Prophets and the Hagiographa, and rejoiced over their contents as though I had been one of those who received the Torah at the foot of Sinai when God proclaimed His word in the midst of fire."â Mid. Songs i.

On the day on which Solomon married Necha, Pharaoh's daughter, the foundation of Romeâ Israel's persecutor and oppressorâ was laid by the angel Michael. â Mid. Songs i.

When Jeroboam erected the two golden calves, they tried likewise to erect two cottages in Rome, but they fell in as often as they were put up. There was near by an old man, named Abbe Kolon, who told the builders that unless water were brought from the river Euphrates to mix with the lime, no building would stand there, and he offered to fetch the water from the Euphrates. He took large casks, and posing as a wine merchant made his way unopposed to the river Euphrates, where he filled his casks with water of that river and returned to Rome. The water being used for the mixing of the lime and sand, the houses were successfully erected. â Mid. Songs i.

Jacob went to Beersheba for the purpose of hewing down the groves which Abraham had planted there. When on his deathbed Jacob was inspired by the Holy Spirit and told that the Shechinah would dwell amongst his descendants when they returned to their fatherland. The middle beam of the Mishkan had to reach from one end to the other, and measured thirty-two cubits (Exod. 26. 28), and was made of the timber which Jacob had hewn down in Beersheba. The Israelites had carried this timber with them to Egypt and preserved some during their captivity. Subsequently they took this timber with them at the Exodus. Thus we have it stated: ' and every man with whom was found shittim wood for the work of the service brought it."â Mid. Songs I.

Formerly learning was a thing sought after, but now we are become spiritually sick we grow dainty, and choose only light reading or what we consider comforting and promising words. So a man when in robust health does not pick and choose his food, but when less robust he must have light morsels such as will tempt his appetite.â Mid. Songs 2.

Israel at the Exodus may well be compared to a prince just recovered from illness. When his tutor suggests study, the king decides to allow his son some time after his convalescence to recover his strength before he begins ' This narrative is seemingly uninteresting, but it seems to me to be given in connexion with what is said about the building of Rome owing to Solomon marrying Pharaoh's daughter. The Mitlrash proceeds to show how the building of Rome extended as the Israelites sunk deeper in sin. Jeroboam having erected the idols caused a further development of Rome. The houses there only became firm when the water of Euphrates, near Jeroboani's wicked monuments, was mixed with the building materials.

to read. Israel did not at once recover from the sufferings they had endured in Egypt, and their Heavenly Father decided to let them have a three months' rest, and feed them with manna and quails, before they approached their school, Sinai, to receive instruction.â Mid. Songs 2.

Nebuchadnezzar was indeed the proverbial gale coming from the north, and sweeping everything before it in the south.â Mid. Songs 3.

Sleep is most agreeable and beneficial in the earlier part of the night.â Mid. Songs 3.

In the plague of hail which was sent on Egypt there were two opposite elements mingled together. There was hail, and fire mingled with the hail (Exod. 9.). It is like a king ruling over various nationalities which are enemies to one another, yet the legions the king sends against an enemy bury their opposition and unite to fight for the king's cause.â Mid. Songs 3.

A preacher must be well conversant with the whole twenty-four books of the Bible. If he is deficient in the knowledge of one of these books it is as bad as if he had no acquaintance with any of them. He must be meek, and even humble; every act of his life should testify to his worth, and withal if his hearers do not like his preaching he is to desist from it.â Mid. Songs 4.

The Psalms were composed by ten individuals: Adam, Abraham, Moses, David, Solomon, Asaph, Heman, Jeduthun, Korah's three sons (taken as one of the composers), and Ezra. But although they were composed by ten different individuals, David's name alone is connected with them. It is like a company of musicians who appear before a king, and are told: ' Although you are, every one of you, efficient in your art, yet I wish the one with the sweetest voice to sing before me."â Mid. Songs 4.

The Sanhedrin were known by the designation, ' The eyes of the community."â Mid. Songs 4.

During the existence of the Temple there were plenty of wicked men such as Ahaz and his followers, Manasseh and his associates, and Amon and his companions. On the contrary, when the Temple was destroyed, the people were conspicuous for the good men amongst them, like Daniel and his associates in righteousness, Mordecai and his followers, and Ezra and his people.â Mid. Songs 4.

Do not, like a simpleton, be deterred from study by thinking ' How can I meet the formidable task of acquiring all that is to be known? ' Rather argue like a wise man, ' Others have done it, so it can be done." Try a little by day and a little by night, and in the course of time your task will be accomplished.â Mid. Songs 5.

The Torah or knowledge increases, and the intellect becomes keener by proper study, and any difficult matter submitted to scholars will find solution; as a structure will be satisfactorily erected by skilful workmen each contributing his skill.â Mid. Songs 5.

The second Temple was deprived of the following five blessings which the first Temple had enjoyed: (i) The fire that came down from heaven for the altar, (2) The anointing oil. (3) The ark. (4) The Holy Spirit. (5) The Urim and Thummim.â Mid. Songs 8.

With the death of the three last of the latter prophets, viz. Haggai, Zechariah and Malachi, the Holy Spirit (prophecy) ceased, but use was made of the bp J12 echo. Once at the assembly of the wise men in Jericho they heard the echo proclaim, ' There is one amongst you who is well worthy of the Holy Spirit, but alas the present generation is unworthy of it." They thought of Hillel the elder. At his death they lamented him with the words, ' Oh that saintly man, that meek man, that pupil of Ezra."â Mid. Song of Songs 8.

The prophet Amos stuttered.â Mid. Eccles. i.

King Solomon was like the clever statesman adopted in the king's house, who when asked by his august master what token of his favour he wished, asked for the king's daughter, Solomon, when asked by the King of Kings for his wish, asked for wisdom.â Mid. Eccles. i.

At the resurrection men will be revived and will have the same infirmities and defects that they may have had during their former life; so that there may be no mistake as to whether those that are resuscitated are the same as those who were known to be dead.â Mid. Eccles. I.

If those who are in authority at present should be inferior men to those who were in authority before them, one is not permitted to slight them on that account, but is bound to pay them the tribute of respect due to their position.â Mid. Eccles. i.

There is no hard and fast rule as to any part with which books in Holy Writ should open.â Mid. Eccles. i.

Man as a rule does not allude to his low estate, except when he comes out of it and gets into an improved position.â Mid. Eccles i.

The Sanhedrin sat at a table in the form of a half moon, or horseshoe, so that they should be able to see each other.â Mid. Eccles. i.

No man dies possessing half of what he wishes to possess.â Mid. Eccles. i.

In one sense there is an advantage in failing memory; if man's memory did not fail, there would be no study of the Torah.â Mid. Eccles. i.

What Solomon meant to convey by the words, ' What profit hath a man of all his labour which he taketh under the sun?" (Eccl. i. 2) is that whatever a man may possess on earthâ under the sunâ he must inevitably part with, but it is dirterent if he provides for himself above the sun, i. e. in heaven.â Mid. Eccles. i.

One does not go to the trouble of examining a pig or camel to see whether it is fit to sacrifice on the altar, but one generally examines a clean animal to see whether it is free from those defects which disqualify it as a sacrifice on God's altar. So one does not criticise the actions or scrutinise the life of' the man in the street," but if one possesses piety and learning and j:)oscs as a religious teacher he must expect to have his life and actions tested and examined, so that it may be known whether they are in harmony with his professions.â Mid. Eccles. i.

If the wind had unbridled sway no human being could stand against it, but God limits its power so that it may not become injurious to mankind. The wind that destroyed Job's property and that which caused shipwreck to Jonah were specially sent and confined to the j)laces where they had to do their work of destruction.â Mid. Eccles. i.

All the waters run into the sea and the sea is not filled; so a man may be possessed of much knowledge and learning and not be overcharged.â Mid. Eccles. i.

Rabbi Janai and Rabbi Ishmael both agree that there is no such thing as Gehinom, but that the Lord will employ the sun to bestow punishment on the unrighteous and reward on the righteous.â Mid. Eccles. i.

The sun rises and the sun goeth down. Ere Sarah died there arose the sun of Rebecca; the sun of Athniel shone before that of Joshua set. So on the day when Rabbi Akiba died Rabbi Judah Hanasi was born, on the death of Rab Adda Rab

Hamomonah saw the light; at Hamomonah's death Rabbi Abbin came into the world; and on the day of R. Abbin's death Abb6 Hoshiah the man of Taria was born.â Mid. Eccles. i.

Rabbi Judah Hanasai made a feast in honour of his son, to which he invited all his fellow-Rabbis, but forgot Bar Kapara, who, in vindication of the slight, wrote on the door, ' After the feast, death." Rabbi Judah then made a special feast to which he now invited his accidentally omitted friend, who however tasted nought of the viands brought on the table; but, as each dish made its appearance, opened a dissertation, taking for his theme the contents of the dish, and so the other guests, their attention being directed to the ready wit and wisdom of Bar Kapara, eat nothing, and every dish was removed untouched. To Rabbi Judah's remonstrance his friend replied that his anger, for not being invited to the former banquet, was not because he was deprived of the food and drink at that feast, but because he could not hold forth on God's goodness in providing good things for man.â Mid. Eccles. i.

Solomon used the word vanity ' seven times, to correspond with the seven stages which man goes through. In his infancy he is like a king, fondled, kissed, and made much of. At the age of two or three years he is more like a pig rolling in the mud, etc. When about ten years of age he is somewhat like a little kid, jumping about and skipping. About the age of twenty he resembles the wild horse in his lusts and desires. When married he is not unlike the ass in his dulness and cheerless-ness and sleepiness. Becoming a parent, he becomes bold like the dog in his anxiety to obtain sustenance for his family. And in his old age, with his furrows and wrinkles, he is not unlike an ape. â Mid. Eccles. I.

When Solomon says ' the wise man's eyes are in his head," he does not imply that the fool's eyes are in his feet, but that the wise man can, at the start, foresee the consequence of every one of his actions. Rabbi Meier was in the habit of calling the finishing of a thing its beginning.â Mid. Eccles. i.

Rabbi Meier, who was an excellent penman, earned three ' seloim ' a week by writing, a third of which he gave away in support of learned men who were poor.â Mid. Eccles. i.

How wonderful is the human heart! It speaks and sees (Eccles. i.), it hears (i Kings 3.), it walks (2 Kings 5.), it falls (i Saml. 17.), it stands (Ezekl. 22.), and it rejoices (Ps. 16.), it cries (Lament. 2.), it is comforted (Isa. 40.), and it grieves (Deut. 15.), it hardens (Exod. 19.), and it softens (Deut. 20.), it saddens (Gen. 6.), it is terrified (Deut. 28.), it breaks (Ps. 51.), it is haughty (Deut. 8.), it rebels (Jer. 8.), it devises (i Kings 12.), and it has imaginations (Deut. 29.), it indites (Ps. 45.), it thinks (Prov. 19.), it desires (Ps. 21.), and it declines (Prov. 7.), it goes astray (Numb. 15.), it supports (Gen. 18.), it is stolen (Gen. 31)., it becomes humiliated (Levit. 26.), it is persuaded (Gen. 24.), it errs (Isa. 21.), it trembles (i Saml. 4.), it is awake (Songs 5.), it loves (Deut. 6.), and it hates (Levit. 19.), it is envious (Prov. 23.), and it is searched (Jer. 17.), it is rent (Joel 2.), it meditates (Ps. 49.), it is like fire (Jer. 20.), and it is stony (Ezkl. 36.), it repents (2 Kings 23.), it is hot (Deut. 19.), it dies (i Saml. 25.), it melts (Joshua 7.), it receives fear (Jer. 23.), it gives thanks (Ps. iii.), it covets (Prov. 6.), it hardens (Prov. 28.), and it is pleased (Judges 16.), it deceives (Prov. 12.), it speaks inwardly (i Saml. i.), it loves bribery (Jer. 22.), it is written upon (Prov. 33.), it is mischievous (Prov. 6.), it receives injunctions (Prov. 10.), it is presumptuous (Obad. I.), and it arranges (Prov. 16.).â Mid. Eccles. i.

Wherever ' eating and drinking' is mentioned in Ecclesiastes it means righteousness and good work, and not material food.â Mid. Eccles. 2.

All the j)eace and happiness here are mere vanity as compared with the abiding peace in the world to come.â Mid. Eccles. 2.

Hadrian said to Rabbi Joshua b. Hananiah, ' I call on you to verify the words of your Torah regarding Palestine being a land that lacks nothing (Deut. 8.), by supplying me with pepper, quails, and silk." Rabbi Joshua complied and brought him the articles demanded from three different towns in Palestine.â Mid. Eccles. 2.

Solomon's saying that there was a ' time to cast away ' was illustrated in the case of a merchant and his son who, travelling over the sea, and having a large sum of money with them, overheard some of the sailors plan to kill both of them and share the spoil. The father and the son decided to pretend to quarrel on deck, and in the rage of the quarrel the older man took the money and threw it overboard and so escaped death. On arriving at their destination the would-be assassins were put in prison, and the merchant brought an action against the owners of the vessel for the recovery of the money. The plea of the defendants that the money was thrown into the sea by its owner himself was of no avail; the judge holding that it was the ' time for casting away," the merchant being justified in throwing the money into the sea to save the lives of himself and his son, which were threatened by the servants of the shipowner.â Mid. Eccles. 3.

If a man does good acts at the close of his life, it shows he is anxious to add these to the many he has done in the course of his life; and vice versa, if at the end of his career a man does a reprehensible act, it tends to show that he is full of such misdeeds, and only required this additional one to complete the sinister list.â Mid. Eccles. 3.

Adam was destined to be the father of the twelve tribes of Israel; but, seeing that of the two sons he had one killed the other, the privilege was withdrawn. The Torah also would have been given through Adam, had he not proved himself unable to observe even one of God's behests.â Mid. Eccles. 3.

MIDRASH ECCLESIASTES loI

That there is a time to be born and a time to die we can have verified in Ezkl. i6. 4 and Num. 14. 36. Equally is there a time to j)lant (Amos 9. 15) and to root out plants (Deut. 29. 27). There is a time to weep (Lament, i. 2), and one to laugh (Ps. i2(). 2) a time to lament (Isa. 22.12), and a lime to dance (Zech. 8.5); a time to cast stones (Lament. 4. i), and a time to gather stones (isa. 28. lo); a time for embracing (Song of Songs 2. 6), and a time to keep away from embracing (Isa. 6. 12); a time to seek (Deut. 4. 29), and a time to lose (Deut. 11. 17); a time to rend (i Saml. 15. 28), and a time to join together (Ezek. 37. i); a time to be silent (Isa. 42. 14), and a time to speak (Isa. 40. 2); a time to love (Mai. i. 2), and a time to hate (Jer. 12. 8); a time for war (Isa. 63. 10), and a time for peace (Isa. 66.12); a time to slay (Lament. 2. 4). and a time to heal (Jer. 3. 6). All these refer to Israel's history; there were proper times for the respective events, enumerated above, to overtake them.â Mid. Eccles. 3.

That King Solomon held the fear of God in high estimation we glean from the fact that his two great books, those of Proverbs and Ecclesiastes, conclude by saying that the fear of God is above everything.â Mid. Eccles. 3.

All souls go uj)wards; but for those of the righteous there is a resting-place, whilst those of the wicked are fugitive.â Mid. Eccles. 3.

The recital of the yr V is better than a thousand burnt offerings.â Mid. Eccles. 4.

An ignorant man who puts forth pretentions to knowledge is best styled a flatterer of the Torah.â Mid. Eccles. 5.

There is stir and noise when man is born, and the same when he dies; he comes to this world weeping, and there is weeping for him when he goes hence. He arrives without knowledge, and departs without knowledge. When born his fists are closed, as if to say, ' I have everything," and when he dies his hands are open, showing that he has nothing.â Mid. Eccles. 5.

There is no death brought about without sin, and no pain without iniquity.â Mid. Eccles. 5.

Are you troubled by evil forebodings, visions, or dreams? Have recourse to prayer, repentance, and charity; for if there is in reality any evil decree against you, the exercise of these great virtues will avert it.â Mid. Eccles. 5.

God says to the prophets, ' Think not that if you do not carry my messages, my will cannot be made known in the world. I have many messengersâ even such as a scorpion, a snake, a frog, or an insect."â Mid. Eccles. 5.

The Israelites were bent on sacrificing, they sacrificed on the high places in the wilderness; hence the Mishkan was erected as soon as was practicable, so that they should bring their sacrifices in that sanctuary.â Mid. Eccles. 5.

If you see cruelty and injustice perpetrated by Romulus in Rome, be not dismayed; remember there is One above the dukes and princes of Rome who executes judgement even by the mere word ' Behold."â Mid. Eccles. 5.

The well of Miriam can be seen from the top of the mountain Jeshimon (Numb. 21. 20), and its waters have healing properties.â Mid. Eccles. 5.

The soul is not attracted by any earthly goods that may be offered to her. She is like a king's daughter, who finds no value in things which to others may seem precious.â Mid. Eccles. 6.

There are additional reasons, besides the one Solomon gives, why it is better to go to the house of mourning than to the house of feasting. In the former case you show respect to the living as well as to the memory of the dead; you can offer consolation and soften the sharp edge of sorrow; you can do all this to the rich as well as to the poor; and you can rely on it that the Lord does not leave acts of charity and kindliness unrewarded. Moses, who took such great care to bury Joseph's remains where the latter expressed his desire they should be re-interred, was buried by God Himself.â Mid. Eccles. 7.

' A good name is better than good oil." Two men (Nadab and Abihu) were anointed with good oil; they went into the place of life (the Tabernacle), but were burnt and did not come out ahve. There were three men with good names, Hananiah, Mishael, and Azariah, who were put into a place of death (the fiery furnace) and came out alive.â Mid. Eccles. 7.

Heart sickness is bad, that of the intestines is worse, but that of the pocket is worse still.â Mid. Eccles. 7.

There are certain things which seek ascendancy over one another. Thus the mighty deep is overshadowed by the high ground, and the mountains are still higher, but they can be levelled by iron. And the iron itself must give way to fire, which can melt it. Fire is extinguished by water, and water is absorbed by the clouds. The wind disperses the clouds, and yet a strong wall defies the wind. Man can pull the wall down, but sorrow pulls man down. Strong drink drowns sorrow, and strong drink is robbed of its effect by sleep. Sleep itself is frustrated by sickness, and sickness is ended by death. A bad woman, however, is worst of all; she is bitterer than death.â Mid. Eccles. 7.

The admonition of a good and sincere preacher is preferable to the expounding of Holy Writ by a quack; however great his enthusiasm, he can only be called a firebrand.â Mid. Eccles. 7.

There are three crowns: that of the priesthood, which fell to Aaron's lot; that of kingdom, which is the jiortion ot the house of David; and the crown of the Torah, which anybody can own; and yet he who acquires it not has acquired nothing.â Mid. Eccles. 7.

Patience is an ornament to a religious teacher, and has mostly a good effect. A Persian called on Rabbi Judah Hanasi to instruct him in the Jewish faith. At the very outset he was shown the first letter of the Hebrew alphabet; the Persian went into debate and asked how we know that the letter is called Aleph, etc. The Rabbi sent him away in disgust. Then he went to Rabbi Samuel and tried the same tiresome trick. When the sage pinched his ear, he cried, ' O my ear." ' How do you know? ' asked the Rabbi, ' that this is an ear? ' With this witty act the Persian was pleased; he acquired knowledge, and was turned away from heathenism.â Mid. Eccles. 7.

A man had the misfortune to have a bad neighbour and a bad wife. His neighbour went out at night to rob, and spent the proceeds in providing a good table for himself and family. Said his wife to him, ' See how our neighbours live, and contrast it with our humble state." ' Shall I then go out at night to rob people? ' replied her husband. ' And what then if you did? ' retorted the woman; ' it would certainly put us beyond the necessity of pinching, as we have to do." She persisted, and kept on nagging at the man so long that at last he resolved to embark one evening on his neighbour s avocation. It so happened that a band of robbers, in whose sphere of operations the man's neighbour carried on his depredations, resolved to put their competitor out of the way, but the man got wind of this and determined to stay at home. The poor man who, at the instigation of his wife, went out to try his neighbour's profession, fell a victim to the plot arranged against his neighbour. Here we have one example of the bitterness of a bad wife.â Mid. Eccles. 7.

Rabbi Judah b. Eleah, having a robust appearance, was told that a certain non-Jew of his acquaintance had expressed the opinion that it was due to good living or to being a usurer. The sage explained to him that his was a very frugal mode of living; as to drink, he had the headache from the Passover night â when he tasted of the four cups of wineâ till the Tabernacles; and with usury he would not stain his life. He ascribed his robust health to the study of the Torah.â Mid. Eccles. 8.

He who rebels against the king has it in him to rebel against God.â Mid. Eccles. 9.

Some of the Rabbis, whilst very assiduous in study and prayer, would not neglect their daily avocations, but had set apart a third of the day for the pursuit of labour, and they were, on that account, known as ' the holy body."â Mid. Eccles. 9.

Abbe, called ' the Saintly," returning home with his bundle of goods from his hawking expedition, one Friday afternoon, saw on the road a sick man unable to walk, who beseeched him to carry him to the town. The poor saintly Abbe was at first perplexed how to act. ' If I leave my bundle with my all in all here, I am undone," he said to himself, ' as far as a living is concerned; if, on the other hand, I do not carry this poor helpless man into town, he may perish in the open field." Humanity, however, was the victor, and the good man, casting his burden on God, took the burden of the invalid on his shoulders, walked with him to town, and housed him where he would be taken care of. As there was yet a little sun in the sky, he ventured out again on the high road in the hope of finding the bundle of wares he had left behind, in which hope he was not disappointed, as he found his scanty stock where he had left it. He now set out in great haste on his return journey, being most anxious to arrive home before sundown and before the Sabbath set in. To his great dismay the shadows of the evening were rapidly setting: when he entered the town and his neighbours saw him coming in with his pack on his back together with the Sabbath, they exclaimed, There comes Abbe, ' the saintly,"who will now be known as Abb6 the Sabbath breaker. When, lo and behold, the sun came out in all his brightness so that to this good man could truly be applied the words of the Prophet Malachi (3. 20), ' Unto you that fear my name shall the sun of righteousness arise."â Mid. Eccles. 9.

Fools, as a rule, look upon all mankind as fools.â Mid. Eccles. 10.

Rabbi Joshua, as was his wont, was on a mission of charity on a hot summer's day, in a glowing sun, without finding a drop of water to quench his thirst. Towards evening he reached a small village, where he espied a girl filling her pitcher at the village well. ' 0 grant me a draught of your refreshing water," he said to the damsel, ' for I am well-nigh perishing of thirst." Like the graceful Rebecca of Holy Writ, the maid handed her pitcher full to the thirsty sage, with the remark, ' Drink, worthy man, to thy full, and I wiu. then also give water to the beast upon which thou camest hither." Touched by the kindly act, the Rabbi said to the maiden, ' I see you understand well how to imitate our pious mother Rebecca." ' And you, I hope," came the quick answer, ' will equally understand how to imitate the faithful Eliezer." ' Quite right, my daughter," replied Rabbi Joshua, struck by the quick-wittedness of the maiden, ' You well deserve golden trinkets for your kindness; but you deserve them, you do not need them, for you possess a jewel in your kindly soul that is the brightest ornament one can possess. The only addition I can give you to it is my prayer that the Lord may aid you to retain your kindly nature through life." With this Rabbi Joshua took his departure.â Mid. Lament, i.

At Sinai the Israelites carried a glorious weapon with the name of God inscribed on it. They were deprived of it after making the golden calf.â Pesichta of Mid. Lament.

Rav Asse and Rabbi Amme went to inspect a town, to see what improvements were required therein. When they came to the place they asked for the protectors of it. The watchmen of the town were presented to them, as being what they asked for. '

These," the Rabbis said, ' are not the protectors of your place. What we want to see is your real protectors: your schools, your teachers and their pupils."â Mid. Lament, i.

Balaam the son of Beor and Abinimos the Gardite, who were considered the wisest men amongst their people at the time, were consulted how to act in order to effect a serious injury to the Israelites. The advice of these two wise men was, to find out whether there were any elementary schools for the instruction of the rising generation amongst the Jews. ' If you hear," said they, ' children's voices studying their Torah, all your efforts to hurt that people will be in vain; if not, you will succeed. For you should remember the words in connexion with the blessings they have received: " the voice is the voice of Jacob, but the hands are the hands of Esau." As long as the voice of Jacob is used in prayer and in study of the Torah, he will defy the hands of Esau."â Mid. Lament, i.

He who trains a bad pupil must expect discredit.â Mid. Lament. (Pesichta).

There was harmony between God and his people when He redeemed them from Egypt. They have sinned and broken that harmony, and become separated from their God.â Mid. Lament. (Pesichta).

At the destruction of the Temple, whilst some of the enemy were busy with the plunder of gold and silver, the men of Ammon and Moab sought to lay hands on the scrolls of the Pentateuch, as it is there written (Deut. 23. 4), ' An Ammonite or Moabitc shall not enter into the congregation of the Lord." So, when a fire breaks out on a slaveowner's premises, while others look for plunder among his valuables, the slave's first care is to look for the contract which binds him to his master and to destroy it.â Mid. Lament, i.

The following story is related of a woman named Miriam, daughter of Nachter, who was made captive with her seven sons. When the chief of the place had her sons brought before an image of an idol and bade them bow down before it, six of the sons, each in his turn, stubbornly declined to do so, each basing his refusal on a different Biblical passage showing the prohibition of idolatry; and each on his refusal to comply with the mandate of the savage paid the penalty of death. When at last the turn of the youngest son came, and he, like his elder brothers, refused to bow down before the idol, the perpetrator of this wholesale slaughter seemed to be overcome with something like pity for the young life, and tried, instead of violence, his persuasive )owers, and argued with the youngster to induce com- )liance with his orders. ' See," he said, ' the fate of your brothers for refusing to do my bidding." ' No," answered the lad, ' I will not bow down to an idol, and I am prepared to meet death with the same fortitude as my brothers." ' But your brothers," argued the heathen, ' did not die before they had seen something of life, and tasted its sweetness; whilst you are so young and have seen nothing of life, you should not be so ready to sacrifice it." ' No " persisted the boy, ' I will not do an act which is offensive to my God and destructive of my soul." ' I am prepared to compromise with you," the savage went on with his subterfuges, ' I will drop my ring in front of the image, and you will bend down to pick the ring up, so that it shall appear to my people that you did my bidding, and they will no longer be able to say that I was defied, not only by your six brothers, but even by one of such tender years as you," When all these devices had failed, the chief adopted other tactics. ' See," he said, ' in my idol you have something tangible, which is more than can be said of your God, whom no one has ever seen and who lias nothing visible about Him. Has your God a mouth, as you see my god has? ' ' He has not a mouth," rephed the lad, ' for He is incorporeal; but by his word the heavens were made (Ps. 33.). He has no eyes, yet I know that the eyes of the Lord run to and fro throughout the land (Zech. 4.). He has no bodily ears, but he hearkens and hears (Mai. 3.). He has no mortal hand, but his hands founded the earth ' (Isa. 48.). ' Then," said the heathen, ' why does He not save you out of my hands? ' ' Because I am destined to die," replied the boy, ' and you are but the instrumentâ as any wild beast, such as a lion, a wolf, or a snake might beâ to bring about the destiny decreed upon me." Hereupon the child was put to death by order of the savage, and his mother, bereft of reason by the loss of all her children, threw herself down from the top of her house. Thus perished the mother and all her seven sons.â Mid. Lament, i.

God in his love and mercy provides the remedy even before the disease visits us. He sent the sweet balm of comfort through one prophet before another of his prophets uttered his lamentations over the woes and sorrows which had overtaken Jerusalem and its people. In the first chapter of the Book of Lamentations Jeremiah pours out his bitter heart in twenty-two verses, alphabetically arranged; but before Jeremiah thus uttered his sorrows the prophet Isaiah anticipated each of his colleague's woes with words of comfort suitable to the complaint.

Jeremiah said, ' How doth the city sit solitary' (Lament. I. i), but in anticipation of this lament Isaiah declares, ' The place is too strait for me, give place to me that I may dwell' (Isa. 49. 20). Against Jeremiah's lament, ' She weepeth sore in the night, and her tears are on her cheeks," Isaiah preceded him with the words, ' For the people shall dwell in Zion at Jerusalem, thou shalt weep no more ' (Isa. 30. 19).

Jeremiah says, ' Judah is gone into captivity," which Isaiah anticipates with the assurance, ' He shall assemble the outcasts of Israel," etc. (Isa. ii. 12). The words of Jeremiah, ' The ways of Zion do mourn," Isaiah meets beforehand with the words, ' Prepare ye the way of the Lord, make straight in the desert a highway for our God ' (Isa. 40. 3). Jeremiah complains, ' Her adversaries have become chiefs ': but Isaiah tells us before this, ' The sons of them that afflicted thee shall come bending their knee' (Isa. 60.14). Jeremiah cries," From the daughter of Zion all her beauty is departed ': Isaiah had already said, ' And the Redeemer shall come to Zion ' (Isa. 59. 20). Jeremiah says, ' Jerusalem remembers in her days of affliction '; Isaiah assures us, ' The former shall not be remembered ' (Isa. 65. 17). Jeremiah says, ' Jerusalem hath sinned '; Isaiah previous to this declares, ' I have blotted out as a thick cloud thy transgressions' (Isa. 44. 22). Jeremiah says, 'Her filthiness is in her skirts '; Isaiah speaks of a time ' when the Lord shall wash away the filth of the daughters of Zion ' (Isa. 4. 4). Jeremiah laments, ' The enemy hath spread out his hands on all her pleasant things '; Isaiah anticipates this lament by assuring us, ' the Lord shall set his hand again the second time to recover the remnant of his people ' (Isa. 11. 11). Jeremiah says, ' All her people sigh, they seek bread '; Isaiah anticipates this complaint with the comforting words, ' they shall not hunger nor thirst' (Isa. 49. 10). Jeremiah asks, 'See if there be any sorrow like unto my sorrow '; Isaiah has it," The Spirit shall be poured out on us from on high ' (Isa. 32. 15). Jeremiah laments, ' From above hath He sent a fire into my bones '; Isaiah brought the message from the

Most High, ' For I will not contend for ever, neither will I be always wroth ' (Isa. 57. 16). Jeremiah complains, ' The yoke of transgressions is bound by his hand '; which Isaiah anticipates with the words, ' Loose thyself from the bands of thy neck," etc. (Isa. 52. 2). Jeremiah cries, ' The Lord hath trodden under foot all my mighty men '; Isaiah comforts us with the words, ' Prepare ye the way of the people, cast up the highway, hft up the standard for the people ' (Isa. 62. 10). Jeremiah says, ' For this I weep, mine eye runneth down with tears '; Isaiah assures us, ' For they shall see eye to eye when the Lord shall bring again Zion ' (Isa. 52. 7). Jeremiah complains, ' Zion spreadeth forth her hands, and there is none to comfort her '; Isaiah had said, ' Comfort you, even I am He that comforteth you' (Isa. 51. 12). Jeremiah declares, 'The Lord is righteous, for I have rebelled against his commandments '; Isaiah declares, 'Thy people also shall be all righteous' (Isa. 60. 2). Jeremiah wails, ' I called for my lovers, but they deceived me '; Isaiah declares, ' But thou shalt call thy walls salvation and thy gates praise' (Isa. 60. 18). Jeremiah cries, ' See, 0 Lord, for I am in distress '; Isaiah declared, ' And when ye see this your heart shall rejoice ' (Isa. 66. 14). Jeremiah laments, ' There is none to comfort me '; Isaiah had previously proclaimed, ' Comfort ye, comfort ye, my people," etc. (Isa. 40. i). Jeremiah finally says, ' Let their wickedness come before thee," etc.; Isaiah had previously said, ' Even them will I bring to my holy mountain," etc.â Mid. Lamentations I.

It seems that the identical word used to describe Israel's sin is employed to particularize the punishment for that sin, and is again made use of as the forgiveness of their transgression. It is, for instance, said that Israel sinned, and with the sin employed the word Ufi l ' head ' in suggesting ' Let us appoint a headâ a leaderâ and let us return to Egypt' (Numb. 14.). In punishing them the same word Wi l ' head' is used (Isa. i. 5), and in comforting them the same word ti K"! ' head ' is employed (Micah 2. 13).

They transgressed with the word ' ear ' (Zech. 7. 11); in punishing them the same word is used (i Saml. 3. 11), and they arc comxforted with the same word (Isa. 30. 21). They sinned with the word ' eye ' (Isa. 3.); they were punished with that word (Lament, i. 16), and comforted with the same word (Isa. 52). They transgressed with the word ' nose ' (Ezkl. 8. 17); they were punished with the word (Levit. 26. 24), and comforted with that word (Levit. 26. 42). They committed sin, and used in connexion therewith the word ' mouth' (Isa. 5.); they were punished with that word (Isa. 9.), and comforted with the same word (Ps. 126.). They erred with their tongue (Jer. 9.); they had their retribution with the same word (Lament. 4. 4), and w ere comforted with the same word (Ps. 126.). They sinned, and used in connexion with their sin the word 'heart' (Zech. 7.); and so they were punished with that word (Isa. i.), and were also comforted with the same word (Isa. 40.). They committed iniquity with their hands (Isa. i.), were punished with the same (Lament. 4. 10), and comforted with the same (Isa. 11.11). They sinned with the word 'foot' (Prov. i.), were punished with the word (Jer. 13.), and comforted with that word (Isa. 52.). They committed sin with the word ' fire ' (Jer. 7), were punished with it (Lament. I. 3), and comforted with it (Zech. 2.).â Mid. Lament. 2.

Rabbi Eleazar, son of Rabbi Jose, says that he saw in Rome fragments of King Solomon's throne.â Mid. Esther i.

As early as the time of creation it was decreed that the following should have precedence, each in his own sphere. Adam was first of man, Cain of murderers, and Abel of the murdered. Noah the first to escape from peril. Abraham held the enviable position of first of the faithful, and Isaac was the first of those ready and willing to sacrifice themselves at the bidding of God. Jacob was the first of plain men, Judah of the tribes, and Joseph of saints; Aaron first of priests, Moses of prophets, and Joshua of conquerors. Samuel was the first anointer, and Saul the first anointed (of kings), David the first singer, and Solomon the first builder; Nebuchadnezzar the first destroyer, Ahasuerus the first seller, and Haman the first buyer.â Mid. Esther i.

Among the vices of Ahasuerus his four cardinal virtues should not be overlooked. (i) Modesty: he reigned three years without demanding a crown or throne. (2) Patience, as he waited patiently for years until he found a wife worthy of his exalted position. (3) He was not too self-reliant, as he did nothing without consulting first those whom he trusted. (4) He was grateful, since any benefit bestowed on him had to be recorded in a book kept for the purpose.â Mid. Esther i.

Ten measures of prostitution were given to this world, of which Alexandria (in Egypt) took nine. Out of ten measures of riches Rome took nine; and of an equal number of poverty Lud took nine. Ten measures of witch- craft were also appropriated to the world, and of these Egypt grasped nine for herself. Out of the ten measures of stupidity, of an equal number of health, and of the same number of strength, Ishmael is the possessor of nine of each. Persia can boast of nine measures of vermin (D'JD ) out of the ten that were sent here below. Media is the happy owner of nine measures of beauty out of the ten that were given to the world. Nine measures each of contempt and ugliness fell to the lot of the East. The Chaldeans had for their share nine out of the ten measures of might, and Judah an equal share of strength. Jerusalem got for her share nine of each of the ten measures of comeliness, flattery, learning, and wisdom.â Mid. Esther i.

The question is raised, whcnce had Ahasuerus his riches? And it is answered that Nebuchadnezzar, who was as rich and as mean as he was wicked, grudged Avilmerodach so much wealth, and therefore had secret caves made on the shores of Euphrates and diverted its waters on to them to cover them. Cyrus, when he decreed to rebuild the Temple, was rewarded by the Lord, who revealed to him the hidden treasures (Isa. 45. 3), of which he took possession, and which eventually found their way to Ahasuerusâ Mid. Esther 2.

Semiramis was the name of Nebuchadnezzar's wife, and she was one of four women who ruled; she and Vashti amongst gentiles, Jezebel and Athalia amongst Jews.â Mid. Esther 3.

A woman's pleasure consists in a fine house and fine clothes rather than in the best of food.â Mid. Esther 3.

When Israelites assemble for eating, drinking, and making merry, they do not omit to offer praise and thanks to God for the meat and drink. With some of the nations it is different; in an assembly of that sort the conversation is confined to the question who are the more beautiful, the Persian or the Median women.â Mid. Esther 3

Rabbi Simon b. Jochua and his son Rabbi Eleazar hid themselves for years in caves to escape death on account of their religion. They suffered greatly from hunger.

Now and then R. Simon ventured to peep out of the cave, and he used to see a hunter shooting at birds with varied success. Sometimes the bird fell, and at times a bird escaped. From this he gained greater resignation to his lot, saying, ' even a bird does not fall to the hunter's bow unless death is decreed for it, and what is decreed we must accept cheerfully."â Mid. Esther 3.

The Hebrew language for speech, Latin for war, and the Persian language for lamentations.â Mid. Esther 4.

The misdeeds of faithless servants sometimes bring about the reward of deserving men, as was the case with Joseph and with Mordecai.â Mid. Esther 6.

The book of memorial of Ahasuerus should remind us of the Book of Memorial of the Most High (Mai. 3.).â Mid. Esther 6.

David's blessing, ' Blessed are they that keep judgment and he that doeth righteousness all the time ' (Ps. 106. 3) is applied to him who adopts an orphan.â Mid. Esther 6.

The fact that the wicked are free from sorrow and wax fat in this world by no means implies their ultimate good. The prosperity of Haman only made him feel his fall all the more keenly. Said the young ass to his elder: How wrong it is on the part of our master to feed that pig of his which does no work, and fatten it up with such care; whilst for us, who work for him, he has but a small measure with which he gauges our food." ' Do not judge things by appearance," answered the older and more experienced animal: ' that very fattening of the pig will cause its destruction. When he is fit and fattened up his master will kill him."â Mid. Esther 7.

The narrative of the sixth chapter of the book of Esther seems to corroborate the tradition that the sleep of Ahasuerus was broken by a dream or vision that Haman was stripping him of his crown and royal attire previous to taking his life; and when Haman suggested putting the crown on the man whom the kingdehghted to honour, he saw in this that his dream was about to be fulfilled.â Mid. Esther 10.

The following is the origin and history of the letters and presents that Merodach-baladan sent to Hezekiah (Isa. 39.). This heathen, a sun worshipper, was accustomed to sleep regularly up to a certain hour of the day. Once an echpse of the sun caused darkness at the hour when he should have risen, and he overslept himself, and was incensed with his courtiers for allowing him to do so. When they pleaded the sun's eclipse and the consequent darkness he seemed amazed at their statement. ' What God is greater than my god, the sun," he asked, ' that could control his movements? ' The God of Hezekiah," they replied, ' is greater than your god." He was struck by their reply, and proceeded to write to Hezekiah a letter to accompany the presents which he sent him. The letter began: ' Peace to Hezekiah, Peace to the God of Hezekiah, and Peace to Jerusalem." He handed the epistle with the presents to the messengers, but they had only gone a short distance when he bethought himself. ' All the honour," he said to himself, ' that I now bestow on Hezekiah is only because of that great God of his, and yet I indited the letter to him, with peace to him first, and then peace to his God." So distressed was he at this serious error that he himself ran after the messengers, brought them back, tore up the original letter, and framed another one which lie headed. ' Peace to the Great God of Hezekiah, Peace to Hezekiah, and Peace to Jerusalem." The Eternal decreed as a reward for him that three of his descendantsâ Nebuchadnezzar,

Avilmerodach, and Belshazzarâ should reign over extensive kingdoms.â Mid. Esther 10.

As the sea throws up its refuse on its shores, so have the wicked their filthiness upon their mouths.â Mid. Psalms 2.

As the billows of the sea, when rushing towards the shores in their violence and fury, threaten to swamp the whole shore, yet when they near the shore their fury and violence are lessened, and at last they meekly spend themselves; so also with those who persecute Israel (likened to the sand on the shore of the sea) and threaten to overwhelm them; they are eventually constrained to lessen their violence and fury.â Mid. Psalms 2.

The wicked try to improve on one another in their acts of wickedness. Cain killed Abel. Esau sought to improve on Cain, who killed his brother whilst Adam was yet alive to beget another son instead of Abel; he would wait till his father died, then he would kill his brother, so that he alone might inherit everything. Pharaoh thought Esau's scheme did not go far enough, because whilst Esau was waiting he allowed Jacob to raise up a family of his own; therefore his design was an improvement on Esau's: better kill the Israelites' males at their very birth; the women would then be intermixed with the Egyptians, and thus Israel would be entirely obliterated. Haman criticised Pharaoh's wisdom, and decided upon the policy of making a clean sweep of all the Jews without distinction of sex. Gog and Magog ridiculed all their predecessors in iniquity, and taking into account that the Jews had a Protector in their Heavenly Father, thought of attacking God Himself.â

Mid. Psalms 2.

All the prophets started with admonitions and ended with words of comfort. Jeremiah alone had no words of comfort to offer.â Mid. Psalms 4.

That the mere mechanical application to the Throne of Mercy is not efficacious is plainly seen from the words of King David, who says God is nigh to all that call upon Him, and, as it were, as a condition, he adds the important words, ' to those who call upon Him iji truth." â Mid. Psalms 4.

The last words of Rabbi Zivry b. Leves were: ' For this let every saint pray to Thee." Those of Rabbi Jos6 b. Pinehas were: ' Better one day in thy court '; and those of Rabbi Joshua b. Levi were: ' How great is thy goodness which Thou hast reserved for those who revere Thee."â Mid. Psalms 5.

A man is bound to pay the same respect to his wife's father as he would to his own father.â Mid. Psalms 7.

With regard to the conduct of life, men may be said to be divided into three sections. There arc men who are thoroughly good, practising righteousness for righteousness' sake. They are thankful to their Maker for having brought them to this life and endowed them with intellect to view the works of creation; they expect and ask for no reward. There is another sect who, when doing any commendable deed, book it, as it were, to their credit and expect recompense in the future life. But there is, alas! a worse section, who neither have nor seek to have any merits of their own, but look for favours to the merits of their ancestors.â Mid. Psalms 8.

If one tells you definitely when the Messiah will come, believe him not.â Mid. Psalms 9.

The following Rabbis were martyrs: Rabbi Simeon b. Gamaliel, Rabbi Ishmacl b. Elisha, Jcshbab the scribe, Chu pas the translator, Jos6 Judah b. Baba, Judah Nachtom, Simon b. Azai, Chanina b. Tradyon. and Rabbi Akiba.â Mid. Psalms 9. David's words clearly show that righteous non-Jews will inherit future bliss. He says: ' The wicked shall go to ' Sheol' and all the nations that forget God ' (Ps. 9. 18), i. e. those of the nations that forget God, but not those who worship God.â Mid. Psalms 9.

A certain philosopher asked Rabbi Elisha:â ' Your prophet predicts about us ' They shall build, but I will throw down" (Mai. i. 4). Now look at Alexandria built by Alexander; at Constantinople, built by Con-stantine; or Antiochia, raised up by Antiochus; at Seleucia, built by Seleucus; or at our Roman empire. The founders and builders themselves are gone, yet their works stand as a monument to their might and wisdom." ' What the prophet means," answered the sage, ' is not the structures of brick and mortar, but your designs against us, in which you will not prevail, but which our God will throw down." ' If it is that," confessed the Roman philosopher, ' to which your prophet alludes, ' then I must admit the truth of it, because I well know what weapons are forged every year, in our councils, for your destruction; and somehow each time some one comes and frustrates our designs."â Mid. Psalms 9.

There would be a serious discrepancy in two parts of Scripture were it not that we know, traditionally, the explanation. In the second Book of Samuel (17. 25) mention is made of ' Ithra an Israehte." In the first of Chronicles (2. 18) the same person is mentioned as ' Ithra the Ishmaelite." The fact is that this man was originally an Ishmaelite who used to frequent the Jewish seminary, when he heard Jesse hold forth on the text in Isaiah (45, 23) ' Look unto Me and be ye saved, all the ends of the earth; for I am God and there is none else." So impressed was this Ithra with the expounding of this text that he became a convert to Judaism, married Jesse's daughter, and was henceforth known as Ithra the Israehte.â Mid. Psalms 9.

1 See also Tosephta Sanhedrin.

Of all the gjod men who arc designed to see God, those that were upright in their hves here stand in the first rank.â Mid. Psalms ii.

Moses' prayer for his people was, ' O that there were such a heart in them," etc. (Deut. 5.), and when his disciple Joshua suggested to him to prohibit any but himself to prophesy, this meek and unselfish man burst out in the l rayer, ' Would that all the Lord's people were prophets, that the Lord would put his Spirit upon them ' (Xumb. II.). Such a prayer from such a man cannot l)e left unanswered, though we must leave it to God's own good time, when these prayers will be brought into fulfilment. By the prophet Ezekiel God's people are promised a new heart (Ezkl. 36.), and through his prophet Joel God promises to pour out his Spirit upon all flesh, and they shall prophesy (Joel 2.).â Mid. Psalms 14.

Most of the blessings that God bestows upon his people proceed from Zion. The Torah, as it is said in Isaiah (2. 3). Blessings in general (Ps. 134.). The blessing of brightness (Ps. 52.), that of support (Ps. 20.), of hfe (Ps. 133.), of greatness (Ps. 98 ), and of salvation (Ps. 14.). â Mid. Psalms 14.

David enumerates eleven attributes which will render a man fit to abide in the Tabernacle of the Lord (Ps. 15.). One of these is, ' he that putteth not his money out to usury." And this applies equally to non-Jews. One is not allowed to take usury from either.â Mid. Psalms 17.

Hillel and Shammai declined to accept remuneration for the instruction tliey gave to their pupils, and truly can we say of them ' they have not put their money out to usury."â Mid. Psalms 15.

He who hears himself abused (or cursed) and does not retaliate may le called a saintly man.â Mid. Psalms 16.

The si. hundred and thirtren commandments which were handed over to the Israelites were reduced by King David to eleven (Ps. 15.). Isaiah further reduced all the commandments to six (Isa. 23- 5, i6). Micah made a further reduction of them to three (Micah 6. 8). Habakkuk reduced the whole to one, that of faith (Hab. 2. 4).â Mid. Psalms 17.

Rabbi Joshua b. Levi mentions a tradition to the effect that when Jacob and Esau met for the purpose of burying their father Isaac (Gen. 35.), Esau at last attempted to carry bis long cherished desire for vengeance on his brother into effect, and took up a threatening attitude towards Jacob; but when Judahâ who with his brothers was present at the burial of Isaacâ saw that Esau's enmity towards Jacob was still smouldering, he prevented any untoward event by killing Esau.â Mid. Psalms 18.

It is much more difhcult to cope with a Jewish enemy than with a non-Jewish enemy.â Mid. Psalms 18.

Good men are meek and humble, and style themselves servants, and they are registered in the book of God's army as servants. Abraham called himself servant (Gen. 18.) and God refers to him as his servant (Gen. 18.); Jacob pronounced himself servant (Gen. 32.), and God calls him his servant (Isa. 44.); Moses refers to himself as servant (Deut. 3.), and God declares him his servant (Numb. 12.); David describes himself as servant (Ps. 116.), and God calls him his servant (2 Saml. 3.). And there are two individuals who had not taken the opportunity of pronouncing themselves servants, but God declares them to be his servants, viz. Isaac (Exod. 32)., and Joshua (Josh. 24.).â Mid. Psalms 18.

A father and his son being on a long journey, the son said that he would like to know when they would arrive at the end of it. The older man replied that when they saw a cemetery they might hope to arrive at the town soon. Similarly our Heavenly Father indicates to us that when heavy persecution and sorrow meet us we may hope to be brought to Him, to a haven of rest and shelter.â Mid. Psalms 20.

The whole of our history tends to show that, when distress was at its greatest, God was nearest. E en when we well deserved God's punishment, as for the making of the golden calf for which our destruction was threatened, yet we find soon after, ' And the Lord repented of the evil which He thought to do unto his people ' (Exod. 32.). When in darkness the Lord hath become our light (Micah 7.). In his anger God yet grants us his mercy (Hab. 2.). The very time of trouble is transposed into a time of joy and help (Jer. 30.), the estrangement to a bringing near (Hosea 2.), the threat of annihilation into exaltation (Esther 4).â Mid. Psalms 21.

Trust in God delivers us from impending peril.â Mid. Psalms 22.

The more good men are exalted the meeker they become. Abraham declared himself dust and ashes (Gen. 18). Moses and Aaron disclaimed all greatness (Exod.

16.). David styled himself a worm and not a man (Ps. 22.). Saul called himself but a child of a Benjaminite (i Saml. q.). Gideon said he was the humblest in Manasseh (Jud. 6.). Not so with the heathen in his brief authority. Pharaoh said, ' Who is the Lord that I should obey his voice? ' (Exod. 5.). Goliath defied the armies of Israel (i Saml. 17.). Sennacherib boasted, ' Who are they among all the gods that have delivered theircountryout of my hands?" (2 Kings 18.). Nebuchadnezzar asked, ' Who is that god that shall deliver you out of my hands? ' (Dan. 3.). Bclshazzar was rebuked by Daniel for having lifted himself up against the Lord of heaven ' (Danl. 5.). Hiram too received a sharp rebuke for having set his heart as the heart of God (Ezkl. 28.).â Mid. Psalms 22.

Woe to any man when death approaches him, to the strong man when he becomes weak, or to him who lo. ses his sight; but woe to the whole generation which is ruled by a woman.â Mid. Psalms 22.

An officiating Priest once scorned a woman who brought a handful of flour as an offering, and, in a vision which he had immediately afterwards, he received a very severe rebuke.â Mid. Psalms 22.

Haman's property was divided as follows: One-third went to Mordecai and Esther, another went to those who separated themselves from the outer world and devoted themselves to study and religion, and one-third towards the building of the Temple.â Mid. Psalms 22.

The Holy Spirit sometimes rested on King David before he commenced singing and playing hymns, and he was in fact prompted to the hymns by the Holy Spirit that rested upon him. At other times the Holy Spirit kept away from him, but came upon him as soon as he gave himself up to hymns and praises.â Mid. Psalms 24.

We Jews surely give practical proof of our faith in God's promises. No resurrection has yet taken place, yet the established ritual throughout Jewry contains the prayers to be said, ' Blessed art Thou, 0 Lord, who quickenest the dead." Our last (chief) redemption has not yet been brought about, but we proclaim twice every day, ' Blessed art Thou, O God, the Redeemer of Israel." â Mid. Psalms 31.

If all your life is given up to the pursuit of earthly things, it is quite consistent for you to look downwards; but if you pursue the higher life, look upwards.â Mid. Psalms 32.

He that feels as though his heart is torn within him on account of his sin may well hope for God's forgiveness. Yet whilst continually thinking of his grievous sin, man must not make a habit of sinning and rely on his sorrow and confession for the expiation of his sin.â â Mid. Psalms 32.

The wicked are, as a rule, brought to judgment when all fear of judgment has left them.â Mid. Psalms 36.

Jerusalem is destined to become the Metropolis of the world. â Mid. Psalms 36.

Israel was in the darkness of slavery in Egypt, and Moses and Aaron were the means of bringing them to the light of freedom. They were in captivity in Babylon; Hananiah, Mishael, and Azariah were the messengers of their freedom. They were oppressed at the hands of the Greeks, and deliverance was brought by Mattathias Hashmonai and his sons. When again brought under the yoke of Edom (Rome) Israel wishes no longer any human agency for his rescue, but looks direct to God to be his light of deliverance (Ps. ii8.). So one enveloped in darkness endeavours to get artificial light time after time, but each time the light becomes extinguished, and he at last resolves to abandon all further attempts to procure light, and to wait for sunrise to bring him natural light.â Mid. Psalms 36.

How flexible is the tongue, and how great is its power! It is related of a Persian king that his physicians ordered him to drink the milk of a lioness, and one of his servants offered to procure the rare medicine. Taking with him some sheep with which to lure the beast, he actually succeeded in obtaining milk from a lioness.

On his journey homewards, being fatigued, he fell into a deep slumber, during which the various members of his body commenced disputing as to which of them had contributed most towards the success of their owner in obtaining so rare a thing as milk from a lioness.

Said the feet: ' There can be no doubt that we are the only factors in this successful undertaking. Without us there could have been no setting out on this dangerous venture." ' Not so," said the hands, ' the facility you offered would have been of no avail had our power not been called into requisition; it is the service we rendered that enabled our owner to procure milk from the lioness." ' Neither of you could have rendered any service," exclaimed the eyes, ' without the sight which we supplied." ' And yet," interrupted the heart, ' had not I inspired the idea, no steps would have been taken to bring any of your powers into exercise." At last the tongue put in her claim, and was utterly ridiculed by the unanimous opinions of all the other contending members of the body.

' You," they scornfully replied, ' you who have not the free power of action which is possessed by all and each of us, you who are imprisoned in the narrow space of the human mouth,â you dare to put in a claim to have contributed to this success!" In the midst of this contention the man woke up, and prosecuted his journey homewards. Being brought before the king with the much desired milk, the man, by a slip of the tongue, said, ' Here I have brought your Majesty the dog's milk." The savage king becoming incensed by this insulting remark, there and then ordered the man to be put to death. On the man's way to execution, all the members of his body, heart, eyes, feet, and hands trembled and were terribly afraid. Did I not tell you," said the tongue, ' that my power is above all the united powers you possess? and you ridiculed me for my trouble. What think you of my power now? Are you now prepared to acknowledge my power to be greater than all yours? '

When all the members of the body consented to the tongue's proposition, the tongue requested and obtained a short reprieve, so that it could make a last appeal for the king's clemency. When the man was brought to the king his tongue started in all its eloquence. ' Is this the reward," it began, ' great and just king, to be meted out to the only one of your majesty's servants who was glad of the opportunity to offer his life to fulfil his king's desire, who gladly carried his life in his hand to obtain for his august master what scarcely ever was obtained by mortal man? ' ' But," replied the king," your own statement was that you brought me dog's milk instead of the lioness' milk which you undertook to procure." ' Not so, O gracious king," replied the tongue, I brought the identical milk that your majesty required; it was merely by an unfortunate mistake in my speech that I changed the name; and in fact there is a similarit ', as the word hi' ' D may mean either lioness or dog. My words will be verifted if your majesty will condescend to make use of the milk I procured, for it will effect the cure your majesty desires." The milk was submitted to the test, and was found to be that of a lioness; and so the tongue triumphantly demonstrated its great power for good or for evil.â Mid. Psalms 39.

View David's career, and you will see both the necessity and the efficacy of repentance.â Mid. Psalms 40.

He that is satiated with tears cannot be expected to have appetite for food.â Mid Psalms 42.

In futurity the righteous will feast on the splendour of the Shechinah.â Mid. Psalms 45.

To Israel's question ' O Lord, when wilt Thou redeem us? ' God's answer is, ' When you have fallen to your lowest depth."â Mid. Psalms 45.

He that puts his sin wilfully away from his eyes has no right to expect or hope for pardon. ' My sin," says David, ' is continually before me." David was like the patient to whom the physician said, ' I am very sorry for you, your illness is a very serious one." ' No," said the patient, ' the reason of my illness is that there may be a reward for curing me." Thus David prayed to God to cure him (to pardon his sins), so that God's great power, his mercy and lovingkindness, might be known, since He had pardoned such great and grievous sin.â Mid. Psalms 51.

He that is deeply sensible of his sin, is in terror of it, confesses it, and is in communion with God concerning this burden of uncleanliness, may hope for forgiveness.â Mid. Psalms 51.

If you intend to put man to rights, put yourself to rights first.â Mid. Psalms 53.

As there is no limit to the evils of a bad wife, so there is no limit to the good that is caused by a good wife. â Mid. Psalms 53.

Men who do not marry deprive themselves of (i) God's blessing, for it was only after Adam became possessed of Eve that God blessed them (Gen. 28.). (2) Life, as King Solomon has it, ' Live joyfully with the wife," etc. (Eccles. 9.). (3) Joy, as it is said, ' Rejoice with the wife of thy youth' (Prov. 5.). (4) Help, ' I will make a helpmate for him ' (Gen. 2.). (5) Good, ' Whoso findeth a wife findeth a good thing ' (Prov. 18.).â Mid. Psalms 59.

If a man should intend committing an evil act, but has not carried out his intention, the Merciful One will forbear punishing him. On the other hand, if a man intends doing a religious deed, and is somehow prevented from carrying it into effect, he will receive his reward as though he had carried out his intention. We find that David was looked upon almost as the builder of the Temple, and the Consecration Psalm (30.) is called ' the dedication of the house of David."â Mid. Psalms 62.

' I am that I am," said God to Moses, by which He intimated that He created the world in mercy, and will always rule the world in mercy.â Mid. Psalms 72.

The great faith manifested by the tribe of Judah entitles it to the dignified position it has attained, that of being the Royal House of Israel. On the banks of the Red Sea the people hesitated to plunge into the water, until the tribe of Judah, exclaiming that there can be no hesitation where one has God's promise of protection, like one man took the initiative and jumped into the sea; then their example was followed by all the other tribes.â Mid. Psalms 76.

One is not to think lightly of a parable or a simile: indeed one is to look upon them in the same sense as psalms, hymns, or prophecy.

Hath not the Lord sent his prophet Ezekiel to put forth a riddle and speak a parable unto the house of Israel (Ezkl. 17.)? and hath not the Psalmist said, ' I will open my mouth in a parable ' (Ps. 78.)?â Mid. Psalms 79.

It seems strange that, out of all the Patriarchs, the Temple should only be called by the name of Jacob (Isa. 2. 3, and Jer. 30. 18). Yet it is but proper that the Temple is styled ' the house of the God of Jacob." A king once intimated to three of his friends his intention of building a palace, and showed them the spot upon which that palace was to be erected. The first friend remarked slightingly, ' there was a mountain on this spot before." The second friend made the disparaging remark, ' This is an open field." The third friend said, ' This is the place for a palace." Abraham, being on the spot where the Temple was destined to be erected, called it the mountain of God (Gen. 22.). Isaac alluded to the spot as a field that God blessed (Gen. 27.). It was left to Jacob to call the place by the proper name when he said, on waking up from his vision, ' This is no other than the house of God, and this is the gate of heaven ' (Gen. 28.). Therefore the Temple was called by his name.â Mid. Psalms 81.

A generation is twenty years.â Mid. Psalms 90.

The coats, or covers, with which God clothed Adam and Eve after their fall were made of the serpent's skin.â Mid. Psalms 92.

Moses and Isaiah alone of all the prophets knew what they were prophesying; all the other prophets, including Elijah and Samuel, uttered their prophecies mechanically.â Mid. Psalms 90.

If you bear in mind that your prayers are directed to the God above, then they will be a blending of joy and awe.â Mid. Psalms 100.

Sing praises unto the Eternal whether you worship Him as a God of judgment or as a God of mercy.â Mid. Psalms loi.

God asks neither for burnt offerings nor for other sacrifices. He asks for earnest prayer.â Mid. Psalms 102.

Rabbi Gamaliel was asked by a heathen to define the residence of God. When the sage stated his inability to do so, the questioner retorted: ' and yet you pray to Him daily without even knowing where He is. Surely our position is a more rational one; we know and we see the god that we worship." ' Now," said Rabbi Gamaliel, ' you ask of me a thing as difficult to comply with as though you had asked me to walk for five hundred years: I will, in return, ask you something by no means so difficult to answer. In which part of your body does your soul reside? ' ' I do not know," answered R. Gamaliel's friend. ' Well then," observed the sage, ' hath David said " Bless the Lord, 0 my soul," for in certain attributes the soul resembles its giver. As God filleth the whole world so the human soul filleth the whole body. God is unique, and the soul is unique. God neither eats nor drinks, neither does the soul. As God is pure, so is the soul (his spark) pure. As God cannot be seen, so the soul cannot be seen."â Mid. Psalms 103.

Prayer is not to be offered in the midst of frivolity or laughter, but with humility and bowed head.â Mid. Psalms 108.

At the redemption of Israel, the nations amongst which they have been scattered, and out of which they will be redeemed, will sing praises to God.â Mid. Psalms 117.

The wicked walk in darkness, but those who have the light of God, the Torah, as their guide are restricted from committing sin even when they have a passing desire to do so.â Mid. Psalms 119.

The fact that special mention is made of the affair of Zimri (Numb. 24. 14) tends to show that the Israelites, in those days, were very chaste, as such conduct seems to have come as a surprise to the whole camp.â Mid. Psalms 122.

Every man gets the wife he deserves.â Mid. Psalms 125.

Repentance is of no avail in a matter of wronging your fellow-man, without first rectifying the wrong done.â Mid. Psalms 125.

Whether in season or out of season, it is a good omen to see white grapes in a dream. With black grapes there is a difference: in their season it is favourable, but if they are seen when they are not in season it is exceedingly unfavourable, and the dreamer should pray for God's mercy.â Mid. Psalms 128.

Water, milk and wine should never be left uncovered.â Mid. Psalms 136.

No one has a right to expect success in his mundane affairs unless he works for it. Moses blessed the works of the hiuids and all of man's doings (Deut. 14. 29).â Mid. Psalms 136.

Let no man say ' My father was a righteous man; I shall be all right for his sake," or ' My brother was a righteous man, and I shall reaj) the benefit of his merits." Abraham could not save Ishmael, and Jacob could not save Esau. Each man must work out his own salvation.â Mid. Psalms 146.

Man should attain sound sense and a feeling of responsibility at the age of twenty.â Mid. Proverbs i.

Man must be attentive to his wife, to his studies, and to his occupation.â Mid. Proverbs 5.

Happy indeed is the teacher who has a disciple that can intercede with Heaven, by his prayer, on behalf of the teacher.â Mid. Proverbs 7.

Do not despise an ignorant man who strives to gain knowledge, or a man of ill repute who strives to redeem his past.â Mid. Proverbs 7.

The Day of Atonement will never be abolished.â Mid. Proverbs 9.

Have a good word for your fellow-man, and the ministering angels will plead for you before the throne of mercy.â Mid. Proverbs 11.

Man has two hands; but he is not to rob with the one and give alms with the other.â Mid. Proverbs 11.

He who, being on friendly terms with another, eats and drinks with him and does not refrain from speaking against him, is designated by God Himself an evil one.â Mid. Proverbs 12.

A man proud of his knowledge is a propagator of folly.â Mid. Proverbs 13.

Here man is able to comprehend things and test them by his senses, such as the sense of sight or the sense of hearing; but he cannot imagine what future bliss means, since it is an abstract idea and cannot be tested either by the sense of sight or by the sense of hearing.â Mid. Proverbs 13.

Consider the great value of righteousness (or charity, the word Hplij may mean either righteousness or charity. The view taken in Holy Writ of giving alms or help to the poor, is that it is nothing more than what is right or just, an act of justice or equity). It atones for the sins, not only of Jews, but also of non-Jews. It is placed at the right hand of God (Ps. 48.). It is God's praise (Isa. 63.). It gives life and honour to its practisers (Prov. 21.). Abraham was praised for it (Gen. 15.). David too was praised for it (i Saml. 28.). And so it is also Israel's praise (Deut. 6.). God will be. e. xalted by it (Isa. 5.). It goes to )repare a place before the departure hence of those who have practised it (Isa. 38.).â Mid. Proverbs 14.

God lends eloquence to the supphant.â Mid. Proverbs 15.

A man of a kindly and charitable disposition is generally blessed with old age, which sits on him like a crown.â Mid. Proverbs 16.

A learned man who has a learned son and a learned grandson may reasonably hope that learning will be the characteristic of his family for generations to come.â Mid. Proverbs 18.

If you want to incur contempt, be extravagant in self-I)raise.â Mid. Proverbs 27.

A judge, like a king, should not depend on anybody's gifts; nor should he, like a priest, live on the people's bounty.â Mid. Proverbs 30.

Alexander of Macedonia overran the whole world like a swarm of locusts.â Mid. Proverbs 30.

What blessings cannot earnest prayer bring down for us from heaven! It was in answer to Hannah's earnest prayer that he was blessed with a son whose name was associated with those of Moses and Aaron (Ps. 99.) as the lights of Israel.â Mid. Proverbs 30.

The virtues of Noah's wife outweighed those of Noah. â Mid. Proverbs 31.

As an example of a good wife, the spouse of Rabbi

Meier may perhaps be mentioned. The learned Rabbi was engaged the whole of one Sabbath afternoon in a discourse in the college, during which time his two sons died. Their mother had them removed to a room and covered up. When in the evening her husband returned from the college and asked for his two sons she gave him some evasive answer and asked him to pronounce the blessing fixed for the departing Sabbath. This done, she set some food before him, of which he partook after persuasion, as his anxiety about his two boys was increasing. When the meal was finished and the good Rabbi insisted on knowing where his boys were, his wife said, ' I will answer your question after you have answered mine. If any one," she asked," has deposited something with you, are you bound to return it to him without any complaint? ' Her husband expressed his surprise that his own wife should ask a question upon a matter so obvious. ' Do you want instruction on this point, and does it not go without saying that you must return what is deposited with you? '

At this she took him gently by the hand, and bidding him follow her, led him to the room where the two corpses lay, and removing the cover from their faces showed him their dead boys. Rabbi Meier showed a tendency to give way to grief, but the good woman checked him. ' Did you not tell me but a few minutes ago that it is our duty to return anything that had been deposited with us? It is our duty not to utter a word of complaint, but to say, "The Lord hath given, the Lord hath taken; blessed be the name of the Lord " ' (Job i.).

Rabbi Meier was glad and grateful to his wife for recalling him to a sense of his duty.â Mid. Proverbs 31.

Behold the greatness of worship. Israel was redeemed from Egypt because of his worship (Exod. 4.). The Torah was given to the Israehtes on account of worship (Exod. 24.). The Temple was built owing to worship (Ps. 99.). The dead will be quickened in consequence of worship (Ps.). The final redemption will be brought about through worship (Isa. 27.).â Mid. Samuel 3.

In naming your children try to perpetuate a good name. You know it is not the custom of the world to name their children after Pharaoh, Sisera, or Sennacherib; rather call them after the Patriarchs or other good men. â Mid. Samuel i.

Prayer is, or should be, the service of the heart.â Mid. Samuel 2.

In the time of Elkanah and Hannah there was a tradition that a wonderful child would be born who would receive the name of Samuel. Many mothers called their newly-born boys by the name of Samuel; but when the Samuel came it was universally acknowledged that this was the one looked forward to.â Mid. Samuel 3.

Faith is a very good thing indeed, but no man has a right to neglect his duty and cast himself on God and say he has faith in Him to do what he himself ought to do. The rabbis taught this practical lesson by their lives. Rabbi Ishmael and Rabbi Akiba were walking through some streets in Jerusalem when a sick man came up to them complaining about his ailment and soliciting their advice. When they told him of a remedy, another man came up to them reproaching them with irrehgion. ' If," argued the man, ' it is God's will that this man should have a certain disease, are you going to counteract God's decision by removing the disease which has been decreed for him? ' ' What is your occupation?" demanded the Rabbis in reply to this piece of philosophy. ' I am a gardener, as you may see by the tools which I carry in my hands." ' But why do you interfere with the earth which God has created? ' continued the wise men. If I were not to manure, prune, and water the trees," retorted the man, ' how could I expect them to produce their fruit? ' ' And man is even like the tree of the field," said the Rabbis; ' he requires tender treatment and attention to his body to make it flourish and keep in good trim."â Mid. Samuel 4.

No wizard or astrologer can produce a human soul.â Mid. Samuel 5.

A religious teacher who in his old age is found not to be what he had always led men to believe that he was, pious and pure, is not to be held up to public derision, but should be made to retire from his duties in a manner which will not detract from his dignity.â Mid. Samuel 7.

Great as is God's mercy, and open as his gates are to admit the prayer of the penitent, a man must not carry his evil deeds too far and rely upon the reception of himself and his prayers, and reckon upon the greatness of God's mercy. The following Scripture quotations tend to confirm our assertion on this point: they would stand in open contradiction to one another were it not that one can detect in them the differences between man's timely repentance and his repenting when the measure of his evil deeds is overfull. Take the following passages and see whether they can possibly be reconciled without adopting the hypothesis which we advance:â ' Have I pleasure that the wicked should die, saith the Lord God, and not that he should return from his way and live? '

Ezkl. i8. 23). Against these comforting words we have these: ' If a man sin against God, who shall entreat for him? ' (i Saml. 2. 25). The Psalmist says: ' O Thou that hearest prayer, unto Thee shall all flesh come' (Ps. 65), but in Lamentations (3. 44) we have it, ' Thou hast covered Thyself with a cloud, that our prayers should not pass through." Again we are assured: ' Out of the mouth of the Most High proceeded not evil' (Lament. 3), and on the other hand, ' Therefore hath the Lord watched evil and brought it upon us ' (Deut. 9.).

Jerusalem is called upon as follows: ' Wash thine heart from wickedness that thou mayest be saved' (Jer. 4.); but the same prophet tells her, ' Though thou dost wash thee with nitre and take much soap, yet thine iniquity is marked before Me, saith the Lord' (Jer. 2.). Again, in Psalms (145.) it is declared ' The Lord is nigh unto all that call upon Him '; whilst in another Psalm (10.) the complaint is uttered Why standest Thou afar off, 0 Lord?" Isaiah's advice is (55.) ' Seek 3 e the Lord while He may be found '; but Ezekiel is charged with the message (20.) 'As I live, saith the Lord, I will not be inquired of by you." Malachi brings the tidings (3.) ' Return unto Me and I will return unto you saith the Lord of hosts '; but Jeremiah says (8.) ' Therefore shall they fall, they shall be cast down, saith the Lord."

By the adoption of our interpretation these passages no longer contradict each other.â Mid. Samuel 7.

The following are dignified with the name ' Precious ': Torah, prophecy, understanding, knowledge, simplicity, the righteous, the death of the righteous, kindness, riches, and Israel.â Mid. Samuel 8.

He that slights his parents may be compared to a knife which one acquires for the purpose of cutting food, but which fails to do this and cuts the owner's hand.â or to a light which one carries in order to help him in the darkness, instead of which it burns his clothes.â Mid. Samuel 7.

Let no man boast of his exalted position. Even so great a man as Samuel received a rebuke for his want oi modesty. His answer to Saul's inquiry was, ' I am the seer ' (i Saml. 9.), and when he was sent to anoint one of Jesse's sons and saw Ehab, who was a fine youth, he decided to anoint him. Then he receives the rebuke for having said I am the seer," when God told him that man seeth with his eyes, but the Lord seeth into the heart, which meansâ Thus much for thy seeing; thou hast seen Eliab's exterior, not his heart.â Mid. Samuel 12.

Immediately a man is born he proceeds into death; when he dies he proceeds into life.â Mid. Samuel 23.

Well has King Solomon said, A good name is better than good oil. Good oil is poured downwards, a good name tends upwards. Oil, however good, gets exhausted; not so a good name. Good oil can only be possessed by the rich; the poor as well as the rich can rejoice in a good name. Good oil we can only put from one vessel into another; whilst a good name circulates everywhere. The best oil if put on a dead body becomes offensive; the good name of a dead man is a glory to his memory. Oil put on the fire will burn; a good name stands proof against fire.â Mid. Samuel 23.

Thl 1 uiali is full of holy tire; it was written with a I)lack hit' upon a white hre.â Tanchum. Bereshith.

The Torah has meekness as its footgear, and the fear of God; ls its crown. Hence Moses was the piroper person through whose hands it should be deliv ered; he was meek, and with the fear of the Lord he was crowned.â Tanchum. Bereshith.

You cannot expect to occupy yourself with the study of the Torah in the future world and receive the reward for so doing in this world; you are meant to make the Torah your own in this life, antl to look for reward in the life to come.â Tanchum Bereshith.

Cain's offering consisted of the seed of flax, and that of Abel of the fatlings of his sheep. This is probably the reason why the wearing of a garment of various materials, as of woollen and linen together, was prohibited.â Tanchum. Bereshith.

As one who finishes the building of his house proclaims that day a holiday, and consecrates the building, so God, having finished creation in the six days, proclaimed the seventh day a holy day and sanctified it.â Tanchum. Bereshith.

If the fraudulent man and the usurer offer to make restitution, it is not permitted to accept it from them. â Tanchum. Bereshith.

The Bible or written law contains unexplained passages and hidden sentences, which cannot be fully understood without the help of the oral law. Further, the written law contains generalities, whilst the oral law goes in for explanations in detail, and is consequently much larger in volume. Indeed as a figure of speech we could apply to it the words in Job (4. 9), 'The measure thereof is longer than the earth and broader than the sea." The knowledge of this oral law cannot be expected to be found amongst those who are bent on enjoying earthly life and worldly pleasures; its acquisition requires the relinquishment of all worldliness, riches and pleasures, and requires intellect aided by constant study.â Tanchum. Bereshith.

There is no evil that has no remedy, and the remedy for sin is repentance.â Tanchum, Bereshith.

Whatever hardships may be imposed upon Jews by the powers that be, they must not rebel against the authorities who impose them, but are to render compliance, except when ordered to disregard the Torah and its injunctions; for that would be tantamount to giving up their God.â Tanchum. Bereshith.

He that stole an ox had to restore fivefold, and he that stole a sheep had to give back only fourfold, because by stealing the ox he may have prevented the owner from ploughing or doing other agricultural work for the time being.â Tanchum. Bereshith.

There is a wall of separation erected between the Shechinah and the following three classes, a wall that can never be razed: The cheat, the robber, and the idle worshipper.â Tanchum. Bereshith.

The meaning of the phrase ' God made man in his own image ' is that, like his Maker, man is to be righteous and upright. Do not argue that the y- r 1 the evil inclination, is innate in you; such argument is fallacious; when you are a child you commit no sin; it is when you grow out of infancy that your evil inclination becomes developed. You have the power of resisting the evil inclination if you feel so inclined, even as you are able to

MIDRASH laNCHUMAII OR YELAMDINU 221 convert the bitter elements of certain foods into very palatable eatables.â Tanchum. Bereshith.

Hadrian, King of (Edom) Rome, having made great conquests, requested his court in Rome to proclaim him God. In answer to this modest request, one of his ministers said, ' If your majesty desires to become God, it will be necessary to quit God's property first, to show your independence of Him. He created heaven and earth; get out of these and you can proclaim yourself God." Another counsellor replied by asking Hadrian to help him out of a sad position in which he was placed. ' I have sent a ship to sea," he said, ' with all my possessions on board of her, and she is but a short distance, about three miles from shore, but is struggling against the watery elements, which threaten her total destruction." ' Do not trouble," replied the king, ' I will send some of my ships well manned, and your craft shall be brought to the haven where she would be." ' There is no need for all that," said the counsellor satirically; 'order but a little favourable wind, and her own crew will manage to bring her safely into port." ' And where shall I order the wind from? How have I the power to order the wind? ' answered Hadrian angrily. ' Has your majesty not even a little wind at your command?" said the king's adviser mockingly, ' and yet you wish to be proclaimed God! '

Hadrian then retired to his own rooms angry and disappointed, and when he told his wife of the controversy he had had with his ministers she remarked that his advisers did not strike on the proper thing which would bring his wish to a hajipy consummation. ' It seems to me," she said mockingly," that the first thing you must do is to give God back what He has given you and be under no obligation to Him." 'And what may that be? ' inquired the heathen. ' The soul, of course," answered his wife. ' But," argued the king, ' if I give l ack my soul, I shall not live." ' Then," said his wife triumphantly, ' that shows that you are but mortal, and cannot be God."â Tanchum. Bereshith.

The slanderer seems to deny the existence of God. As King David has it, ' They say, our lips are with us, who is Lord over us? ' (Ps. 12.)â Tanchum. Bereshith.

Let us not lose sight of the lesson that it is meant to convey to us by the expression, ' And the Lord came down to see' (Gen. 11.), namely that we are not to judge merely by ' hearsay' and to assert anything as having taken place unless we saw it.â Tanchum. Bereshith.

Elijah quickened the dead, caused rain to descend, prevented rain from coming down, and brought lire down from heaven; but he did not say ' I am God."â Tanchum. Bereshith.

When Noah set out to plant the vine, Satan encountered him and asked upon what errand he was bent. ' I am going to plant the vine," said Noah. ' I will gladly assist you in this good work," said Satan. When the offer of help was accepted Satan brought a sheep and slaughtered it on the plant, then a lion, then a pig, and finally a monkey. He thus explained these symbols to Noah. When a man tastes the first few drops of wine he will be as harmless as a sheep; when he tastes a little more he will become possessed of the courage of a lion and think himself as strong; should he further indulge in the liquid produced by your plant he will become as objectionable as a pig; and by yet further indulgence in it he will become like a monkey.â Tanchum. Noah.

Because the Torah mulcts the thief in double, and in some cases more than double, the value of what he has stolen, one is not to conclude that he is allowed to steal when in want, with the intention of paying back double and more than double the value.â Tanchum. Noah.

The promise to Abraham that he should become a great nation was fulfilled when the Israelites became the recipients of God's laws. Moses, on account of their being the possessors of the Torah, styles them ' a great nation ' (Deut. 4.).â Tancluim. Lech Lecho.

Blessings proceed from Zion (Ps. 134.), the dew is blessed from Zion (Ps. 133.), so does help come from Zion (Ps. 20.), and salvation (Ps. 14.). The future blessings of Israel will proceed from Zion (Ps. 133.), and Zion itself will receive God's blessings.â Tanchum. Lech Lecho.

The comparison in Ix auty of any woman to Sarah is like comparing monkeys with men.â Tanchum. Lech Lecho.

' This shall not be thine heir, but he that cometh forth out of thy loins shall be thine heir'(Gen. 15.4). There is a story of a man blessed with learning, wisdom, and riches, who had an only son, to whom he naturally gave the best education, and whom he sent to Jerusalem for the purpose of completing his education. He had all arrangements made for his bodily comforts, and took every care that the young man. who was very promising and on whom he doted, should want for nothing. Shortly after his son's departure, he took to his bed, from which he rose not again.

His death caused immense regret in the place of his residence, for in him the poor had lost a real support, and many a man a wise counsellor and adviser. It was felt that the town in general had lost one whom it would be difficult to replace.

The funeral and the days of mourning over, a friend who was known to be the executor of the dead man's last will, and who had duly informed the son by letter of the sad death of his father, proceeded to break the seal of the will and see its contents. To his great astonishment, and no less to the astonishment of every one who learnt the nature of its contents, the whole of the dead man's property, personal and othcnvise. moveable and immoveable, after leaving considerable amounts to various charities, was left to his negro slave; there was but a saving clause that his beloved son should have the privilege of choosing one thing, but one only, out of the whole estate.

The son, though duly informed of the details of this strange will, was so immersed in grief at the loss of his father that his mind could not be diverted to anything else; and it was only when his teacher alluded to his father's death and the inheritance which he might expect, and advised him to use it for the same laudable purposes, that the young man informed his beloved master that by his father's will he had been reduced to a beggar. Meanwhile the negro slave of the departed man, having gone through all the formalities and proved his title, lost no time in taking possession of his dead master's property. He was ready and willing enough to grant the son one thing out of his late father's goods, whenever he should come and claim the object of his choice. The acute rabbi, on reading the will, saw at once the drift of the testator's intention, and told his pupil that he should proceed to his native town and take possession of his property. ' But I have no property to take possession of," pleaded the young man, except one article of my late father's goods." ' Well then," replied the teacher, unable to conceal a smile, ' choose your late father's negro slave out of his estate, and with him will go over to you all he possesses, since a slave can own nothing, and all he has belongs to his master. That indeed was your father's clever device. He knew that if the will were to state that all was left to you, the negro, being by the force of circumstances in charge of everything that was left, would probably in your absence take for himself and his friends all the valuables on which he could lay his hands; whereas if he knew or thought all belonged to him, he would take care of everything that was left. Your wise father knew that the one thing he gave you the power to choose would be no other than his slave, and with him you would become the just and rightful owner of everything." â Tanchum. Lech Lecho.

You cannot be too careful about prayer, and you should never omit to pray. Prayer eclipses all other services, and towers above sacrifices; and the sinful man may receive God's grace through prayer.â Tanchum. Vaayro.

As one is prohibited from reciting any portion of the Torah by heart, but must read it out of the written scroll, so is he who expounds any portion thereof not allowed to read his exposition from anything wtitten, but must deliver it by word of mouth.â Tanchum. Vaayro.

When God's creatures incur punishment, the Merciful One looks for one to plead for the guilty people, to ojicn a way, as it were, as was the case in the time of Jeremiah. (See Jer. 5.)â Tanchum. Vaayro.

The proverb says, ' If you rub shoulders with the anointed you will become anointed." Lot, being associated with Abraham, became hospitable; whilst his character does not indicate inclination to hospitality on his own part.â Tanchum. Vaayro.

You must not in any way mislead your fellow-man, not even to the extent of asking the price of anything he may have for disposal, so as to make him believe that you are a likely purchaser, whilst you have no intention of jmrchasing the article.â Tanchum. Vaayro.

The righteous are put to more and severer trials than the unrighteous. So the owner of flax will beat out the good flax often and severely, so as to make it purer, but does not treat the inferior article in the same way, lest it fall away into small pieces.â Tanchum. Vaayro.

The following tend to make a man prematurely old: Fear, war, trouble from his children, or a shrew of a wife. â Tanchum. Chaya Sarah.

As there is a regularity in the position of the sun daily tliree times: in the morning he is in the east, at noon between east and west, and in the evening in the west, so must there be an inflexible regularity with every Jew in reciting his prayers three times daily, morning, afternoon, and evening.â Tanchum. Chaya Sarah.

A widower with unmarried sons is advised to see his sons married before he marries again.â Tanchum. Chaya Sarah.

Adrianus (Hadrian), discussing with Rabbi Joshua the innumerable adversaries that the Israelites had to encounter, said ' Great is the sheep that can withstand seventy wolves." Rabbi Joshua replied, ' Greatest is the shepherd who enables the sheep to outlive the constant attacks of the wolves."â Tanchum. Toldous.

There is merit and even dignity in handicraft.â Tanchum. Vayaitza.

Do not say, I need not work for my living, but cast my hope on God who supports all living creatures. You must work for a livelihood and look up to God to bless the work of your hands. Jacob, in alluding to the delivery from Laban's house, says, ' God hath seen the labour of my hands ' (Gen. 31.).â Tanchum. Vayaitza.

A homely domesticated wife is like the altar in the Temple; and she is even an atonement as the altar was.â Tanchum. Vayishlach.

Isaiah committed sin by saying, ' In the midst of a people of unclean lips do I dwell' (Isa. 6.). For this, the slander which is compared to fire, he was punished with fire, with the live coal taken from the altar (Isa. 6.).â Tanchum. Vayishlach.

However adverse one's opinion may be of any one placed in a high position, he is bound to pay him the respect due to his position. Rabbi Judah Hannasi, when writing to Antoninus, invariably used the phrase, 'Judah, thy servant, sends greeting."â Tanchum. Vayishlach.

A modest woman is worthy of being the wife of a high priest, for she is like an altar in her home.â Tanchum. Vayishlach.

God wishes man to ask forgiveness, and not to see him in his guilt.â Tanchum. Vayishlach.

So exceedingly handsome was Joseph that when the friends of Potiphar's wife visited her, and the hostess proffered them fruit, the Egyptian women cut their fingers instead of the fruit, as they could not take their eyes off the wonderfully handsome Hebrew slave; and they sympathized with their friend when he scorned her advances.â Tanchum. Vayaishev.

Give me the admonition of the old in preference to the flattery of the young.â Tanchum. Vayaishev.

When Moses said to the people ' After the Lord your God shall ye walk ' (Deut 13), they took alarm at the formidable, or rather impossible, task imposed upon them ' How," said they, ' is it possible for man to walk after God, who hath his way in the storm and in the whirlwind, and the clouds are the dust of his feet ' (Nahum i.) 'whose way is in the sea and his path in the great waters '? (Ps. 77.). Moses explained to them that to walk after God meant to imitate humbly his attributes of mercy and compassion by clothing the naked, visiting the sick, and comforting the mourner.â Tanchum. Vayaishev,

A fatality seems to have been attached toshechem in connexion with Israel's sorrows. The capture of Dinah took place at Shechem. Joseph was sold there into slavery. David's kingdom was split in Shechem; and the advent of Jerolxjam also took place in Shechem.â Tanchum. Vayaishev.

C) woman, what mischief thou causest! Even the worshipping of idols did not cause such trouble and loss of life as a woman caused. The making and worshipping of the golden calf caused the loss of three thousand men (Exod. 32.); but through a woman at Sliittim twenty-four thousand were the victims. â Tanchum. Vayaishev.

Good men lift up their eyes and look one straight in the face; bad, wicked men drop their eyes.â Tanchum. Vayaishev.

' Should not a man pray every hour? ' asked Antoninus of his friend Rabbi Judah Hannasi. He demurred on receiving a reply in the negative. After a while the Rabbi called on Antoninus, and was as careful as always to address him with considerable deference.

After about an hour he came again, and addressed him again carefully with all the titles he was wont to use, and so the Rabbi repeated his visits and expressions of homage about every hour during the day. When, at last, Antoninus told his friend that he felt himself slighted instead of honoured by the frequency of the visits, and the expressions of homage with which Rabbi Judah meant to honour him, ' Therein," the sage said. ' lies my reason for telling you that man was not to address the throne of mercy every hour as you contended, since such frequency savours of contempt."â Tanchum. Miketz.

There is a most remarkable identity between the occurrences in the life of Joseph and those in the history of Zion and Jerusalem, and a remarkable similarity in the phrases employed in describing the respective events of each, whether in their adversity or in their prosperity. We read: ' Israel loved Joseph' (Gen. 37.), ' The Lord loveth the gates of Zion ' (Ps. 8y.). Joseph's brethren hated him; ' My heritage is unto Me as a lion in the forest, it crieth out against Me, therefore I hate it' (Jer. 12.). Joseph speaks of making sheaves; there are sheaves in connexion with Zion (Ps. 126.). Joseph dreamed; ' When the Lord turned again the captivity of Zion we were like them that dream' (Ps. 126.). Joseph was asked, ' Wilt thou rule over us? ' ' Say unto Zion thy God ruleth' (Isa.52.). Joseph was asked whether his father and brothers would prostrate themselves before him. ' They shall bow down to thee with their face towards the earth ' (Isa. 49.). Joseph's brethren were jealous; ' Thus said the Lord of Hosts, I was jealous for Zion with great jealousy' (Zcch. 8.). Josej)h went to inquire about the peace of his brothers; Zion was to seek the peace of the city where she is captive (Jer. 29.). Joseph's brethren saw him from the distance; the same is said about Zion (Ezkl. 23.). Joseph's brothers contemplated his destruction; so the nations contcnij)lated the destruct ionof Zion (Ps. 83.). Joseph was stripped of his coat of many colours; concerning Zion, the prophet says, ' They shall strip thee of thy clothes ' (Ezkl. 16.). Joseph was put into a pit; ' They have put me alivt- into the dungeon' (Lament.3.). The pit into which Joseph was put contained no water. In connexion with Zion, Jeremiah was put into a pit where there was no water (Jer. 38.). Joseph's brothers sat down to their meal; ' We have given the hand to Egyptians and to Assyrians to be satisfied with bread ' (Lament. 5.). Joseph was pulled up from the pit; Jeremiah, who in connexion with his prophecy about Zion was put into a dungeonâ as stated aboveâ was drawn up from the dungeon (Jer. 38.). Lamentations were raised alx)ut Joseph; ' And in that day did the Lord call for weeping and mourning ' (Isa. 22.). In the case of Joseph consolation was rejected. ' Labour not to comfort me ' (Isa. 22.). Joseph was sold; ' the children of Judali and of Jerusalem have you sold unto the Grecians ' (Joel 4.). Joseph is described as handsome; ' Beautiful for situation, the joy of the whole earth, is mount Zion' (Ps. 48.). Joseph was the greatest in his master's house; ' the glory of the latter house shall be greater than the former' (Hag. 2.). The Lord was with Joseph; ' Now mine eyes shall be open and mine ears attcnt unto the prayers that are made in this place ' (2 Chron. 7.). Grace and lovingkindness were shown to Joseph; concerning Zion God says, ' I remember the kindness of thy youth, the love of thine espousals ' (Jer. 2.). Joseph was rendered presentable by changing his clothes, etc.; ' When the Lord shall have washed away the filth of the daughters of Zion ' (Isa. 4.). The throne of Pharaoh was above Joseph; ' At that time they shall call Jerusalem the throne of the Lord' (Jsr- 3-)- Joseph was clothed in grand garments; ' Awake, awake, put on thy strength, O Zion, put on thy beautiful garments ' (Isa. 52.). Joseph was met by an angel; ' Behold I will send my messenger, and he shall prepare the way (Mai. 3.). The name of Joseph and the name Zion are the same in numerical value DV 156, V2i 156).â Tanchum. Vayigash.

There is a tendency with every man to become humble when near his death.â Tanchum. Vaychee.

It matters not where the body is buried, the spirit goes whither it is destined.â Tanchum. Vaychee.

Jacob's objection to being buried in Egypt was due to the fact that the Egyptians practised witchcraft by means of dead bodies, and he would not have his body utilized for such abominable practices.â Tanchum. Vaychee.

There is no death to the righteous.â Tanchum. Vaychee.

The righteous bless their offspring before they depart hence.â Tanchum. Vaychee

David was descended from Judah.â Tanchum. Vaychee.

' Behold how good and how pleasant it is for brethren to dwell together'â or in unityâ (Ps. 133.). ' 0 that thou wert as my brother' (Songs 8.). There are brothers and brothers. Cain and Abel were brothers, but the former slew the latter. Ishmael and Isaac were brothers, but there was no love lost between them. Jacob and Esau had no brotherly love for one another, nor did Joseph and his brothers show much love between them. David and Solomon had in their minds Moses and Aaron as typical brothers. One of the reasons why Moses so persistently hesitated to be the messenger to Pharaoh was his consideration for his brother Aaron, who was older and more eloquent than he, so that he hesitated to usurp what he considered should be Aaron's function. God, who knows the innermost thoughts of man, knew the real motive of Moses' refusal to accept the mission. Therefore we find God telling Moses, ' Behold Aaron the Levitc, thy brother, I know that he can speak well, and also behold he comcth forth to meet thee, and when he seeth thee he will be glad in his heart ' (Exod. 4.), And as Aaron's delight at his younger brother's elevation was so greatâ for the phrase ' glad in his heart ' conveys his great delightâ he was rewarded in that the Urim and Thummim were on his heart (Exod. 28.). When Aaron met his brother in the mount of God he kissed him (Exod. 4.).â Tanchum. Shemous.

The staff of Moses had the initials of the names of the ten plagues written on it, in order that Moses should know in which order they were consecutively to be brought on Pharaoh and the Egyptians. These initials were formed into three words, 2ni3, ly, 1!Â 1.â Tanchum. Voairo.

When we are told that Pharaoh took six hundred chosen cliariots with which to pursue the Israelites, we are naturally met with the question whence he got those six hundred chosen chariots. He could not have obtained them from his people the Egy tians, for we find that 'all the cattle of the Egyptians died' (Exod.9). They could not have l)een his own, for his own cattle also perished (Exod. 9.). Nor did the Israelites supply them, since they left with all their cattle, there Wcis not a hoof to be left.

The explanation is found in the fact that those who feared the word of the Lord among the servants of Pharaoh made their cattle flee into the house when the hail was predicted (Exod. 9.), and these ' fearers of the word of tile Lord ' among the Egyi"tians supplied Pharaoh with their animals for the jurpose of pursuing the Israelites. Bv the character of those among the

Egyptians who ' feared the word of the Lord ' that of the nation can be judged.â Tanchum. Beshallach.

' Fear not thou, worm Jacob," says the prophet (Isa. 41.). Why was Israel compared to a worm? As the insignificant worm is able to destroy a big cedar with no other weapon than its small weak mouth, even so is Israel able to prevail against his great persecutors with no other weapon but the prayers emanating from troubled hearts and uttered with the mouth.â Tanchum. Beshallach.

How great is faith! It secures happiness and salvation. Abraham's faith was accounted to him as righteousness. It was the faith which the Israelites had that redeemed them from Egypt (Exod. 4. 31). Their faith on the bank of the Red Sea carried them over that sea and brought them to the land of promise. The Lord keepeth the faithful (Ps. 31.). The righteous liveth by his faith (Habak. 2.). The last redemption of Israel will only be effected through faith. See how King David values faith (Ps. 105.). Concerning faith, David says, ' This is the gate of the Lord, the righteous shall enter therein."â Tanchum. Beshallach.

The lifting up of Moses' hands did not defeat Amalek, nor did the copper serpent stay the biting of the burning serpents. It was the directing by these of the hearts of the Israelites, with their prayers heavenwards, that defeated Amalek and caused the fiery serpents to cease. â Tanchum. Beshallach.

If you have acquired knowledge, do not simultaneously acquire a haughty spirit on account of your knowledge; and if you intend to expound God's word, recite to yourself twice or thrice what you intend saying. Even so great a man as Rabbi Akiba, when once called upon in the assembly to get up and preach, declined to do so, on the ground that he never preached unless he rehearsed his intended speech twice or thrice to himself.â Tanchum Jethro.

Whilst man is not to seek public notoriety and dis- tinction, he is not to err on the side of modesty and seclusion, and refuse to give his services in communal matters. Rabbi Asy when approaching death was visited by his nephew, who found the patient very depressed. ' Death," said his nephew, ' should not in your case be attended with feelings of alarm. Think what you leave l ehind you, the learning you have acquired and imparted to an army of students, the charity you have practised, and the kindly acts you have done; is there any good that it was in your power to do that you have left undone? And you have been so modest withal; you have always eschewed putting yourself forward or seeking notoriety, and have not mixed in disputes and in communal matters."

' This," replied the good man, ' even if all the good you said about me were quite correct, this alone would )C sufficient cause for my depression, for I might perhaps have been able to render some service, had I not kept to myself but taken upon me the burden of communal affairs."â Tanchum. Jethro.

With idol worshipik'rs it is the habit to treat their gods according to the circumstances in which they find themselves, which they attribute to the actions of their gods. If their condition is favourable, they pay tribute to their god. ' Therefore they sacrifice unto their net, and burn incense unto their drag, because by them their portion is fat and their meat plenteous," says the prophet (Habak. i.). If, on the other hand, adversities overtake them, they vent their anger on their gods. ' And it shall come to pass," the prophet tells us, ' that when they shall be hungry they shall fret themselves and curse their king and their god' (Isa.8.). Not so shall you do, my people, whose destiny is shaped out by the Creator of heaven and earth. Whatever Ix falls you, give thanks and praises unto your God. Are you in j rosperity? do not forget the (iiver do not say in your heart, ' My power and the might of mine hand hath gotten me this wealth," but hke David say, ' I will lift up the cup of salvation and call upon the name of my God." If adversity overtakes you, if sorrow and trouble overtake you in the midst of the smooth current of your affairs, take up David's words again and say ' I found trouble and sorrow, then I called upon the name of my God."â Tanchum Jethro.

The altar of God was to prolong man's life, and iron is a metal which can destroy man's life; therefore it was forbidden to use iron in the erection of the altar.â Tan-chum. Jethro.

Shght no man. Every man was created in God's image.â Tanchum. Jethro.

Onkeles, the nephew of Hadrianâ his sister's sonâ being anxious to embrace Judaism, yet being afraid of his uncle, told him that he wished to embark on a certain enterprise. When Hadrian offered him some money he refused to accept it, but said he wanted his uncle's advice, as he was inexperienced in the ways of the world. ' Purchase goods," replied his uncle, ' which do not, at present, command a high price, and are not favourites in the market, but for which there is reason to believe a demand at higher prices will eventually arise." Onkeles betook himself to Palestine, and gave himself up to study. After a time Rabbi Eliezer and Rabbi Joshua recognized in him the face of a student; they took him in hand, solved all the difficult problems he put before them, and generally befriended him. On his return home he again visited his uncle Hadrian, who, noticing that his nephew did not look as well as was his wont, inquired whether he had met with any monetary reverses in his new enterprise, or had been injured in any way. ' I have met with no monetary losses," said Onkeles, ' and as your nephew I am not likely to be hurt by any one." Being further pressed for the reason of his poor looks, Onkeles told his uncle they were due to his excessive studies and to the fact that he had under- gone circumcision. ' And who told you to do such a thing as to undergo circumcision? ' demanded Hadrian. ' I acted on your advice," replied Onkeles. ' I have acquired a thing that stands at a low jnice just now, but will eventually rise in value. I found no nation in such low esteem and so sure to rise in value as Israel. For thus said the Lord, tlic Redeemer of Israel and his Holy One, to him whom man despiseth, to him whom the nation abhorreth, to a servant of rulers, kings shall see and arise and princes also shall worship, because of the Lord that is faithful and the Holy One of Israel, He shall choose them ' (Isa. 49.). One of Hadrian's counsellors advised his master to visit his nephew's misdeed with death, for which advice the adviser received such a sharp rebuke from Hadrian that he committed suicide. Hadrian, after the death of his minister, further discussed with his nephew the matter of his conversion, and again asked for the reason of circumcision, Onkeles asked his uncle whether he had ever bestowed any distinction on any of his army who were not willing and ready to fight for his majesty and for the country at the risk of hfe. ' Neither could I be received into the fold of those to whom God has given his behests and statutes without having the seal of those great statutes put on me even at the risk of my life."â Tanchum. Mishpotim.

Whilst the Torah teaches peace and goodwill to one's fellow-man, it likewise teaches the necessity of standing up against evil deeds and even rebuking the evil-doer. Moreover, though all reverence and deference are due to one's teacher, yet in the matter of censurable conduct it becomes the pupil's duty to protest against it. Bad conduct is contaminating. One is apt to fall into the same error if one sees any evil act and docs not lift up one's voice to protest against it.â Tanchum. Mishpotim.

He who rebukes his fellow-man with a sincere desire to make him hetti-r comes within the inner walls of the heavenly pavilion.â Tanchum. Mishpotim.

You are not permitted to select injunctions of the Torah which you consent to observe, and reject others for the observance of which you can find no reason. In accepting God's word one is bound to imphcit obedience to it.â Tanchum. Mishpotim.

The rich should ever bear in mind that his wealth may merely have been deposited with him to be a steward over it, or to test what use he will make of his possessions. Not less should the poor remember that his trials may have been sent as a test of his fortitude.â Tanchum. Mishpotim.

Poverty outweighs all other sorrows.â Tanchum. Mishpotim.

' If you have taken a pledge from the poor," says God to the rich, ' do not say he is your debtor and you are therefore justified in retaining his garment. Remember you are my debtor, your life is in my hand. I return you all your senses and all your faculties after your sleep every day."â Tanchum. Mishpotim.

Jewish litigants are to bring their disputes for adjustment before a Jewish court, and not to have recourse to outside tribunals.â Tanchum. Mishpotim.

Although witnesses have always to give their evidence standing, yet an exception may be made in the case of a distinguished (learned) man, who may be allowed to sit whilst giving evidence. Should he consider it beneath his dignity to give evidence at all, he may be exempted. This only applies to any suit regarding money matters (civil cases), but in criminal matters he is not to be exempted.â Tanchum. Mishpotim.

God's works accommodate one another without asking any interest. The day accommodates the night, and the night the day (according to season). The moon borrows from the stars, and the stars from the moon. The higher wisdom borrows from the simple or common sense; kindness borrows from charity, the heavens from the earth, and the earth from the heavens. The

Torah borrows from righteousness, and righteousness from the Torah; all without charging any interest. Is man. and man only, not to extend a helping hand to his fellow-man without exacting usury for a kind act?â Tanchum. Mishpotim.

Regarding the giving of alms, judgment and discretion should ye exercised. Obviously, poor relatives have a prior claim to any other, and the poor of your town claim priority over those of another town.â Tanchum. Mishpotim.

' He who hath pity on the poor lendeth unto the Lord," says Solomon (Prov. 19.). It is surely good enough for you, O man, to be God's creditor. Not that He will return to you exactly the coin you give to the poor; He will look even farther into your deed. The poor man was perhaps famishing, and your timely help may have rescued him from an untimely death; God, whose creditor you have become when you helped the helpless, will rescue you and yours from danger when it is near.â Tanchum. Mishpotim.

He who by usury and ill-gotten gain increaseth his substance, it shall be taken from him by him who pities the poor (Prov. 28.). When a non-Jew wants to borrow of you, you will perhaps say that since you are not permitted to take usury from your own compatriot you may take it from a non-Jew. Be assured that such ill-gotten gain will be taken from you; probably by the autliorities, to erect baths or other sanitary buildings ' for thf j)oor or the strangn-.â Tanchum. Mishpotim.

Why, asked Turnus Rufus, a heathen king, of Rabbi Akiba, have we incurred the hatred of your (iod so that He says, ' I hate Esau '? (Mai. 3.). The Rabbi said he ' It is said in the Taltnud. Haba Mczia y K that ("hebore. King of Persia, laiil liis Jewish subjects under special tribute, and with the money thus raiseil he built dwellings and other accommodations for the ptwr. Hence the expression of the Midrash. 'it will be taken from you, probably, by the authorities, to erect baths or other sanitary buildings.

would reply to the question the next day. On his making his appearance the following day, the king, thinking that Rabbi Akiba had postponed the answer the day before in order to invent meanwhile some lame explanation, said to the sage satirically, ' Well, Akiba, what have you dreamt during the night? ' Rabbi Akiba, taking the very question as the text for his reply, said, ' I dreamed I became possessed of two dogs which I named Rufus and Rufina (the names of the questioner and his wife).

The king, in a great fury, asked Rabbi Akiba how he dared offer him and his queen so gross an insult as to name his dogs by their names. ' Wherefore this indignation? ' returned R. Akiba calmly; ' you and yours are God's creatures, so are dogs God's creatures; you eat and drink, produce your species, live, decay and die; all this is also the case with dogs. Yet what umbrage you take because they bear the same name as you! Consider then that God stretched forth the heavens and laid the foundations of the earth, is the Creator, Governor and Ruler of all animate and inanimate things; yet you make an idol of wood and stone, worship it and call it by the name of God. Should you not then incur his hatred? 'â Tanchum. Troomah.

A distinguished scholar was on a voyage at sea, and on board the same ship were some merchants with their goods. In the course of conversation they asked the scholar what was the nature of his goods. ' My goods," he replied, ' are invaluable." Knowing, however, that there was no cargo of his on board the ship, they ridiculed his assertion. After sailing some distance from shore the ship was overtaken by pirates, who robbed the ship of its cargo and took the very clothes the passengers were wearing so far as they were of any value. Passengers and crew were only too thankful to escape with their lives and to clothe themselves with the rags which the pirates rejected. The scholar, as he did not wear any valuable clothes, was spared by the pirates as not being worth robbing, and landed at a small town, together with his fellow-passengers, who made a sorry sight in the lags that served them as clothes. The learned man, whose reputation had gone before him, was asked and consented to deliver lectures on various scientific subjects, which he handled in a niiisterly fashion. The lectures excited great interest, and attracted large audiences from all the neighbouring towns, with the result that the man not only found his lectures remunerative from a pecuniary point of view, but soon won the friendship of the leading men of the place, where he settled down and became an influential member of the community. Fate did not smile quite. so kindly on his former fellow-pa-ssengcrs, who, having unfortunately lost all their possessions, having no trade or profession, and being clothed in rags, found it impossil le to get employment. Seeing the great position the professor held in the town, they called upon him and solicited the favour of his intluence on their behalf. This he unhesitatingly and ungrudgingly gave them; he procured employment for them, and reminded them how perfectly justified he was in styling his goods invaluable.â Tanchum. Troomah.

On several occasions the Israelites were numbered, a census taken. For as the owner of a flock of sheep is an. xious to know how many he possesses, when anything untoward hapi)ens, when a wolf has Ixien in their midst, he is again anxious to ascertain what loss has lieen sustained by the mishap. Thus Moses had the jieojile numbered to see what loss there was after their punishment for making the golden calf.â Tanchum. Kee Sisso.

Poor ignorant man, you want to find out God's ways; e. xplain first the phenomenon of your own eye; it consists of white and black, and according to all rea. son the white should supply light, but in reality the little spot in the centre of your eye is the lens to give you sight.â Tanchum. Tezaveh,

A man never so learned should not preach if his preaching is not agreeable to his audience.â Tanchum. Kee Sisso.

A public teacher (preacher) must not only be thoroughly conversant with the twenty-four books of the Bible, but must be known to his flock as modest and distinguished for his virtues.â Tanchum. Kee Sisso.

Moses, in spite of his being the mediator between God and his people in promulgating God's behests to them, and knowing God's intention of giving his law to his people Israel, in spite of all his varied and most wonderful qualities, and his having been in the mountain forty days and forty nights, during which he eat no bread and drank no water, in spite of all this, he is but styled U1, and is only looked upon as an earthly, a mortal being, the greatest of men, but only a mortal man.â Tanchum. Kee Sisso.

There were forty thousand of the mixed multitude, who forced themselves on the Israelites at the Exodus and came out with them from Egypt. Amongst them were the two great Egyptian magicians of Pharaoh who imitated Moses' miracles before Pharaoh. Their names were Junus and Jumburius.â Tanchum. Kee Sisso.

The living always have to arrange for the dead, such as bringing them to their resting-place, etc., but the dead are not called upon to provide anything for the living; yet behold, when any serious trouble or threats overtook the Israelites, though there were many righteous men in the camp, Moses in his intercession had no recourse to them, but fell back upon those who had long since departed. ' Remember," he prayed, ' thy servants Abraham, Isaac, and Jacob." Solomon alluded to this when he said, ' Wherefore I praised the dead which are already dead more than the living, which are yet alive' (Eccles. 4.).â Tanchum. Kee Sisso.

The ' Mishna ' would have been incorporated with the

MIDRASn TANCHUMAH OR VELAMDINU 24I written Torah, but God saw that the Torah would eventually be translated into Greek and published as though it were the code intrusted to Greeks. Had the Mishna been together with the written law, the nations would have claimed to be the custodians of the whole of God's word. But the oral law, the key to and interpreter of the written law, being intrusted to Israelites only (which could not have been done had It been written) the Jews have the whole of God's word with the interpretation in full.â Tanchum. Kee Sisso.

Wisdom is granted by God to him who already )os-sesses knowleilge, not to the ignorant. A certain matron was arguing with Rabbi Jos6 b. Chlafta on this point of God giving wisdom to men of understanding. This, she thouglit, was paradoxical, as it would be more proper if God granted wisdom to simpletons, who are more in want of it than wise men.

Rabbi Jos6 put a simple question to her. ' If two men," he asked, ' were to appear before you, one wealthy and the other poor, each asking you for a loan of money whom would you be more inclined to trust? ' ' Surely the one possessed of wealth,' she replied. ' God in his dispensation," said Rabbi os6, ' giveth wisdom to the man of imcu'rstanding, who possesses and knows the value of it, and will make profitable use of the augmentation: like a man whom you would prefer to trust with your money, knowing that he has facilities to employ j jrofit-ably what you lend him; whereas the fool intrusted with wisdom would abuse the precious gift and convert it into folly, like the poor man whom you would not care to trust, lest the money should be lost through his inability to emj loy it profitably."â Tanchum. Kee Sisso.

Rabbi Eliezer b. Jos6 stated that he saw in Rome the Mercy-seat of the Temple. There was a bloodstain on it. On inquiry he was told that it was a stain from the blood which the High Priest sprinkled thereon on the Day of Atonement.â Tanchum. Vayakhail.

The Tor ah was given in the wilderness, and hke the wilderness it is free and open to all comers without formalities or introductions: all that wish to do so can enter into it.â Tanchum. Vayakhail.

The boards for the Mishkan were made from shittim-wood, from a tree that does not bear fruit; thereby man is taught the virtue of economy: he should not waste anything of greater value when the same can be obtained by using articles of lesser value. Even the Mishkan was not to be made out of fruit trees, since it could be made equally as effective out of trees bearing no fruit.â Tanchum. Vayakhail.

It is but right and proper that one should be right in the sight of God, but it is also desirable so to act as to be just and right in the eyes of man.â Tanchum. Pekudai.

Slander no one, whether thy brother or not thy brother, whether a Jew or not a Jew.â Tanchum. Pekudai.

In connexion with the poor man's sacrifice, that of a handful of flour, and not in connexion with the rich man's sacrifices (of bulls and rams) do we find the expression ' and if any soul." God looked upon the poor man's offering of a handful of flour as though he had offered his life.â Tanchum. Vayikra.

The righteous stand on a higher level than angels.â Tanchum. Vayikra.

Those who aim at greatness do not always get it. Moses fled from it, but it was forced upon him.â Tanchum. Vayikra.

God consulted the Torah when about to create man, but the Torah was dubious about calling man into existence, for since his days would be so short and his ways so perverted he would require much forbearance, God's reply was, ' By thee (Torah) I declare myself as a God merciful, longsuffering, and abundant in goodness and in truth."â Tanchum. Pekudai.

'Swear not at all, not even to tlie truth."' â Tanchum. Vayikra.

Future bliss can neither be imagined, explained, or described. We know nothing of its nature, form, greatness, or beauty, its quantity or quality. This much one should know, the phrase N H Db y, ' the world to come ' does not imply that it is a world yet to be called into existence; it exists already, but the phrase is employed to describe the life into wliich those who are in the present stage of existence will bo transposed when they throw off this mortal coil.â Tanchum. Vayikra.

The leper, the blind, the abject poor, and those who have no j rogeny, are as though dead.â Tanchum. Tsav.

Kabbi Judah Hanasi, arriving at a place called Semunia, was entreated by the community to select a rabbi for them. He sent them Rabbi Levi b. Sissyas, a learned and able man. Not long afterward the newly appointed Rabbi came to R. Judah Hanasi, the donor of his living, and whilst thanking him for the appointment expressed the fear that his position was not tenable. On Ix'ing questioned for his reasons he answered that Scriptural passages were submitted to him for solution by his congregants which it was above his capability to solve. Amongst others he mentioned the passage, ' I will show thee that which is written, and which is true '(Dan. 10.). Hence they argue that there must be something written and which is not true. Rabbi Judah Hanasi then explained: ' Man," he said, ' incurs retribution if he leaves matters as they are, and does nothing to avert the punishment decreed upon him. In this case what is written Is true: his punishment will overtake him. But on the other hand, if he reflects and thinks over his evil ways, becomes contrite, repents and asks his merciful Father for forgiveness, and the deserved punishment

Maimonides in hls nptnn T hold. s a contrary opinion. He says, one â. houu swear to trutli and mentions y2L"n 1DC'31, "By his name thou shalt swear" (Deut. 10. 21) as a commandment.

is held back, in this instance what is written is not true."

By this hypothesis you are to reconcile some seemingly contradictory passages in Scripture, such as in i Saml. (2. 25), where in connexion with Eli's sons we have it that they hearkened not unto the voice of their father because the Lord wanted to slay them. But through the prophet God sends us a message, As I live, saith the Lord, I have no pleasure in the death of the wicked ' (Ezkl. 33.). The answer is that there are sinners and sinners, those who do and those who do not repent.â Tanchum. Tsav.

There is a good reason why the secret comes out when the wine goes in, 'Â wine is in numerical value seventy, and so is the word Tld secret: one seventy in, the other seventy out.â Tanchum. Sheminee.

Two sheep and two tenth parts of flour were demanded as an offering, whereas of wine only the smallest possible quantity was to be offered. This was a hint that wine is always to be used sparingly, as indulgence in it leads to mischief.â Tanchum. Sheminee.

The guardian angels are always near God's throne, but the accusing ones are kept at a distance.â Tanchum. Sazrea.

Have no undue compassion for tyrants, and you will not become a tj ant over those who deserve compassion. â Tanchum. Metzora.

As an example of good manners and the virtue of considering the feelings of others, a story is related of a distinguished man who invited friends to his son's marriage. During the feast the bridegroom himself went to the cellar to fetch some very old and costly wine for the guests, when he was fatally bitten by a snake which was hidden under the casks. When the host learned the shocking news of his son's death he refrained from disturbing his guests' enjo)mient, and when the feast was over and prayers after meat were about to be pro- nounced, he told the assembly that there would be burial j)rayers for his son, who had met his death by the bite of a snake.â Tanchum. Metzora.

At Sinai the women received and accepted the Decalogue before the men.â Tanchum. Metzora.

Palestine is destined to be the centre of the globe.â Tanchum. Kedoshim.

Sceptics argued with Rabbi Simlua that from the words D'l 'lip D"n':'S (Josh. 24. 19) a plurality of gods is clearly deducible. Rabbi Simlua dispelled their contention by pointing out that the word that follows is Kin, ' he is," and not rtDH, ' they are." As for the word D"lt'TTp, which is plural, he explained that God's holiness does not consist in being holy in one thing only, but that the whole of his doings are full of holiness. Hence the D'l which indicates the j lural; that is to say, every one of his actions is holy, all his words are holy, all his ways are holy, his revelations, his manifestations, are all holy, and He is perfect holiness in all his nature and properties.â Tanchum. Kedoshim.

Before man had yet made his appearance on earth, the angels sanctified God's name and sang hymns before Him in antici )ation of man's advent. The words they used for their hymns were, ' Blessed be the Lord God of Israel from everlasting to everlasting." When Adam made his appearance they asked, ' Is this the human creature in anticipation of whose advent we sang hymns? ' They were told that this was not the one, as he would prove to Ixj dishonest. At Noah's birth the angels exclaimed, ' This time we behold the man." ' No," they were told, this one will le given to ' drinking " Nor did they guess well when they suggested Abraham was the right man when he made his ajipcarance, for his irogcny was Ishmael. Again they were undeceived when they hit upon Isaac as the man for whose coming they had sung hymns, for did he not beget Esau whom God hated? At the appearance of Jacob they again ventured a guess, and this time God said to them, ' You have fixed on the right man." He shall be named Israel, and his descendants shall be called by his name." Hence God said to Moses, Tell the children of Israel that they were sanctified before they were called into existence, and must therefore remain holy, even as their God is holy. So a king when bringing his newly-married bride into his palace might say to her: ' You are now united to me. I am king, therefore be you henceforth queen."â Tanchum. Kedoshim.

' When you come into the land you shall plant all manner of trees for food' (Levit. 19.). Although you will find ' the land filled with all good things," yet you are not to abstain from labour, especially agriculture; you are to occupy yourselves in these pursuits. Even the old who have no reasonable expectation of eating of the fruits of their labour shall participate in the work of cultivating the ground.â Tanchum. Kedoshim.

The caution which King Solomon utters, ' Rob not the poor' (Prov. 22.) would seem superfluous. Who is likely to rob a poor man who has nothing to be robbed of? But his words go farther than they seem to go at first sight. They mean that if you are in the habit of apportioning some of your substance to the poor it should not enter your mind to discontinue doing so. If you are tempted to say, why should I give my substance to others? remember that by your discontinuance you are robbing the poor. He and you are mine, and I may reverse the condition of things.â Tanchum. Behar.

Regarding the ceremony of the red heifer (Numb, ig.), Rabbi Jochanan b. Zakkai explained to his pupils that its ashes could not render any unclean person clean. But as this is a statute of the Torah, we must inquire for no reason. If we refused to do anything that God commands without a definite reason, we should no longer be paying Him simple obedience.

In addition, he continued, supposing one of the child-

MIDRASn TANCHUMAH OR YHLAMDINU 247 ren of the king's servants had soiled the king's palace, the mother would naturally be fetched and asked to wash out the stain which her child had made. So the mother of the calf with which the Israelites polluted God's world is called into requisition to purify the pollution made by her offspring.â Tanchum. Chookas.

Apart from the essential qualifications for the office of High Priest, he had also to be handsome, healthy, in a good financial ixsition, a man of mature judgment, and of advanced age. When he was poor, but otherwise qualified, he was placed in a position beyond want. One Pinchus, ' the stonecutter," being in every respect eminently fitted for the office of High Priest except that he was poor, the priests amongst themselves contributed enough to make him actually a man of affluence.â Tanchum. Emmur.

Out of certain classes of things God has chosen one. Of days, the seventh was chosen and sanctified. Of years too the seventh was chosen as the Sabbatical year; and out of seven Sabbatical years one was selected as the Jubilee. Of countries, God made choice of Palestine. Of the heavens, the 7112 1 Aroboth was chosen for God's tfirone. Of nations, Israel was the choice, and of the tribes of Israel, that of Leviâ Tanchum. Bamidbar.

God blessed Adam, Noah and Abraham, but He endowed Abraham with the power of blessing which the Lord will endorse.â Tanchum. Nosou.

During the twenty-six generations that passed from the creation to the giving of the Torah, the world was upheld by God's lovingkindness, which was, so to speak, the pivot upon which the world existed. When the Torah was given to and accepted by Israel, an additional support was given to the world upon which it could stand, and yet it was only like a lxnch standing upon two feet, not very well supported. N 'ith the erection of the Mihkan the world received a substantial support. So a stool which only stood upon two legs receives a third, and is rendered firm.â Tanchum, Nosou.

At the Exodus a compact was made with the Israehtes, by which they undertook to erect the Mishkan for the Shechinah to dwell amongst them, and this is indicated in the 29th chapter of Exodus, ' And they shall know that I am the Lord their God that brought them forth out of the land of Egypt that I may dwell among them." â Tanchum. Nosou.

In order not to cause jealousy as to who should be the seventy elders, Moses cast lots by taking seventy-two slips representing six of each tribe, writing the word ' elder ' on seventy of the slips and leaving the two odd ones blank. Seventy-two men then drew out each of them a slip, and those who drew blanks had to give up their claims.â Tanchum. Behaaloscha.

The harp upon which the Levites played had seven strings.â Tanchum. Behaaloscha.

Priests and prophets are designated by the name of IJ ' 'D, which simply means messenger. â Tanchum. Shelach.

God's behests were to be the guiding principle of the Israelite in all his doings throughout his earthly career. Ploughing, sowing, reaping, threshing: these have all their laws by which he is to conduct them. In the making of dough, in killing meat, in the fruit of his trees, he has his laws, also about the hair of his head, his apparel, the building of his house, and the burying of his dead.â Tanchum. Shelach.

Orientals have some commendable habits. When they kiss they kiss the hand, not the mouth. They do not handle meat with their hands, but use knives. When they have to consider any important public matter, they assemble in the open outside the town.â Tanchum. Chookas.

The ' Shekel' when mentioned in the Pentateuch

See also Moreh Nebuchim, vol. i, cap. 27, and vol. 2, caps. 6 and 42.

means one ' sela '; in the prophets it amounts to five and twenty ' selaiin '; but those mentioned in the Holy Writings (Hagiographa) are one hundred selaim. There is an exception in the case of the shekohm which Ephron the Hittite asked of Abraham for the ' cave of Machpelah ': they also were one hundred selaim each.â Tanchum Balak.

Midian and Moab were enemies from time immemorial; but for the purpose of injuring the Israelites they overlooked their long-standing enmity: just as two dogs will very quickly desist from fighting if they see a wolf approaching, and will unite their strength against the advancing enemy. Balaam's services were so anxiously sought after because the Israelites and their leader, Moses, were known to have immense power with their'mouth (prayer); therefore they wanted one who also had great power with his eloquence.â Tanchum. Balak.

When man confesses and says, ' O God, I have sinned," the very messenger sent to punish him for that sin has his power paralysed and his hand stayed.â Tanchum. Balak.

To entice a man to sin is tantamount to taking his hfe. â Tanchum. Pinchos.

If Moses had been a selfish man and had only considered himself and his own interest, he would have delayed to avenge the Israelites on the Midianites as long as possible, because the duration of his earthly life was fixed for the time when he should have brought about vengeance on Midian (Numb. 31.). But like a faithful shepherd, unselfish and self-sacrificing as he was, he strove to consummate all his work without regarding his own life or his own interest, and as soon as that part of his duty was ripe for performance, and when it was to the advantage of his flock, he set himself to do the work, knowing well that when that work was finished his earthly career was finished.â Tanchum. Mattos.

' Ye shall keep my statutes and my judgments, which if a man do he shall live in them ' (Levit. i8.): live in them, says God, but not die by them.â Tanchum. Massa.

God gave the Torah to Israel, but all nations are to benefit by it.â Tanchum. Devorim.

Jews are under an oath not to reveal the time of redemption (those who may know it), not to prolong its consummation by their unrighteousness, and not to rebel against the ruling power.â Tanchum. Devorim.

Moses was born and died on the same day of the month, namely, the seventh day of Adar.â Tanchum. Voes-chanan.

Moses prayed to God to show him his glory, and in compliance with that prayer God says, ' I will pass all my goodness before thee ' (Exod. 33.). Because God's goodness is God's glory; mercy and goodness are the brightest jewels in God's crown.â Tanchum. Voes-chanan.

Death is designed for man from time immemorial. When the hour of man's departure hence arrives, nothing will save him from it. If he had the wings of an eagle and could soar high up above the earth, he would, of his own accord, come down to meet his fate.â Death is a new gate for the righteous to enter in.â Tanchum. Voes-chanan.

Do not weigh, as it were in scales, the importance or the insignificance of your acts, as long as they are acts of righteousness; and do not speculate and say, ' I will not do this or that because it is only a small or light act in the scale of God's commandments; I will therefore rather perform a more important act, and my reward will be correspondingly greater." For this reason God hath concealed the nature of the reward for carrying out his statutes. A certain king hired workmen to cultivate his garden, but did not tell them what the reward would be for raising each kind of fruit or plant, for if he had done so the workmen would one and all have endeavoured to produce the fruit for wliich the higlu-st wage was promised, and the other products would have been neglected. Yet there are two commandments, one apparently of slight and the other of great importance, for which precisely the same reward is promised, (i) That of sending away the dam and retaining its young, for the carrying out of which well-being and long life are promised (Deut.22.); and (2) the honouring of parents, for which the same reward is assured. This tends to endorse what we maintain, that it is not for man to define the smallness or greatness of a godly act, or the nature and quality of the rewards. It is suf cient to know that the doing of God's will carries with it reward for faith and for doing it simply because we are told to do so.â Tanchum. Ike v.

Let not the Israehtes be haughty and say that they only are the people who possess and live up to the commandments of God, for other nations, though not the recipients of God's laws, also have the commandments of the Lord as their life's guide, and glorify his nameâ Tanchum. Ikev.

No affliction overtakes man without his having first some foreboding or warning of its coming.â Tanchum. Reai.

No evil-doer can plead ignorance; for the two ways, the good and the evil, are so distinctly marked that it is impossible to mistake the one for the other. Moses was like the old watchman who sat on the high road where two paths, a stony and a smooth one, met, and constantly warned wayfarers which one to take.â Tanchum. Reai.

God will eventually reveal his glory to all mankind as unmistakably as though He had placed his throne in the centre of the heavens, and then moved it from one extreme end to the other, so that everybody should see and know it.â Tanchum. Shoftim.

No one can imagine the reward of him who accepts all his sorrows and reverses with religious resignation. â Tanchum. Kee Saizai.

Rabbi Akiba, in defiance of the mandate of the Grecian authorities who prohibited the study of the Torah, was found by his friend, Prysus b. Judah, with a host of disciples, diligently pursuing his wonted research. ' Knowest thou not," asked his friend, ' the great danger thou art facing by thus defying the authorities? Take my advice and desist from thy studies."

' Your advice," returned Rabbi Akiba, ' seems to me like the advice of the fox who on seeing fishes swimming in a river here and there, told them to come out, and he would show them a resting place in the rocks. " Are you the wise one amongst the beasts of the field? " retorted the fishes. "If in our own element we can find no rest and safety, how much worse will it be with us when we are out of it? " With us Jews the Torah is our very life (Prov. 4). In pursuing its study I may incur the risk of losing my earthly life; in relinquishing it I face the certainty of moral and spiritual death."â Tanchum. Keesovou.

The heart and mind of the Priest when conducting Divine service was not to be diverted by anything else, his whole heart and mind was to be concentrated upon the service.â Tanchum. Kee Sovou.

It is not too much to say that discretion should be exercised regarding the names one gives to his children. There are instances in which a name implying evil qualities has been given to a child, and the child, when grown up into manhood, has exemplified by his life the meaning of his name.â Tanchum. Haazenu.

Hope is held out here for man for everything. If he is in abject poverty, he may become rich; if he is sickly, it is not beyond the range of possibility for him to become robust; if he is captive, he may regain his liberty. Death is the only thing which man cannot hope to

MIDRASn TANCHUMAH OR YELAMDINU 253 escape. But let man take comfort in the thought that even so great a man as Moses, who spoke with God face to face, the head of all prophets, the greatest of men, did not escape death.â Tanchum. Berocho.

Lightning Source UK Ltd.
Milton Keynes UK

173602UK00001B/106/P

9 781152 044357